"Glenn Pearson does a masterful job making the complexities easy and understandable, while providing industry outsiders with recommendations on how to navigate the inner workings of health systems. What I truly like about this book is that both a seasoned health care executive and someone new to the industry would find it equally valuable."

Peter D. Banko
President & CEO Centura Health

"Peter Drucker believed that healthcare was the most complex of human organizations. This book goes a long way to explaining that complexity and making it simpler for a seller to market its products or services to the healthcare market place. Glenn's experiences with the healthcare field lead to accuracy in a commentary that can't be beaten by works written by less experienced writers. He knows what he is writing about!"

J. Larry Tyler, FACHE, FHFMA, CMPE
CEO of the Practical Governance Group
Chairman Emeritus of Tyler & Company

"Interesting, engaging and informative with good examples. As Chief Medical Officer of a biotech startup that has to sell into the C-suite, I will be buying copies for our entire sales team."

Bob Lubitz, MD, MPH, FACHE, MACP
Chief Medical Officer, 3Oe Scientific, Inc.

"One of the underlying principles in this book is the importance of integrity and honesty in business dealings. Never say anything that you don't believe or cannot support."

William Cleverley, Ph.D.
Professor Emeritus, Ohio State University
Chairman and Founder
Cleverley & Associates

"*Thriving in the Healthcare Market* offers real solutions and innovative approaches to dealing with our country's complex and often-confusing healthcare market. The book promises to be a helpful and important addition to healthcare thinking."

Nancy Desmond
Co-founder and Former CEO of the
Center for Health Transformation

"I often cringe at the lack of financial analysis and credible forecasting I see in many companies' presentations. The ROI discussion in *Thriving in the Healthcare Market* nails it! Any entrepreneur can use it to produce projections that will stand up to scrutiny and demonstrate value to both investors and customers."

Jason Rupp
Executive Director
Southeastern Medical Device Association

"Glenn's expansive knowledge and in-depth industry experience is evident in "Thriving in the Healthcare Market." Add that to a clever writing style interwoven with anecdotes and analogies, and it makes the reading fun and educational. Hockey great Wayne Gretzky said "You miss 100% of the shots you don't take," and Glenn scored on this one. A book sure to be shared by many a salesperson and industry leader. GOAL!!!"

Robert Budman, MD
MBA CDI-P, Board Certified ABFM and
ABPM Informatics
CMIO Nuance Healthcare and former
CMIO Piedmont Healthcare

"One of the best ideas for a book I've heard in a long time. It should be required reading for all vendors. Reading this book would be one of the smartest things a healthcare salesperson could do for their career."

O.J. Booker
Healthcare Consultant and Hospital CEO

"Glenn delivers a well-organized narrative that demystifies the many complexities and hidden pitfalls preventing entrepreneurs from finding success today. This is a <u>must-read</u> for any investor, entrepreneur or technologist inspired to disrupt healthcare!"

Michael A. Levy
CEO and Co-Founder, Bluedoor Health
Co-Founder Digital Health Institute for Transformation

"The reader will know Glenn Pearson has 'been there and seen that.'"

William Moore
Retired Hospital CEO
President, Moore Business Groups, LLC

"This would be a great book for anyone preparing for a career as a healthcare executive."

Jeffrey Whitton, FACHE
Senior Director, Physician Practices
LifePoint Health

"This is wonderful. I got a good chuckle out of his scenarios. This will be so helpful for those trying to 'sell us.' We see right through all these ROI pledges from vendors. They make us not trust the salesperson."

Cathy H. Dougherty, FHFMA
Vice President, Revenue Cycle Management
Gwinnett Health System

"Pearson applies his high level of intellect to this book, yet he presents his material in a way that is easy to digest."

Jerry Fulks, FACHE
Retired President
WellStar West Georgia Medical Center

"Glenn Pearson's explanation of how the healthcare system is funded goes a long way towards helping the reader understand the complexities of both the current environment and legislative proposals being floated."

Russ Lipari
Founder and CEO
Health Connect South

"The chapter on approaches for reforming the healthcare system is a real highlight. I love the concepts he presents. Great ideas!"

Lance B. Duke, LFACHE
Healthcare Executive

"Glenn Pearson is like a one-man think tank."

Joel Pieper
Atlanta Office Managing Partner
Womble Bond Dickson law firm

"Great book!"

Kathy Reep, MBA
Vice President, Financial Services
Florida Hospital Association

Thriving in the Healthcare Market

Strategies from an Industry-Insider for Selling Your Product

Thriving in the Healthcare Market

Strategies from an Industry-Insider for Selling Your Product

Glenn E. Pearson, FACHE

CRC Press
Taylor & Francis Group
Boca Raton   London   New York

CRC Press is an imprint of the
Taylor & Francis Group, an **informa** business

A PRODUCTIVITY PRESS BOOK

CRC Press
Taylor & Francis Group
6000 Broken Sound Parkway NW, Suite 300
Boca Raton, FL 33487-2742

International Standard Book Number-13: 978-0-367-18329-5 (Paperback)
978-0-367-18331-8 (Hardback)

Visit the Taylor & Francis Web site at
http://www.taylorandfrancis.com

and the CRC Press Web site at
http://www.crcpress.com

To all the wonderful professional colleagues I've
been blessed to work with over the years

Contents

Acknowledgments

This book has been greatly improved through the generous involvement of the following people: Liza Behles, Ed Bonn, O.J. Booker, Marie Cameron, Jay Dennard, Nancy Desmond, Cathy Dougherty, Lance Duke, Will ElLaissi, Matt Ethington, Larry Emmelhainz, Kay Floyd, Wes Foote, Jerry Fulks, Andy Goodwin, Rosty Gore, Stephanie Gore, Liz Hansen, Dr. Denise Hines, Bill Jacobsen, Pete Kane, Doug Keir, Michael Lank, Michael Levy, Russ Lipari, Dr. Robert Lubitz, Dr. Dominic Mack, Stephanie Meier, Jason Miller, Bill Moore, Dr. Mike Mull, Erich Murrell, Chuck Orrick, Andy Pearson, Joel Pieper, Bill Radler, Kathy Reep, Brian Regan, Hal Robbins, Chris Rohrbach, Greg Schaack, Dr. Ray Snead, Aron Starosta, Carie Summers, Rob Vachon, Dr. Nizar Wehbi, Jeff Whitten, and Tiffany Wilson.

About the Author

Glenn Pearson has worked in the hospital industry for more than 35 years and now, as Principal of Pearson Health Tech Insights, LLC (PHTI), applies his vast experience to bridge the gap between the healthcare field and emerging, disruptive, and transformational technologies.

Before founding PHTI, Glenn was Executive Vice President at Georgia Hospital Association for 19+ years where he led:

- Finance
- Data
- IT
- mHealth
- Public relations
- Communications
- Entrepreneurial ventures
- Vendor endorsements

For three years, Glenn served as elected American College of Healthcare Executives (ACHE) Regent for Georgia, representing the state's 1,500 affiliates to the international association. In addition to chairing or being on six ACHE committees, he also chaired and/or served on many other national, regional, statewide, and local boards, committees and organizations including:

- Association of Healthcare Enterprises
- Allied Association of Hospital Accountants
- The Center for Health Transformation
- Southern HIPAA Administrative Regional Process
- Technology Association of Georgia Health Society
- Georgia Department of Community Health
- Georgia State University Institute of Health Administration
- Leadership Atlanta

He was also the founding president of what is now the Georgia Health Information Network and, in addition to chairing the Financial Sustainability Committee, continues to serve on its executive committee and as treasurer.

Glenn graduated magna cum laude and with honors from the Syracuse University Honors Program and was elected to Phi Beta Kappa and Phi Kappa Phi international honor societies. He went on to earn a Master of Health Administration degree from the Ohio State University where he received the Faculty Award for Outstanding Scholarship.

Outside the work environment, Glenn is a professional blues/bluegrass/rock harmonica player who has performed in nearly 1,000 events on five continents and has a number of recording projects to his credit. He also actively mentors a number of younger men both professionally and personally and is a cycling and fitness enthusiast.

He can be reached at: glenn@pearsonhti.com

See also www.PearsonHTI.com

Introduction

At 18% of GDP, healthcare represents a hugely attractive market for suppliers and vendors. Any sector this enormous requires support from dozens of entities: legal services organizations, design and construction companies, pharmaceutical suppliers, utilities companies, information technology vendors, food services suppliers, consulting firms, medical equipment manufacturers, and many others.

However, just having a great product or service is no guarantee of success. The selling organization must know how to fine-tune its offerings to match providers' operational preferences, present a bold case for how their product will be advantageous to the purchaser, and effectively communicate with potential customers. The right product is a must, but it's not enough. To recast a well-known phrase: "If you build it, they might not come."

People from outside the healthcare industry attempting to sell to hospitals, physicians, and other providers can achieve great success, but they often get sidelined if they don't know the sector's unique protocols, clinical requirements, financial dynamics, and operating procedures. Even seasoned veterans sometimes stumble over an unexpected speedbump. *Thriving in the Healthcare Market: Strategies from an Industry-Insider for Selling Your Product* provides specific and actionable insights into problems faced by those offering products and services to the healthcare world.

Why This Book?

I've always been a "bridging" person, able to understand where different people are coming from and communicating the needs of one sector to others. *Thriving in the Healthcare Market: Strategies from an Industry-Insider for Selling Your Product* draws on my 35 years of experience working within the hospital industry. Most of my activities have been in "mainstream" executive leadership, but I have always had a special appreciation for technology as a possible source of new ideas to breathe innovation into some of the traditional ways we do business. Over the years, I have been instrumental in helping open doors for numerous healthtech initiatives. This book taps into my love for bridging the gap between healthcare executives and the technology world.

Thriving in the Healthcare Market: Strategies from an Industry-Insider for Selling Your Product presents 84 pitfalls I've personally observed and, in some cases, personally fallen victim to. These are not theoretical problems. Every one of them has bitten more than one entrepreneur, and my objective in this book is to point them out to help you minimize their impact or, even better, avoid them entirely whenever possible.

The Sources

This book blends three experience streams:

1. My 35 Years as a Healthcare Executive

Right out of graduate school, I did a two-year administrative fellowship at Michigan Medicine: University of Michigan where I spent one year working for the medical center CEO and the second year assisting the medical school dean. This was followed by four years in the planning department of an acute care hospital in the Midwest. Those six years gave me a deep understanding of the inner workings of large healthcare organizations and physician groups and provided several anecdotes that made their ways into this book. For the next five years, I worked at a regional hospital association in western Michigan focusing largely on data projects and the relationship between the business community and hospitals.

In 1995, I moved to Atlanta to become Executive Vice President at Georgia Hospital Association (GHA) where I led the following areas for the next 19+ years:

■ Finance
■ Data
■ IT
■ mHealth
■ Public relations
■ Communications
■ Entrepreneurial ventures
■ Vendor endorsements

The mainstream focus of my job was policy, finance, data, and communications, but a small part of my efforts at both GHA and the hospital association in Michigan involved evaluating and working with companies that wanted to become endorsed vendor partners. This interaction brought me face-to-face with hundreds of organizations where I observed what some of them did really well and where others were lacking.

Additionally, over my career at the two hospital associations, I established a number of successful entrepreneurial programs. I personally developed 100% of two data programs in the Midwest, taking them from identifying the opportunity to:

■ Fleshing out the concept
■ Aligning the resources
■ Designing the offerings
■ Determining the pricing

- Developing the marketing strategy
- Selling the products
- Actually operating the programs
- Helping users receive maximum value from the reports

At GHA, I also led teams that designed major offerings around:

- Health Insurance Portability and Accountability Act (HIPAA) legal compliance
- Helping hospitals assess, within the limits of antitrust regulations, the levels of their payments from managed care plans by specific product lines in light of what others in the market were being paid
- Completely reformulating our statewide discharge data program by bringing it in-house instead of continuing to outsource it
- Y2K preparation through a nationwide, technology-delivered educational series that was endorsed by the American Hospital Association and 41 state hospital associations

Each of these was a big success both in terms of addressing member hospital needs and generating additional revenue for GHA. Lest I create the impression that we did everything right, though, I must tell you that we attempted a few other products that didn't make it.

The reason I mention these entrepreneurial ventures is to let you know I thoroughly understand how complex it is to take a product from concept to success. And I also know the exhilaration of success and the heartbreak of seeing something wither away. Sometimes the most important lessons come through failure.

So, all these efforts have informed my understanding of how to succeed in selling into the healthcare marketplace.

2. My Experience as a Consultant

Through my company Pearson Health Tech Insights, LLC, I help entrepreneurs and others entering the healthcare market create their strategies for product development, pricing approaches, communications strategies, message formulation, and navigation through health system politics. When I first began my consulting business, I decided to write down the pitfalls I had seen plague vendors throughout my career. That first list consisted of 14 items, and as I worked with my clients over the years and heard their tales of woe, I both recalled other pitfalls I hadn't previously written down and learned about some new ones my clients faced. The list now contains 84 pitfalls, all of which are addressed in this book.

3. Supplemental Insights from Leading Healthcare Experts

One of the blessings of having a long career is knowing hundreds of wonderful, talented healthcare people all over the country. As I was getting close to bringing this book in for a landing, I reached out to many colleagues in various subsections of the healthcare world asking them to provide a "reality check" for my observations and recommendations. They generously offered their time, and their input both validated my conclusions and offered truly helpful supplemental thoughts, examples, and anecdotes that really help bring life to many of the principles in the book. These ideas have translated some of the pitfalls from theoretical possibilities to 3D examples of what can go wrong, adding a tremendously helpful "edge" to the book.

Among my reviewers are healthcare CEOs, CFOs, COOs, CIOs, physicians, an innovation center director and his staff, a healthcare think tank leader, hospital association executives, healthcare consultants, an insurance benefits consultant, graduate school professors, and healthcare sales executives. Having this diverse group weigh in provides additional assurance that these are reality-tested recommendations. I'm thankful for my reviewers.

Who This Book Is For

Although this material emphasizes healthtech, it's really applicable for anyone who interacts professionally with the healthcare world. This group includes:

- Technology innovators and entrepreneurs
- Companies in verticals other than healthcare with viable tech products that can be adapted to healthcare applications
- International healthtech companies that would like to bring their products to the US market
- Established companies (sales or otherwise) already operating in the healthcare world
- Healthtech incubators and accelerators
- Investors either:
  - Considering supporting new healthtech product so they know what questions to ask to make sure end users will really buy the products they are considering funding, or
  - Looking to improve the performances of companies in which they have already invested
- Employees within healthcare organizations who understand the transformational potential of technology and who could benefit from strategic advice on how to get others within their organizations onboard
- Students and anyone else entering one of the healthcare delivery professions as executives, physicians, nurses, therapists, etc.

Although the recommendations in this book are addressed to the first four categories, the insights gained are applicable to all eight groups.

How the Book Is Organized

The bulk of the book describes 84 things I've personally seen go wrong for people interacting with the healthcare universe. However, in order to provide context for these pitfalls, I inserted four preliminary chapters that provide insights into the healthcare field's unique operating environment, which is sometimes dysfunctional. Some of what we do either doesn't make sense or is sub-optimal. But I believe that rational people respond rationally to the settings in which they operate, even if they are not rational. So, there are reasons – many of them even good – for why we do some of the surprising things we do. Chapters 1 and 2 delve into a few of the more pressing problems.

But rather than just complain with no ideas for improvement, I want to present some common-sense suggestions based on my decades of observing and being part of the system. I've always said if you want to change the outcomes, change the inputs and incentives you offer. Chapter 3 describes three ideas that could fundamentally solve some of the most vexing problems in our healthcare system.

Since one of this book's primary targets is the healthtech sector, I devoted Chapter 4 to describing and analyzing the many promising possibilities technology offers. So much of what we do in healthcare amounts to rearranging the chaos, but healthtech affords the opportunity to truly improve patient care, increase efficiency, and maximize cost-effectiveness. So, this chapter points toward a future made brighter because of the efforts of people – like many of my readers – devoting themselves to using technology to bring about clinical and operational breakthroughs.

Reading Plan

There are several ways you can read this book. Of course, every author thinks every single word he writes is worth reading. So, one way to read this book is from cover to cover. This may not be reasonable for leaders with jam-packed schedules, so you might try one of these approaches instead:

■ Regardless of how much time you have, everyone should read Chapter 1 – "The Jacked-Up World of Healthcare Financing." Finances drive everything in every industry, and this chapter is a "must" if you want to understand the world you are relating to.

■ Read the key pitfalls chapters next – The three areas with the greatest potential for scuttling any change initiative are financial (who stands to gain or lose financially), relational (how the change personally affects the people involved), and operational (what systems or ways of doing things must change). Therefore, if you are tight on time, I suggest you start with the following chapters:
  – Chapter 12 – "Return on Investment Pitfalls"
  – Chapter 13 – "Other Financial Pitfalls"
  – Chapter 16 – "Internal Political Pitfalls"
  – Chapter 17 – "Organizational/Operational Pitfalls"

■ Alternatively, you can start with the "Top 10" pitfalls – As I indicated, I've identified 84 different things that can derail a new initiative. Sometimes, all it takes is one, and it can be any one of the 84. So, they're all important. However, there are some that are far more common or serious than others. As you read through the book, you will notice the following icon: ⇛ Top 10. This icon identifies that pitfall is one of the Top 10. If you want to dive into the greatest threats first, start with the ten pitfalls I consider having the highest likelihood of creating problems for you:

⇛ Top 10 *28. Introducing System Security and/or Privacy Vulnerabilities*

⇛ Top 10 *33. Not Being Able to "Break Through the Clutter" and Even Get a Hearing*

⇛
Top 10 *45. Thinking a Healthcare Organization Will Embrace Your Product or Service Even If You Don't Have a Clear, Demonstrable ROI*

⇛
Top 10 *46. ROI Fallacy 1 - Not Realizing How Difficult It Is to Actually Capture Potential Savings*

⇛
Top 10 *54. Not Fully Understanding Overall Financial Incentives*

⇛
Top 10 *55. Not Appreciating the Misaligned Financial Incentives between the Environment Asking for Greater Care Coordination Utilizing the Lowest Acuity Interventions Possible and Most Payers Reimbursing on a Fee-for-Service Basis*

⇛
Top 10 *68. Playing into Professional Rivalries*

⇛
Top 10 *69. Threatening Someone's Job or Stature within the Organization*

⇛
Top 10 *76. Not Recognizing the High Threshold Required for Decisions and Action due to Organizational Complexities*

⇛
Top 10 *77. Underestimating the Complexity of Streamlining a Process or Changing Procedures, Especially If It Creates Additional Workload Requirements for Some Departments or Individuals*

A Disclaimer

I believe one of this book's strengths is its extensive inclusion of real-life examples drawn from my experience in the hospital industry and with my clients. Some of these examples are positive, and others, not so much. Whenever authors include real-life examples, they run the risk of embarrassing some of their subjects. In order to avoid this, I am following the standard practice of announcing that I have changed – sometimes substantially – the details of many of my stories to protect the privacy of those involved.

A Final Thought on My Perspective

Although I am an industry-insider, I am not a blind cheerleader for hospitals or the rest of the healthcare delivery system. I know the flat spots as well as the next person. However, I have a deep appreciation for the dedication of the thousands of fine people working in this field, and my complaints are probably more akin to a family quarrel than to someone lobbing grenades from the sidelines. I try to be honest but kind in my comments, and I have done my best to avoid joining the "blame game," pitting different parts of the industry – hospitals, physicians, insurance companies, etc. – against each other. I also avoid making overtly political statements. The purpose of this book is to equip you to maximize your interactions with the healthcare system, not raise a clenched fist over everything that is wrong with it.

May this book assist you as you devote yourself to helping the healthcare delivery world more effectively serve its patients and do their best to restore them to full health.

Chapter 1

The Jacked-Up World
of Healthcare Financing

Every industry has its quirks. Healthcare may be among the
quirkiest. And perhaps the most complicated. Far from being
a fairly cohesive industry like retail sales or manufacturing, the
healthcare world is made up of overlapping types of service
providers, occasionally coordinated but usually not. The two
most influential groups are physicians and hospitals.

Physicians

Physicians provide the backbone of medical care and are the
primary drivers of the diagnostic and caregiving decisions and
processes. Although healthcare information and/or interventions
for less serious conditions are available through public health
centers, pharmacies, nurse helplines, and other places, physicians
determine the treatment path for the most serious medical issues.
They're the only ones who can admit a patient to the hospital and
approve their discharge, they determine the care decisions during
an inpatient stay, and they set the course for post-discharge care.
Nothing happens unless a physician writes an order.

About one-third of the nearly 625,000 US physicians who spend the majority of their time in direct patient care are primary care doctors: family physicians, general practitioners, internists, pediatricians, obstetricians/gynecologists, and geriatricians. The rest are specialists and sub-specialists. Primary care physicians generate 51.8% of all office visits.[1] The fact that this one-third of the physicians is responsible for half the visits makes sense. Many office visits are for relatively less severe conditions and are appropriately treated by primary care doctors.

Historically, most physicians worked either alone or in relatively small group practices. Over the last few decades, though, more and more individual doctors and groups have joined together to form larger entities, or they have been acquired by hospitals. The days of the small-town family doctor in solo practice are quickly fading.

Hospitals

Hospitals are the other major factor in the healthcare ecosystem. According to the American Hospital Association, there were 6,210 hospitals in the United States in 2017.[2] Hospitals are either not-for-profit, governmental entities, or investor-owned. Most are general "community" hospitals while others are considered Academic Medical Centers (AMCs), which combine patient care services, medical education, and academic research. Other hospitals focus on care for selected groups like children or for specific clinical areas like cancer care, behavioral health, or rehabilitation services. In the late 1990s, the federal government established a new category of small, rural hospitals designated as Critical Access Hospitals (CAHs), which are limited-service institutions with 25 or fewer beds. Because of the vital roles they play in their communities, they benefit from slightly enhanced payment terms to help keep them solvent.

People unfamiliar with the inner workings of a hospital can underestimate their complexity. None other than management expert Peter Drucker has called hospitals "the most complex human organization ever devised."[3]

Perhaps hospitals' most significant oddity is the fact that historically the people who run the enterprise rarely control what happens within the organization. Typically, a company's top executive has great authority to control the transactions that affect its core business. Although hospital leaders can set policies that influence doctors' decisions in a general way, the final determination about each individual patient rests solely with the physicians. They decide who will be admitted. They decide what tests and procedures will be done. They decide when a patient can be discharged. Every one of these choices carries operational and financial implications for the hospital, and they are made by people who are not always employed by the organization.

Some analysts have likened a hospital to an airport. Airports exist because planes need a place from which to operate and because passengers need a place to connect with the airlines. Each airline is an independent organization that contracts with the airport for various services. Although the airport sets certain broad policies, it doesn't control the airlines' specific internal operations or activities. Each airline company sets its own human resources rules, work require-ments, investment strategies, etc. All this is very parallel to the traditional relationship between hospitals and physicians. The hospital "sets the table," but the physician provides the meal.

However, this semi-independent relationship is beginning to change. In recent years, insurance companies – including the governmental Medicare and Medicaid programs – have encouraged greater coordination among hospitals, physicians, rehab facilities, and other providers. Rather than paying each provider separately and for each individual service they deliver to a patient, they are moving toward a more coordinated sin-gle payment where the provider organizations assume increas-ing financial risk. These new financial incentives foster more resource alignment.

One way this happens is through a single bundled payment to an entity such as an Accountable Care Organization (ACO) that assumes clinical and financial responsibility for a patient's episode of care. The ACO either owns the necessary resources or contracts with others to access them. A related concept is value-based payment where patients are encouraged to use services that can demonstrate superior and cost-efficient care. The best way to achieve these goals is through greater coordination among all the organizations providing care. And many hospitals have concluded that the best way to manage care is through owning the "assets," in this case physician practices. As a result, many hospitals have purchased practices or have developed stronger contractual relationships with them.

Although this movement toward bundled payments or value-based care has been growing, the vast majority of healthcare is still paid on a piecemeal, fee-for-service basis where every time a physician or hospital provides a service, they get paid for that specific intervention. Typically, procedural-based activities (i.e., "doing something" for a patient like replacing a hip) are more lucrative that the medically based ones (such as hospitalizing a patient while they recover from pneumonia). A 2018 survey of health system executives reveals that 78% of care is still covered under a fee-for-service arrangement. However, the remaining 22% that is paid under some kind of value-based care arrangement is growing and is expected to rise to 25% in 2019.[4]

The Three-Legged Stool

One of the keys to understanding the operating dynamics within the healthcare industry is recognizing that it is like a three-legged stool where all three legs are equally important and must be kept in balance. The three legs of the healthcare delivery stool are access (both geographic and financial), quality, and cost. It's easy to get two of these right but very tough to keep all three in perfect balance.

- A given region may generally offer high-quality, affordable care for most things but may have an undersupply of certain medical specialists or other services. This can be especially problematic in rural or impoverished areas.
- Affordable care may be within a patient's reach, but if it's of poor quality, people will avoid it unless they have no other choice.
- Patients may have physical access to great quality care but if they can't afford it – either because they don't have insurance coverage or because they can't pay for it out of their own pockets – it does them no good. Also, a healthcare industry whose costs continue to spiral out of control is unsustainable in the long run.

So, this is the challenge to the healthcare field: figuring out a way to keep these three needs in equilibrium.

Now let's take a more detailed look at the inner workings of healthcare financing.

How Healthcare Is Paid For

Because of the extensive debate leading up to passage of the Affordable Care Act of 2010 (ACA – also known as Obamacare), most Americans realize that we are about the only major "first world" nation that does not provide universal healthcare coverage for our citizens. Many countries offer a single-payer system where the government operates a publicly funded insurance plan. In some cases they also own the hospitals and employee all personnel.

By contrast, the United States has a patchwork of public and private insurance programs. Figure 1.1 shows the percentage of the US population covered under various insurance arrangements as reported by the Kaiser Family Foundation.[5]

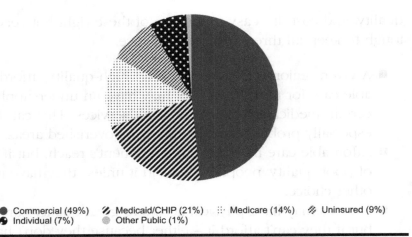

Commercial (49%)   Medicaid/CHIP (21%)   Medicare (14%)   Uninsured (9%)
Individual (7%)   Other Public (1%)

Figure 1.1   Health Insurance Coverage of the US Total Population – 2017.

Source: Kaiser Family Foundation

Forty-nine percent of the population is enrolled in private commercial insurance programs. The public programs cover 36% of the total, broken down as follows:

- Medicaid (the program for low-income individuals)/ Children's Health Insurance Program (the program for low-income children) – collectively 21%
- Medicare (the program for the elderly) – 14%
- Other public programs – 1%

Let's look at how well the major public programs (Medicaid and Medicare) cover the cost of care for their enrollees. Before we do so, however, I would like to comment on the different ways healthcare population, utilization, and economic statistics are presented. Readers are often confused when they see various statistics, studies, articles, or news stories that show conflicting numbers.

First of all, each type of insurance program's percentage of the market varies depending on what data is being reported:

- Percentage of the *population* enrolled in each type of coverage – This is what is presented in Figure 1.1.

- Percentage of *hospital admissions* – Since Medicare patients are almost exclusively elderly and older people are admitted more frequently, they tend to account for a far greater percentage of hospital admissions than their proportional representation in the population.
- Percentage of *days patient spend in the hospital* – Similarly, Medicare patients represent a greater proportion of hospital days than their percentage of the population, both because they tend to be admitted more frequently and because they also tend to stay longer than younger patients.
- Percentage of *revenue* – Again, Medicare tends to be over-represented for the reasons stated above. As an example, in the state of Georgia, Medicare patients were only 12% of the 2016 state's population but represented 42% of 2016 hospital revenue. Conversely, during that same year, those with no insurance made up 12% of the state's population but only contributed 3% of total hospital revenue.[6] This also makes sense because, by definition, they have no insurance, and many of them are unable to pay their bills.

Just as it's important to clarify which statistic – population coverage, admissions, patient days, or revenue – is being reported, we should also clearly define various aspects of hospital financial condition and performance. There are several different measures, and results range wildly, depending on which number is being reported:

- Total margin – This represents excess of revenue over expenses (or profits) for the entire corporate entity. Included here are margins from:
  - Inpatient care
  - Outpatient care
  - Owned nursing homes
  - Other medical services – durable medical equipment, home health services, retail pharmacies, and all other related clinical services

- Other non-clinical offerings – real estate, gift shops, parking, and any other type of business
- Investment income
- Any other sources

Within any given year, some of these are profitable while others may lose money. The total margin rolls all these together to show a single bottom line income.

■ Patient care margin – This reports only the profits from direct patient care.

■ Inpatient margin – As the name implies, this reflects only activities for inpatient services. Over the last few decades, more and more care is being shifted to outpatient settings, so although it's still central to a hospital's financial results, this number is becoming slightly less relevant than it was in the past. In fact, a recent *Modern Healthcare* article reports that hospital revenue from outpatient care is catching up to revenue from inpatient care and may soon surpass it. In 2017, outpatient services accounted for 48.7% of all patient care revenue.[7] Just reporting margin from inpatient activity only tells part of the story and leaves off the increasingly important outpatient activity and all the other services included under total margin.

■ Margins from individual sources of payment:
  - Medicare – This can be further confused by which Medicare services are being reported: *all* Medicare services or just inpatient, just outpatient, just other service areas, or some combination of all the above. Results obviously differ depending on what is being measured.
  - Medicaid – This number can be tricky too. In addition to the issues of whether just inpatient or if both inpatient and outpatient results are included, some reports fold in activity related to the Children's Health Insurance Program (CHIP). Furthermore, there are

some supplemental payment programs such as the Disproportionate Share Hospital Program (DSH) that pay hospitals beyond the direct Medicaid payments. DSH and other supplemental payment figures are sometimes rolled into Medicaid numbers, raising the reported Medicaid margin.
- Other government sources such as the Veteran's Administration or the Tri-Care program for military families.
- Private insurance including Anthem, UnitedHealthcare, Aetna, and dozens of others.

So, it's important to read reports very carefully to understand exactly which set of statistics they are using. Depending on the data source, different sectors of the healthcare world can appear to either be ready to crash and burn or be doing fairly well.

Now, let's look at the economic realities of the various payer categories.

Medicaid

The Medicaid program covers certain children, pregnant woman, senior adults, and people with disabilities who are designated as low-income. Medicaid is jointly funded by the federal government and individual state governments. The national Centers for Medicare and Medicaid Services (CMS) sets certain broad national coverage requirements, and then each state can set up its own program that meets the necessary coverage, adding additional services if they wish.

Through a provision called the Federal Medical Assistance Percentage (FMAP), the federal government matches at least one-for-one each dollar a state spends on Medicaid. This is the minimum match, and, depending on the services provided and the populations served, the FMAP can be considerably higher.

One of the provisions of the ACA was a guarantee that, for the first few years, the federal government would pay 100% of the costs of Medicaid recipients *newly enrolled* through the expansion of the state's Medicaid program. (Already-enrolled patients remained under that state's original FMAP formula.) After the first few years of Medicaid expansion under the ACA, the federal ACA match started phasing down and will stabilize at 90% in 2020 and thereafter.[8] Since Medicaid expansion was deemed optional by the Supreme Court, several states declined, stating they were concerned about their long-term ability to match the 10% requirement once the 100% federal coverage wound down. Some critics of this position likened it to refusing to let someone buy you dinner if you have to pick up the tip.

A program that is related to Medicaid is the Children's Health Insurance Plan (CHIP), which expands coverage to additional children from low-income families. As shown in Figure 1.1, Medicaid and CHIP cover 14% of the nation's population.[9]

Unfortunately, Medicaid rarely covers the full cost of care. According to the American Hospital Association, hospitals in 2017 received on average only 87% of what they actually spent – not what they charged or what they wanted to get, but what they actually spent – caring for Medicaid patients. Although some hospitals did have their costs covered or even earned a profit from Medicaid, 62% lost money.[10]

This Medicaid net loss situation has not always been the case. Between 1990 and 1997, every state Medicaid program was obligated to operate under a congressionally mandated policy called the Boren Amendment, named after the Oklahoma senator who sponsored it. Essentially, the Boren Amendment required each state's Medicaid program to, in the aggregate, pay the cost incurred in caring for Medicaid patients by "efficient and economically operated facilities."[11] This didn't guarantee that every hospital and nursing home would break even, but the concept was that if you added up the amount every Medicaid provider in the state spent caring for Medicaid patients, it would equal the total amount Medicaid paid them.

From a budgetary standpoint, Medicaid is often seen as a bottomless pit. It is a huge line item in both the federal budget and every state's budget. And since healthcare inflation has exceeded the general inflation rate for many years, elected officials are alarmed about the long-term implications of this trend. They are always on the lookout for ways to rein in what some see as out-of-control spending.

In 1997, Congress passed a sweeping piece of legislation called the Balanced Budget Act (BBA) which had a huge impact on the way healthcare was paid for. One of its provisions was repealing the Boren Amendment, thus removing the require-ment that each state's Medicaid program fully covers its costs.

I was Executive Vice President at Georgia Hospital Association (GHA) during the time the BBA was being debated. I remember commenting to some of my colleagues that if we lost the Boren Amendment, that could spell the beginning of the end for hospitals' long-term financial viability. We did lose it, and my observation may have been prophetic. As we have seen, rather than paying 100% of costs, Medicaid now only pays 87%. And these shortfalls have proven to be a significant drag on hospital finances.

While at GHA, I often spoke to various community and civic groups on the status of the state's healthcare industry. Like any speaker, I try to think of ways to help my audiences emotionally relate to my points, and I came up with this scenario that explains what hospitals are up against when it comes to Medicaid payments.

"Suppose," I would say, "you are the owner of a road con-struction company, and the State of Georgia and the federal government come to you and explain that Interstate 75, which runs north-to-south through the state, needs to be repaved. Since yours is a Georgia-based company, they would like you to take this on. In fact, since you are based in the state, they decided you are *required* to do so. *And*, the government will even pay you 87% of what you spend to complete the job. How many of you would jump at this opportunity?"

Of course, no fiscally responsible person would do cart-wheels over these terms. Yet, this scenario pretty closely approximates hospitals' deal with Medicaid. And since Medicaid represents a significant proportion of each state's population, the underpayments add considerable financial stress.

As a reminder, Figure 1.1 shows that 14% of the population nationally is covered under Medicaid. However, this level can be much higher. In fact, fully 31% of New Mexico's population is covered by Medicaid.[12] And if the statewide *average* in New Mexico is 31%, there are undoubtedly some hospitals that approach the mid-30% level or even higher. Obviously, with a shortfall for every Medicaid patient on average, the higher the Medicaid volume, the greater the financial burden. Greater-than-average Medicaid volumes are typical for inner city and rural facilities, and as we will see below, these hospitals are under enormous financial stress.

Hospitals in Georgia also face a quirky payment system for outpatient Medicaid care that *guarantees* they will lose money. In the early 2000s, because of funding challenges and as a result of a budget cut, the state enacted a policy that limited hospital outpatient payments to 85.6% of costs.

Under this policy, the Georgia Department of Community Health (DCH) took its historical data on the level of payments for outpatient care each hospital typically got and paid an estimated amount to each hospital via installments throughout the year. At the end of the year, the hospital submitted documentation on how much it actually spent caring for Medicaid outpatients. DCH then calculated 85.6% of that amount. If there was a shortfall in what the hospital should have been paid, Medicaid cut a check to make up the difference. If the hospital received more than 85.6%, the check went the other way. For the record, the cost coverage amount was raised to 95.7% in 2010, but the principal remains the same. Hospitals are guaranteed to lose money.

Think about that. There is absolutely no way under this policy that the hospital can ever cover its Medicaid outpatient costs. Many of the payment programs enacted by various insurance programs (like Medicare, Blue Cross, and other payers) have the stated objective of encouraging more efficient care delivery. That's impossible with this 85.6% (now 95.7%) payment policy. If a Georgia hospital really streamlines its operations and cuts its Medicaid outpatient costs by 10%, guess what? Its payment also goes down 10%. No matter how efficient it becomes it will *always* lose money taking care of Medicaid outpatients. How messed up is that?

On the Medicaid physician side, according to a Forbes article entitled "Why Many Physicians Are Reluctant to See Medicaid Patients," physicians are paid, on average, 61% of the *Medicare* physician payment levels,[13] which, as we will see, is not all that great. Since physicians are not required to take Medicaid patients, many opt out. And, because payments are so low, even those who do take Medicaid sometimes limit how many they accept. Patients often report major access issues, especially when trying to locate super-specialists like pediatric surgeons.

Medicare

Medicare's payments are generally considered better than are Medicaid's, but many – if not most – hospitals still lose money caring for Medicare patients. The Medicare Payment Advisory Commission (MedPAC) reports that 2017 overall Medicare margin slipped to −9.9% down 0.2% from the previous year.[14] Put another way, Medicare is only paying 90% of the total cost of care. This would be like going into a car dealership with documentation of what the dealer actually paid for the car you ordered, and writing a check for 90% of that amount.

Unfortunately, Medicare losses have been growing and are projected to continue to rise. A recent MedPAC action testifies to the inadequacy of current Medicare payments. As it was considering its Fiscal Year 2020 hospital payment adjustment, the organization took the unusual step of recommending a boost larger than the current policies require. That's because it was concerned that even high-quality hospitals were losing money. MedPAC Executive Director Jim Matthews stated, "When a hospital or provider is being efficient and still can't stay in the black in Medicare, that is cause for concern."[15]

But hospitals' financial wellbeing at the hands of the federal government gets even worse. Recent years have seen several additional cost-cutting initiatives that continue to chip away at hospital payments. Besides inadequate Medicare and Medicaid payments, hospitals face cuts from the following multi-year legislative or regulatory items:

■ Patient Protection and Affordable Care Act of 2010
■ Budget Control Act of 2011
■ Middle Class Tax Relief and Job Creation Act of 2012
■ American Taxpayer Relief Act of 2012
■ Bipartisan Budget Act of 2013
■ Protecting Access to Medicare Act of 2014
■ Veterans COLA – 2014
■ Medicare and CHIP Reauthorization Act of 2015
■ Bipartisan Budget Agreement Act of 2015
■ Bipartisan Budget Act of 2018
■ Various CMS Regulatory Changes[16]

Each of them removes funding, and collectively they will reduce hospital payments by billions and billions of dollars between now and 2026.[17]

Let's turn now to Medicare physician payments. Just how well are doctors paid? The answer varies, depending on which specialty you are considering. In general, all payers – including Medicare – tend to pay specialists like cardiologists, oncologists, etc. better than they do primary care physicians, like family physicians and internal medicine physicians.

The following is an anecdote, and policy should be driven by data and not anecdotes. However, this story typifies how many physicians feel about Medicare payment levels. My primary care physician of about 15 years is a family practitioner. We developed a good rapport, and because he knows I work in healthcare, we often have fairly extensive conversations about the state of the industry.

About ten years ago, he told me about an analysis his practice conducted. They used national average statistics regarding physician productivity, primary care cost structure, and Medicare payments and estimated per physician take-home pay assuming their physicians:

▪ Saw the average number of patients a family practitioner sees a day,
▪ Had the same cost structure as the average family medicine practice, and
▪ Were paid only the amount that Medicare pays per visit

I thought that was an interesting and relevant question, and I was surprised to hear their analysis estimated a physician's take-home pay under those assumptions at only about $40,000 per year. That's pretty shocking when you consider the many years of advanced training physicians have, the huge debt loads many carry, and the amount of liability they assume in caring for patients. Accounting for inflation, that take-home number would probably be closer to $55,000 in today's dollars, but that's still terrible. Is it any wonder physicians have mixed feelings about Medicare payments?

According to the Forbes article cited above, *Medicaid* physician payments are only 61% of *Medicare* physician payments.[18] If we apply this statistic to the take-home numbers calculated by my primary care physician's office ($55,000), this translates to something like $33,000 per year if they treated only Medicaid patients and were only paid the Medicaid rates. Clearly, no one would spend all those years necessary to become a physician with this type of financial return.

The Uninsured

In the early 2000s, one of the factors that convinced the public that we needed healthcare reform was alarm over the growing percentage of the population under 65 without healthcare insurance. That momentum ultimately culminated in passage of the ACA in 2010. The number of uninsured kept creeping up through the early 2000s and reached its peak of 17.8% in 2010, the year the ACA passed. It declined over the next few years and stood at 10.2% in 2017.[19] Despite a marked improvement, 10% of non-elderly population without health insurance – 27.4 million people – is still high. So, even though the ACA made a big dent in the number of uninsured, it only achieved a 43% reduction in the number of people who lacked coverage.

Most people without insurance have limited financial resources, and many have major challenges paying large medical bills. Statistics are difficult to access, but many hospital financial experts estimate that the percentage of payment they receive from the uninsured is roughly 25% of actual cost. If this number is accurate, it means that hospitals must absorb about 75% of what they spend caring for the uninsured.

The Need to Shift Costs

The above discussion describes the incredibly challenging financial climate hospitals and physicians operate in. Often, the economic numbers from the major public programs – Medicaid and Medicare – and from the uninsured are presented in isolation from each other. Some news stories discuss financial stress the uninsured place on hospitals. Others present some of the difficulties created by Medicaid payment shortfalls. But what happens when we try to get our arms around the full range of the underpayment situation?

Let's use the American Hospital Association number – 87% – for Medicaid's cost coverage. And let's assume the *Medicare*

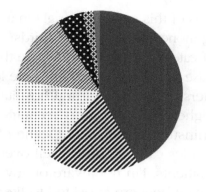

● Medicare (40.9%) ▨ Medicaid (17.2%) ⣿ Private Pay (16.5%) ▨ HMO/PPO (14.0%)
◓ Self Pay (4.9%) ❁ Workers Comp (2.0%) ● Other (1.2%)

Figure 1.2 US Hospital Discharges by Payer – 2009.

Source: Becker's Hospital CFO Report/National Hospital Discharge Survey

cost coverage is about 90%, as reported by MedPAC. Just how big a problem does this create?

As we have said, the percentage of discharges each hospital gets from each payer type varies considerably depending on its location, services offered, number and type of physicians, and many other factors. Figure 1.2 shows the 2018 *national* distribution of hospital discharges by source of payment.[20]

It shows that 40.9% of patients were covered by Medicare and 17.2% were covered by Medicaid. An additional 4.9% had no coverage.

The table below summarizes the combination of the percentages of patients covered by each source and the shortfalls from each:

Payment Source	Percentage of Discharges (%)	Percentage Loss (%)
Medicaid	17.2	13
Medicare	40.9	10
No insurance	4.9	75

The implications of this are staggering! On average, hospitals are literally losing money on nearly two-thirds - 63% – of all their patients. The best category is Medicare where they are "only" losing 10%. In the case of the uninsured, they are losing about 75%.

To make matters worse, many rural hospitals and inner-city hospitals have higher-than-average percentages of Medicare, Medicaid, and uninsured patients. For some of those hospitals, these three categories can add up to well over two-thirds or more of their inpatients. I'm not aware of any other industry sector where its members are expected to literally lose money providing services to such a huge part of their client base. Over the long haul, there are only two possible outcomes of this type of financial arrangement. Hospitals can either:

1. Go out of business, or
2. Get someone else to make up the difference

Many have succumbed to option 1, and option 2 has resulted in something called cost shifting. This is where commercially covered patients end up paying considerably more – estimated by some at about 30% – than would otherwise be necessary in order to make up the shortfall from the public programs and people without insurance. Cost shifting amounts to a hidden tax on patients with commercial insurance and/or the companies that buy this insurance for their employees.

There is another dimension of cost shifting: using profits from certain profitable service areas within the hospital to cross-subsidize other ones that lose money. Historically, areas like behavioral health, patient education, and post-acute care have been financial drains on the income statement. The way hospitals have been able to continue offering them is through subsidizing them with profits from other areas like neurosurgery and interventional cardiology. However, the growing financial pressures have forced some hospitals to curtail these needed but unprofitable services to the detriment of the communities they serve.[21]

The Impact of These Dynamics on Hospitals

These Medicare and Medicaid shortfalls have put great financial pressure on the delivery system with sometimes devastating results. Many hospitals have been forced to close over the last two decades, and many others have been severely weakened by many consecutive years of financial loss. Recently, respected healthcare consultant Paul Keckley commented, "About 18% of the hospitals in the country are at or near insolvency."[22]

Rural and inner-city hospitals have been particularly hard-hit. The University of North Carolina's Cecil G. Sheps Center for Health Services Research reports that since 2010, 102 rural hospitals have closed.[23]

The February 25, 2019 edition of *Modern Healthcare* ran a story entitled, "Fewer independent hospitals can weather operating headwinds." Here's an excerpt:

> More than half the nation's stand-alone hospitals (53.2%) have lost money on an operating basis for each of the past five years, which is more than twice the share of system-owned hospitals (25.9%)... Rural stand-alone hospitals are most at risk, with 60.5% having lost money on an operating basis in each of the past five years, compared with 42% of their urban counterparts.[24]

Just five days earlier, *Becker's Hospital CFO Report* highlighted a Navigant study that predicted that 21% of the nation's rural hospitals are at risk of closure, and 64% of those hospitals are considered essential to their communities.[25] Losing them would wreak havoc downstream.

Some people who think we probably have too many hospital beds might not see these hospital closures as all bad. In their minds, reducing the supply could lower overall healthcare expenditures. The problem with this view is that closures are not planned out rationally. Instead they are haphazard, and losing too many hospitals in the same geographical area can create real access problems, thereby throwing the three-legged stool off kilter.

Furthermore, hospitals are usually the largest employer in small towns, and losing one often takes the whole community down. *Huffington Post* recently ran an extended story called, "A Hospital Crisis Is Killing Rural Communities. This State Is Ground Zero" that highlights the wreckage left in the wake of the shuttering of three Georgia rural hospitals. After its hospital closed in 2014, the town of Glenwood, Georgia was decimated financially. The town's mayor told *Huffington Post*, "I tell folks that move here, 'This is a beautiful place to live, but you better have brought money, because you can't make any here.'"[26]

There is little doubt that the long-term impact of serious underpayments to hospitals year after year stresses the provider system, results in unnecessarily inflated premiums for commercially insured patients, and can have a strongly negative trickle-down impact on some of the communities whose hospitals disappear.

Earlier, I stated that various reports on hospitals' financial state are all over the place. The February 25, 2019 *Modern Healthcare* article mentioned above that indicates how many hospitals have lost money year after year and the Becker's story predicting one in five rural hospitals closing seems at odds with statistics from other sources. For example, data from Modern Healthcare Metrics reports that total hospital margin nationally in 2017 was 3.83%.[27] That doesn't seem too bad. Most organizations can do just fine with that type of profit. But remember that this is an *average* number. There is tremendous variation among the results of the country's 6,210 hospitals. As we saw, even though many have positive margins, many others operate in the red. In some cases, for many years.

My intention in this book is to remain as politically neutral as possible, but I feel compelled to point out the following. The healthcare reform debate regularly includes various versions of a single-payer system. The latest incarnation is Medicare for All (M4A). The concept behind M4A is that everyone would be covered by a single, federally operated health program, thus essentially eliminating both Medicaid and the private insurance industry. M4A would set payments for *all* patients at the Medicare level,[28] thereby replacing the Medicaid 13% shortfall and the uninsured 75% shortfall with the Medicare shortfall that is "only" 10%. That's better, but it's still a 10% loss. And don't forget these loss numbers are averages. Many hospitals would undoubtedly lose more, sometimes through circumstances beyond their control. M4A would also eliminate the excess of revenue over expenses hospitals currently earn from commercially insured patients that currently keeps many institutions afloat.

Out of fairness, M4A proponents predict cost savings through restructuring administrative processes, allowing hospitals to deal with just one insurance program instead of dozens and dozens. Furthermore, M4A supporters predict the government would be able to negotiate significant savings on pharmaceuticals. These savings could possibly happen, but it would take a lot of streamlining and some powerful negotiations with drug companies to make up for an average 10% loss on every single patient.

There is much to be said for providing care to everyone, but I have to remind you of the troubling past performance of the two existing major public programs – Medicare and Medicaid. I don't believe anyone in either state or federal government is maliciously underfunding these programs. When budgets are developed each year, representatives of the healthcare community remind politicians that the programs aren't carrying their weight financially and urge them to at least bring them up to break-even. In response, the elected officials express sympathy over providers' plight but tell them they just don't have the funds.

What this means is that healthcare payments are no longer policy driven or designed to maximize access, quality, and cost-effectiveness (the three-legged stool). Instead, they have become strictly subject to budgetary forces. Just refer back to my Georgia Medicaid outpatient example explained above where it's impossible for hospitals to not lose money. Everyone knows the policy has to result in a financial loss. As much as the politicians might like to fully cover costs, they just can't. In light of this depressingly consistent history of underfunding of both Medicare and Medicaid year after year, why would we think that payments under M4A would fare any better?

Several analyses of Senator Bernie Sanders' 2016 version of M4A estimate a jaw-dropping price tag. A George Mason University study predicted costs at $32.6 *trillion* over 10 years. This number is in the same ballpark as other analyses' projections. According to *U.S. News and World Report*, even doubling all federal individual and corporate income taxes wouldn't fully fund Sanders' plan. Former Clinton admin- istration senior health policy advisor and Emory University professor Kenneth Thorpe – hardly a right-wing spokesman – said, "Even though people don't pay premiums, tax increases are going to be enormous. There are going to be a lot of people who'll pay more in taxes than they save on premiums."[29] A senior executive at one ambulatory surgery company reports that his organization estimated the implica- tions if they had to operate under M4A. They concluded that 23 of their 24 sites would be bankrupted.[30] And, finally, an analytical piece in the respected publication *HealthLeaders* sports the headline "Medicare for All Could Reduce Hospital Revenues by 16%." This article also references a *JAMA* report that concludes M4A would "do little to encourage hospital efficiency." A parallel analysis by the consulting firm Navigant concludes some hospitals would experience a margin decline of more than 22%.[31]

Given the government's track record, if M4A somehow managed to survive what could be the political fight of the century, how likely is it that the program would fully cover the cost of care in the long run? I shudder to think what would happen if we carried over the current Medicare program's 10% loss to M4A and the "promised" administrative and drug savings didn't materialize.

Did You Notice?

As an interesting side-note, you may have picked up that I have not used the word "reimbursement" anywhere in this chapter. That's because neither hospitals nor physicians are really *reimbursed* for the care they provide. They are *paid*. Reimbursement, by definition, involves someone spending money for a given purpose, submitting documentation for their expenditure, and then receiving the entire amount back. As we have seen, that's not at all the way it works in healthcare. With the public programs like Medicare and Medicaid, the federal or state governments decide the amount they will pay for a given treatment, the provider submits the required documentation, and then the program pays whatever amount they have determined. And the statistics I have presented demonstrate that, most of the time, the payment falls short of what the care actually costs. So, no, these are not reimbursements, they are payments. And they don't adequately cover what it costs to provide the care.

In the same vein, most private insurance companies like Blue Cross, Cigna, Humana, Coventry, and others typically pay set amounts rather than truly reimbursing providers. Fortunately, though, these payments are usually more generous.

Final Thought

This chapter describes the bleak financial climate hospitals and physicians must operate in. If you are selling products or services into the healthcare world, you must be sensitive to the financial challenges it faces. And you must develop your strategies and messaging with this jacked-up world in mind. Providers respect vendors and others who appreciate the difficulties they experience because of environmental factors beyond their control.

End Notes

1. The Agency for Healthcare Research and Quality, "The Number of Practicing Primary Care Physicians in the United States," https://www.ahrq.gov/research/findings/factsheets/primary/pcwork1/index.html, accessed April 1, 2019.
2. American Hospital Association, "Fast Facts on U.S. Hospitals – 2018," https://www.aha.org/statistics/fast-facts-us-hospitals, accessed April 1, 2019.
3. Rick Pollack, "How hospitals are redesigning care delivery to serve changing needs," *Modern Healthcare*, September 26, 2015, https://www.modernhealthcare.com/article/20150926/MAGAZINE/309269977/how-hospitals-are-redesigning-care-delivery-to-serve-changing-needs, accessed March 3, 2019.
4. Kelly Gooch, "Health system executives expect 25% of care delivery payments to be value-based in 2019," *Becker's Hospital CFO Report*, February 21, 2019, https://www.beckershospitalreview.com/finance/health-system-executives-expect-25-of-care-delivery-payments-to-be-value-based-in-2019.html, accessed March 8, 2019.
5. Kaiser Family Foundation, https://www.kff.org/other/state-indicator/total-population/?currentTimeframe=0&sortModel=%7B%22colId%22:%22Location%22,%22sort%22:%22asc%22%7D, accessed March 7, 2019.
6. Georgia Hospital Association, *Hospitals 101*, 8th edition, 2019, page 17, www/gha.org, accessed March 8, 2019.
7. Tara Bannow, "Outpatient revenue catching up to inpatient," *Modern Healthcare*, January 7, 2019, page 6.
8. Laura Snyder and Robin Rudowitz, "Medicaid Financing: How Does it Work and What are the Implications?" https://www.kff.org/medicaid/issue-brief/medicaid-financing-how-does-it-work-and-what-are-the-implications/, accessed March 7, 2019.

9. https://www.kff.org/interactive/medicaid-state-fact-sheets/, accessed March 7, 2019.

10. American Hospital Association, "Underpayment by Medicare and Medicaid Fact Sheet – January 2019," www.aha.org, accessed March 7, 2019.

11. The Urban Institute, "Repeal of the Boren Amendment," https://www.urban.org/research/publication/repeal-boren-amendment, accessed March 7, 2019.

12. Kaiser Family Foundation, https://www.kff.org/other/state-indicator/total-population/?currentTimeframe=0&sortModel=%7B%22colId%22:%22Location%22,%22sort%22:%22asc%22%7D, accessed March 7, 2019.

13. Peter Ubel, "Why Many Physicians Are Reluctant to See Medicaid Patients," November 9, 2013, www.forbes.com, accessed March 7, 2019.

14. Rich Daly, "Hospital Medicare Margins Decline Further," December 10, 2018, https://www.hfma.org/Content.aspx?id=62592, accessed March 20, 2019.

15. "MedPAC wants to boost Medicare acute-care hospital payments 2.8%, *Modern Healthcare*, March 18, 2019, page 2.

16. https://www.gha.org/News/Reference-Guides, accessed March 20, 2019.

17. ibid.

18. Peter Ubel, "Why Many Physicians Are Reluctant to See Medicaid Patients," November 9, 2013, www.forbes.com, accessed March 7, 2019.

19. Kaiser Family Foundation, "Key Facts about the Uninsured Population," December 7, 2018, https://www.kff.org/uninsured/fact-sheet/key-facts-about-the-uninsured-population/, accessed March 9, 2019.

20. Molly Gamble, "America's Payor Mix by Region," *Becker's Hospital CFO Report*, April 9, 2012, https://www.beckershospitalreview.com/finance/americas-payor-mix-by-region.html, accessed August 3, 2019.

21. "Tough Economic Times Motivate Hospitals to Migrate Away from Unprofitable Clinical Service Lines," *the DARK Daily*, March 7, 2012, https://www.darkdaily.com/tough-economic-times-motivate-hospitals-to-migrate-away-from-unprofitable-clinical-service-lines-30712/, accessed March 21, 2019.

22. Alex Kacik, "Financial concerns may lead to high-margin service line imbalance," *Modern Healthcare*, June 3, 2019, p. 17.

23. https://www.shepscenter.unc.edu/programs-projects/rural-health/rural-hospital-closures/, accessed March 20, 2019.
24. Alex Kacik, "Fewer independent hospitals can weather operating headwinds," *Modern Healthcare*, February 25, 2019, page 16.
25. Keely Gooch, "1 in 5 rural hospitals at high risk of closing, analysis finds," *Becker's Hospital CFO Report*, February 20, 2019, https://www.beckershospitalreview.com/finance/1-in-5-rural-hospitals-at-high-risk-of-closing-analysis-finds.html, accessed March 8, 2019.
26. Lauren Weber and Andy Miller, "Hospital Crisis Is Killing Rural Communities. This State is Ground Zero," *Huffington Post*, September 22, 2017 and updated June 4, 2018, https://www.huffpost.com/entry/rural-hospitals-closure-georgia_n_59c02bf4e4b087fdf5075e38, accessed March 20, 2019.
27. Reported in Susannah Luthi, "Grassley back at it, ramping up scrutiny of tax-exempt hospitals," *Modern Healthcare*, March 11, 2019, page 12.
28. Merrill Goozner, "M4A isn't the only way to go," *Modern Healthcare*, March 18, 2019, page 24.
29. Ricardo Alonso-Zaldivar, "Study: 'Medicare for All' Projected to Cost $32.6 Trillion," *U.S. News and World Report*, July 30, 2018, https://www.usnews.com/news/business/articles/2018-07-30/study-medicare-for-all-bill-estimated-at-326-trillion, accessed April 3, 2019.
30. Thomas Mallon, "Cost shifting makes Medicare, Medicaid look good," *Modern Healthcare*, February 18, 2019, page 28.
31. Jack O'Brien, "Medicare for All Could Reduce Hospital Revenues by 16%," *HealthLeaders*, April 5, 2019, https://www.healthleadersmedia.com/finance/medicare-all-could-reduce-hospital-revenues-16, accessed April 28, 2019.

Chapter 2

Six Things That
Don't Make Sense

After reading the last chapter, some readers may be bewildered by the complexities of how healthcare is organized and paid for. To put it mildly, the whole thing is a mess. I have said many times that if I set out to design a totally confusing and dysfunctional way to deliver and finance healthcare services, it might be tough to come up with anything better than what we have.

I am profoundly thankful for my decades-long association with the healthcare world, but due to its dysfunctionality, I have also experienced many frustrations. This chapter is designed to help you further understand a few things that aggravate some of the healthcare people you will interact with. Although I could probably fill an entire book listing things that don't make sense, I will present just six in this chapter.

1. Fundamental Confusion about Who the Customer Really Is and How That Drives the Purchasing Decision

In most industries, the person who orders and pays for the product or service is clearly the customer. There may also be a middleman, but that person essentially acts as an extension of the decision-maker.

When it comes to clinical services, though, there are really three customers:

1. The physician, who is the only one who can authorize ordering the care
2. The patient, who is the actual recipient of the care
3. The insurance company that pays for the care

With so many parties with varying interests involved, it's not surprising that conflicts often arise. The well-intentioned physician wants to offer all the diagnostic tests and interventions they feel are necessary for optimal outcomes. The payer wants to assure that only the clearly medically necessary services are offered and, therefore, often erects speed bumps to authorize only the care it deems appropriate. Patients are often caught in the middle and generally lack the medical knowledge to influence the decision. In recent years, pharmaceutical manufacturers have capitalized on the patients' role and have successfully increased demand for some of their products through direct-to-consumer advertisements.

As one health system CEO puts it, "What other business model exists where the person ordering the service doesn't use it, the person receiving the service doesn't pay for it, and the entity paying for the service doesn't use it? It's a strange economic model but one that must be understood!"

2. The Underfunding of Medicare and Medicaid

This is right at the top of the list of things that doesn't make sense. I think I made a pretty strong case in the last chapter that the inadequacy of payments from the two largest public payers cascades down through the entire care delivery system. I need not say more but did want to spotlight it here since it represents such a major issue for everyone you encounter as you try to sell your products or services.

3. Unfunded Mandates and Overbearing Regulation

This one is almost as bad as Medicare and Medicaid underfunding.

Oversight to protect all parties is necessary for any industry, especially one as personal as healthcare. Policies and programs designed to maximize patient safety and operational efficiency are to be applauded. But responding to these requirements costs money. Unfortunately, payment seldom accompanies the mandate. Or if there is funding, it only covers part of the cost. Let me highlight just a few of healthcare's unfunded mandates.

Emergency Medical Treatment and Active Labor Act of 1986

Back in the 1980s, there were several highly publicized cases where patients who had presented to hospital Emergency Departments (EDs) were not adequately treated and were subsequently sent away. A few of them died, one even in an ED parking lot.

The public understandably got up in arms over this, and their concern fed into a public policy stream that eventually resulted in the passage of the Emergency Medical Treatment and Active Labor Act of 1986 (EMTALA). This law requires hospitals to evaluate and stabilize every patient who goes to the ED, regardless of their ability to pay.

This is an entirely appropriate requirement. It's unthinkable that somebody in a medical crisis would be turned away. Most hospitals go beyond EMTALA's strict requirement and treat patients beyond just evaluating and stabilizing them.

Although EMTALA provides a lifeline to many people who otherwise have no options, there are two problems with this policy:

1. There are absolutely no payment dollars attached to this requirement. The hospital must provide the care but often receives no payment whatsoever. As we saw in the last chapter, hospitals already experience significant financial challenges, and this just makes the problem worse.

2. A small percentage of patients has figured out that this is their all-access pass to free care. Several years ago, I had a conversation with some Emergency Medical Technicians (EMTs) – who also operate under similar requirements to provide their service to all – where they told a discouraging story of someone milking the system. Bertha was one of their "regulars" who frequently called for transportation. Just the previous week, Bertha had called 911 saying she had a medical emergency. By law, the EMTs had to go to her house, and when they arrived, they discovered that her "emergency" was that she had a doctor's visit in a medical office building next to her "regular" hospital.

   "Bertha," they told her, "you know that we can't take you to your doctor's appointment. That's not a real medical emergency." Suddenly, Bertha clutched her chest and exclaimed, "Oh, my goodness. I'm having chest pains." That was her "taxi" ticket to the hospital. Once there, she walked over to her physician's office.

This is a somewhat extreme and perhaps rare case, but many providers feel they are regularly being taken advantage of because of mandates like this.

Health Insurance Portability and Accountability Act of 1996

The Health Insurance Portability and Accountability Act of 1996 (HIPAA) set in motion incredibly complex and detailed requirements around patient information privacy. Among the requirements for healthcare organizations HIPAA set in motion were the following:

- A pre-emption analysis comparing state law and judicial case requirements with the new federal ones to determine which is more restrictive
- A thorough analysis of existing internal policies to determine what changes are required
- The lengthy legal review and renegotiation of most outside contracts
- Assessment of existing information systems and security policies and the remediation work required to bring everything into compliance
- The extensive and ongoing training of all personnel to ensure compliance
- Updating notices of privacy practices
- Updating breach notification practices
- Updating business associate agreements

HIPAA regulations provided no direct funding for any of this.

A few years ago, *Modern Healthcare* published in "Outliers," its light-hearted back page feature, an article entitled "3,500 years of HIPAA." The author calculated that each year providers and patients spend about 30.7 *million* hours complying with *just* HIPAA's notice of privacy practices requirements. The story summarizes the situation like this: "Think of it as 35 centuries worth of bureaucracy."[1] Maybe this article isn't that light-hearted after all.

Other Regulatory Requirements

Here's just a smattering of other unfunded or seriously underfunded mandates:

- Changing from the ICD-9-CM medical coding system to the ICD-10-CM system – This massive effort affected every single medical encounter for every physician in the country.

- Achieving "Meaningful Use" of Electronic Health Records (EHRs) – Despite the significant federal funding provided, *Becker's Health IT & CIO Review* reports that the incentives only covered 20–25% of the total cost to implement EHRs and achieve meaningful use status.[2]
- Participating in numerous overlapping, duplicative quality reporting programs required either by governmental agencies, different insurance companies, or private groups trying to control healthcare spending.
- Complying with the Americans with Disabilities Act.

These are just a few of the many, many requirements driven by external forces and which receive little or no financial support.

In November 2017, the American Hospital Association released a document called "Regulatory Overload Report." Here are some highlights:

- Hospitals and health systems face 629 separate regulatory requirements across nine domains overseen by the Centers for Medicare & Medicaid Services (CMS), the Office of the Inspector General (OIG), the Office of Civil Rights (OCR), and the Office of the National Coordinator for Health Information Technology (ONCHIT).
- Hospitals and health systems spend nearly $39 *billion* a year to comply with all these regulations.
- An average hospital must fund 59 Full-Time Equivalents (FTEs) for compliance purposes. More than 25% of these employees are highly trained – read "expensive" – physicians and nurses.
- The fraud and abuse laws – which impose very strict rules governing financial incentives hospitals can offer physicians – were written in another era and are counterproductive to the current emphasis on great coordination among all caregivers.[3] On the one hand, hospitals and physicians are told to more closely coordinate care, but

on the other hand, anti-fraud and anti-kickback regulations restrict the type of incentives they can implement to fully support this.

Again, it's hard to argue against the need for regulations that maximize safety and protect patients. But many in the healthcare industry feel that regulators have gone way overboard and have unnecessarily added complexity. The whole situation would be far more palatable if those mandating the activities compensated those charged with complying. It's easy to mandate something but another thing to carry it out. This situation reminds me of one of my favorite sayings in life: "Nothing is impossible for the man who doesn't have to do it himself."[4]

4. Being at the Mercy of Others

This item is related to the previous one. Allow me to share some anecdotes that illustrate how providers are often downstream of other people's troubling actions.

A Statewide, Retrospective Audit of Inpatient Cases

Whoever pays the bills has the right to define the rules and demand accountability. But sometimes their oversight goes too far.

Soon after I started my job at Georgia Hospital Association (GHA), we learned that the Medicare program was conducting a massive audit of all the hospitals in the state to see if they were overbilling for a certain inpatient diagnosis. In 1984, Medicare started paying for inpatient care under a system called Diagnosis-Related Groups (DRGs). The idea is that most patients with the same medical conditions should require roughly the same type of treatment and resources for their care. So, rather than pay for every test, procedure, medication, etc. done while the patient is an inpatient, Medicare now pays the same amount for each admission for the same category of problem. They came up with an initial list of about 500 separate reasons people are admitted to a hospital, and they pay according to whichever bucket the patient ends up in, based on the medical codes on the patient's record. (The list of DRGs has since expanded to about 1,000.)

The DRG system does recognize that there is some variation in patient conditions and needs. Not every pneumonia case is simple. Patients sometimes have other conditions at the same time. Consequently, there are some "pairs" of DRGs where simpler cases are given the "regular" DRG designation, and more complex ones are assigned to a DRG "with complications." From the start of the DRG system, regulators were concerned that hospitals might be tempted to "upcode" cases, making them look more severe than they really were in order to get higher payments.

There are pretty clear definitions of the differences between a DRG with complications and a DRG without complications. But, because no two cases are identical and because there is a certain amount of judgment involved when assigning individual diagnostic and condition codes on the medical record, it is possible for a more "aggressive" medical coder to end up coding in such a way that the patient is assigned to the "with complications" DRG when that might be pushing things.

The allegation behind the statewide audit in Georgia was that hospitals were either intentionally gaming the system and upcoding patient records or were mismanaged and unaware of faulty coding. In either case, they would be inappropriately collecting more than they were due. Virtually every hospital in the state was required to submit extensive documentation on every "with complications" patient discharged during the period of time in question for the particular condition being investigated.

Hospitals were understandably concerned for two reasons:

1. Their integrity was being questioned – A GHA spokesman pointed out in a newspaper interview that the implication of the extensive audit was that almost all the hospitals in the state were either acting fraudulently (if they were knowingly overcharging) or were lacking appropriate oversight (if their governing boards were unaware of the sloppy management that allowed inaccurate billing). Either case would be an unwelcomed reproach of the hospitals' governing boards and seems unlikely considering that boards are populated by respected pillars of their communities. How likely was it that hundreds of recognized leaders all across the state were either so dishonest or inept?
2. Hospitals spent several months and large sums of money providing the required documentation. Besides having to hire additional staff to pull medical records, review charts, and possibly conduct additional coding, they also incurred considerable legal and consulting expenses preparing their documentation and defenses.

When all was said and done, of the more than 100 hospitals investigated, only one received a fairly significant fine, and a second one got a slap on the wrist. Every other institution drawn into the investigation was completely exonerated, but this scrutiny cost Georgia's hospital millions and millions of dollars.

When it comes to investigating fraud, there are four categories that sometimes get muddled in people's minds:

1. Fraud – These are obvious illegal activities, like sending bills from a fictional clinic using the address of a Chicago airport parking deck as its location, or a solo practitioner physician billing for 80 procedures a day when each procedure takes 30 minutes. This is clearly impossible

mathematically. Fortunately, this level of blatantly dishonest activity is rare.

2. Abuse – This is where a provider discovers a loophole that allows an activity that is technically allowable but still inappropriate. The audit of possible upcoding of DRG pairs, as in the case just cited, would probably fall into this category.

3. Mistakes – Any complex process is subject to errors. The number of inputs involved in generating and submitting a hospital bill is formidable, and honest mistakes sometimes happen.

4. Confusion over regulations – Whenever there is a significant regulatory change, it can take some time to figure out all its nuances. I remember fielding questions at GHA from members asking how to interpret a particular new requirement that could be taken two or more ways. Since we hadn't written the regulations in question, we didn't know, so we contacted the appropriate agency. Sometimes they were unable to answer the questions either. We carefully documented their answers (or lack of an answer), but this was always a bit troubling. Over my career, I saw the high turnover rates at various governmental agencies. The future leaders wouldn't always feel compelled to abide by their predecessors' interpretations, especially if their interpretations were somewhat unclear. We always feared that a few years down the road, a different bureaucrat would retroactively reinterpret a regulation in a way that would deem, after the fact, a hospital's action as being out of compliance and potentially fraudulent.

If you prepare your own income tax returns, haven't you discovered after filing that you made an innocent mistake (as in 3 above) or misinterpreted a policy (as in 4 above)? After I received my second audit notice from the IRS because of honest mistakes on my part, I decided hiring a tax expert is well worth the cost.

People who oversee the regulatory process sometimes fail to distinguish among these four categories and can conclude that every violation or mistake is willful fraud. Hospitals and physicians resent this.

Questionable Interpretation of Definitions of What Constitutes a True Medical Emergency

Like many other states, Georgia moved many of its Medicaid patients into managed care arrangements several years ago. The state was trying to rein in overall costs, so part of the strategy was to only pay for ED visits that were true emergencies. Cases that were not deemed emergencies were paid a very modest fee, initially $50 and later increased a bit. Fifty dollars doesn't even come close to covering the hard costs of an ED visit.

There were two problems with this policy:

1. EMTALA – As we saw above, every patient who goes to an ED – for any reason at all – must be screened and stabilized. The hospital has absolutely no control over their decision. And since many people lack access to physician care, they end up using the hospital ED as their primary care provider. Why should the hospital be penalized because some patients have no other recourse or if others abuse the system?
2. The determination of whether a case was truly an emergency was left to each managed care organization, and their judgments were sometimes questionable at best. The "average person" is not medically trained and wouldn't necessarily know what constitutes a true medical emergency. Therefore, federal requirements state that a condition that a "prudent layperson" would consider a true emergency should be paid as such.

Not soon after the Medicaid $50 payment for a non-emergency visit was enacted, our hospitals started

complaining loudly that the care management organizations were denying full payments for cases that anyone
would consider true emergencies. Here are just a few
examples:

- A pregnant woman who was experiencing vaginal
  bleeding
- A young man who crashed his pickup truck and
  bashed his head through the windshield
- A two-year-old who had a high fever in the middle of
  the night, had been seen by a pediatrician earlier that
  day, and whose mother was told to seek care immediately if the fever got worse

None of these was deemed an emergency, and the hospitals
were initially paid $50 for each case.

Suffering Huge Payment Delays Because of a Botched IT System Conversion

Providers in one Western state experienced a months-long
nightmare when its state's Medicaid program converted
to a new IT system. Capacity requirements were woefully
underestimated, and the system crashed immediately upon
implementation. Hospital billing departments could seldom
log on to the system, and when they could, lag times were
horrendous. Many hospitals resorted to paying staff for
extensive overtime hours or hiring temporary personnel to
constantly monitor traffic level and jump onto the system the
moment capacity opened up. Others had billing staff report
at 3:00 a.m. when traffic was lighter. All these efforts added
significant unbudgeted expenses for a program that – as we
saw in the last chapter – already failed to pay the total cost
of care.

Since insurance programs don't pay claims without submis-
sion of accurate data, and since the IT system was essentially
non-functional, this situation created massive payment delays.

It got so bad that eventually the Medicaid program started cutting checks based on estimated volumes rather than tying payments to actual individual cases. This made some hospitals nervous about the possibility of a future Medicaid official attempting to reconcile payments to actual claims, being unable to do so, and challenging the appropriateness of certain payments. The entire system conversion was a disaster, and providers were left holding the bag.

These are just three examples of how hospitals and other healthcare providers are often at the mercy of other people's actions and decisions that create chaos downstream.

5. Programs That Look Good on Paper but Which Might Make No Sense in the Long Run

The most effective way to get doctors and hospitals to change their behavior is to change how they are paid, an approach CMS has been using for years. Many of these initiatives are designed to be budget-neutral. CMS decides on an outcome designed to either improve patient care or save money and then changes incentives to encourage the desired end. This typically results in additional payment to those who successfully respond to the new incentives, but in order to keep the program budget-neutral, CMS penalizes others who are less compliant.

One recent CMS initiative – the Medicare Hospital-Acquired Condition (HAC) program which is designed to reduce infections – contains a stick but offers no carrots. It imposes a penalty for poor results without offering a reward for superior performance. Hospitals in the bottom performance quartile are financially penalized on all their future Medicare discharges for a certain period of time. Performance is evaluated each year and new penalties are imposed for subsequent periods.

On the surface, this seems like a reasonable way to encourage hospitals to improve: get better, "or else." This is a great theory, except for two things:

1. The approach would be valid if every hospital were starting from the same point with the same chance to be a top performer. That would be a fair horse race. However, this is not the case. For a variety of reasons – including geography, strength of medical staff, level of resources, payer mix, and other factors – some hospitals start with a distinct disadvantage. This is like lining a dozen runners up at the start of a 5K race and placing ankle weights of various sizes – some quite considerable – on some of the participants. Starting conditions are not equal for all.
2. There is a compounding effect of the penalties. By definition, 25% of hospitals *have* to end up in the lowest quartile every year, thereby being penalized. If objection 1 is valid and some institutions are unfairly handicapped, at least some of the penalized hospitals may end up at the bottom due, at least in part, to factors beyond their control. The good news is that each year offers a new opportunity to improve.

    However, if *every* hospital takes the program seriously and does all it can to improve, low-performing providers are at a continued disadvantage. Even if a bottom-tier facility reduces its HAC rate, all other hospitals may do so as well. If everyone – including this year's bottom performers – improves by, say, 1 percentage point, this year's bottom-tier hospitals will still be there next year despite their improvement. The only way out is to leapfrog hospitals in the next category up, improving *more* than the next tier hospitals do. But how likely is that? Some of the lowest group hospitals are already disadvantaged, and now the program further reduces their payments making it even less likely that they can escape from the basement. Despite their improvement, they will continue to be penalized. Going back to the 5K analogy, this would be like going to one of the runners who had a 10-pound weight on each leg and who finished at the back of the pack and putting 15-pound weights on for the next race.

So even though the theory of a financial penalty seems sensible, it can contribute to a long, slow death spiral for some of our most vulnerable hospitals. Is this what we really want?

This is just one example of a zero-sum program that, although well-intentioned, may not make sense in the long run.

6. The Lack of Uniform IT Communications Protocols

This one is pretty esoteric, and the only people within the healthcare provider's world who probably "get" this one are IT professionals.

About 15 years ago, I had an inkling that right about now, the healthcare technology world would look back to a very unwise regulatory decision made concerning EHRs. I was having coffee with a friend who was a fairly senior leader at the Department of Health and Human Services and asked, "Why aren't you guys defining the technical communication standards and protocols for EHRs? Right now, each vendor has its own specs and uses proprietary programming. This means EHRs from different vendor companies can't communicate with each other."

"Well," he answered, "our philosophy is that the federal government shouldn't micromanage the standard-setting process. We think the free market should address this."

I hope I hid my shock at hearing this totally nonsensical answer. That would be like saying that local electrical coops should feel free to determine voltage output to suit their personal preferences. Why not produce 230-volt current like European countries do instead of the US standard of 120 volts?

Why not 400 volts? Allowing this variation would be fine as long as two conditions exist:

1. The local power company is a closed system with no need to connect to the larger electric grid.
2. All of the power company's customers are OK with their appliances frying from the catastrophically elevated electrical output if it plugs in a device designed for the wrong system.

Since the federal government offered billions of incentive dollars to encourage broader adoption of EHRs with the end of greater data portability, wouldn't it have made sense – to shift metaphors – for everyone to speak a common language instead of some speaking Portuguese, others speaking English, and still others speaking Hungarian?

The other thought that went through my mind was that the federal government regulates seemingly everything hospitals and physicians do, from EMTALA rules regarding screening and stabilizing all ED patients, to Occupational Safety and Health Administration requirements, to compliance with Medicare billing protocols. Why not set technical communications protocols that would allow for easy transfer of relevant data among providers?

Earlier in this chapter, I railed against over-regulation. Isn't it ironic that now I'm suggesting that there should have been more regulation in this arena? This is one area where strict requirements would have actually helped. The federal government should have convened a group of healthcare IT professionals to define the best technical communications standards and protocols and then pick a target date – perhaps five years out – for full migration to those standards. Essentially, the message to vendors would have been, "You're free to write to any technology communications standards you like, but if you want your customers to buy your products, we suggest you migrate toward these standards since everyone else will be using them. And you have five years to get there."

Unfortunately, this was not the path chosen, and we could have been much further down to road toward truly useful interoperability. What a missed opportunity!

Final Thought

As I said, there are many, many aspects of the healthcare delivery system that seem to defy logic. I'm not including these just to "ventilate" over these frustration points. Having some sense of the environment clinicians and executives operate in may help you understand their frustrations and interpret some of the reactions you may get as you present your products or services to them. If you can describe your product as a solution – or at least a partial solution – to one of these problems, you will be welcomed with open arms.

End Notes

1. *Modern Healthcare*, "Outliers: 3,500 years of HIPAA," https://www.modernhealthcare.com/article/20130907/ MAGAZINE/309079915/outliers-3-500-years-of-hipaa, September 7, 2013, accessed April 29, 2019.
2. Michael Sinno, "8 Problems Surrounding Meaningful Use," *Becker's Health IT & CIO Review*, April 28, 2011, accessed March 29, 2019.
3. American Hospital Association, "Regulatory Overload Report," https://www.aha.org/guidesreports/2017-11-03-regulatory-overload-report, November 2017, accessed March 25, 2019.
4. Arthur Bloch, *Murphy's Law and other reasons why things go wrong 1* (Los Angeles: Price/Stern/Sloan, 1978), page 80.

Chapter 3

Three Ideas to Make Things Better

So far, I have painted a pretty gloomy picture of our health-care system. I outlined in Chapter 1 the less-than-ideal way it's financed, and I described in Chapter 2 a number of providers' major frustration points. Just to recap, here is the list of things that don't make sense to hospitals, health systems, physicians, and other clinicians:

1. Fundamental confusion about who the customer really is and how that drives the purchasing decision
2. The underfunding of Medicare and Medicaid
3. Unfunded mandates and overbearing regulation
4. Being at the mercy of others
5. Programs that look good on paper but which might make no sense in the long run
6. The lack of uniform IT communications protocols

The first one is an inherent part of the system and will probably never change. Numbers 2 through 5 will only be fixed if those in charge change their policies and approaches. I don't expect that to happen any time soon. Concerning number 6, we've already burned many years when we could have been developing IT technical standards, and I'm not hearing anything that leads me to believe that the federal government will suddenly reverse course.

However, when it comes to reforming the system, all is not lost. There may be some creative ways to rethink how we finance care delivery. The old cliché tells us to follow the money, so let's do that. The fiscal incentives in today's system have created the system we have. To change the endpoint, we need to look upstream.

The three proposals in this chapter are not magic bullets, and nothing is ever as easy as it seems. Although these ideas only address part of the problem, implementing them could bring us at least part way down the road. *These concepts are not necessarily designed to be implemented together. Each is* extremely *complex in its own right, and trying to link them for simultaneous adoption would almost certainly sink the entire effort. I am presenting these as discussion points which need extensive fleshing-out.*

Idea 1 – Develop a Truly Effective Preventive Care Approach

One of the most frequent and valid criticisms of our current system is that we focus far more on treating people rather than helping them avoid medical problems in the first place. Trying to prevent illness – or at least intercepting it as early on as possible – is both better for the patient and, in many cases, cheaper in the long run.

The reason that I qualify my comment about being cheaper is that some preventive interventions – even if they are relatively inexpensive – may not necessarily be truly cost-effective. There are two reasons for this:

1. Actually realizing theoretical savings from preventive programs can be difficult
2. People sometimes confuse *unit* cost and *total* cost

Let me explain what I mean through the following example. I had a cousin who, unfortunately, had major mental health issues: schizophrenia and manic depression. He spent many years drifting through various levels of lucidity. There were times when he was able to function fairly well on his own, but other times when he needed to be hospitalized. During one of his hospitalizations, he gradually improved to the point that he was almost – but not quite – capable of living on his own. The state where he lived was considering expanding its halfway house program where patients could live in an environment where their living circumstances would be monitored and they would receive medication supervision. Beyond that, they would otherwise be free to come and go as they pleased, get a job, and try to live somewhat normal lives.

My cousin's dad loved this concept and started a campaign to expand the program. In the course of his activism, he uncovered some statistics he felt supported his case. At the time, an inpatient day in the state mental hospital cost about $400 while the cost of the halfway house was closer to $175. The implication was that by moving a patient from an inpatient unit to the halfway house, the state could save $225 a day. Wouldn't that make sense?

Maybe yes, maybe no. Let's take a closer look at the two factors I mentioned above:

1. The difficulty of truly capturing savings – If my cousin moved from the inpatient facility, how much would the state truly save? Almost nothing. His inpatient psychiatric unit would still be open. The building's utility bills wouldn't go down. The hospital director's salary would be unchanged. Reducing patient census by one person wouldn't even have enough impact on the direct staffing needs to cut down on frontline personnel.

   However, if several patients *from the same unit* could move into the new program, some inpatient staffing positions could be eliminated, and you could begin to reduce costs. If enough patients transferred, the hospital might be able to close down a unit or possibly even an entire building. But saving money by moving all those patients would only work if they were currently housed together. This is not always the case for patients with differing care needs. If they were not "clustered" within a single unit but were instead scattered throughout the facility, capturing savings would be harder.

Even if whole units or even an entire building were closed, the true savings probably wouldn't approach $225 per day. When a hospital reports total cost per day that includes *every* cost element divided by the number of patient days. Total expenses include the salaries of executives who oversee the entire facility, the cost of compliance with mandated reporting, expenses for maintaining and upgrading the IT system, and many other items. Additionally, although a building may be out of service, it still requires a minimal degree of maintenance, including some level of utilities, groundskeeping, etc. So, if part of a facility shut down although there could be substantial cost reduction, the daily savings wouldn't be $225 per patient day.

2. Confusion over unit cost and total cost – Healthcare often experiences something called "The Woodwork Effect." This is where people who currently receive no care "come out of the woodwork" to get help when a new option is offered. Having a halfway house for psychiatric inpatients who no longer need to be institutionalized would certainly be beneficial for them, and it could possibly save a decent amount of money if – as described above – the program were big enough to truly realize significant cuts in operational costs. Such an alternative would also undoubtedly be of great value to some community-based patients who might otherwise be at risk of inpatient admission.

However, would the net impact of expansion on the total cost of the state's psychiatric program be positive or negative? It all comes down to the numbers. Would enough inpatients be able to transfer to the new care level to save substantial money on the inpatient side? How many non-institutionalized patients would pursue the halfway house option? What would adding all those new halfway house residents do to the state's global psychiatric care budget? Of those community-based patients who enter the halfway house program, how many *would have* been admitted as inpatients had they not sought placement in the halfway house? Would that "anticipated savings" from avoided inpatient admissions be enough to offset the cost of the new program option? These are all tough questions to answer.

(As an aside, one way to counteract the Woodwork Effect in this example would be to limit eligibility for the halfway house to patients moving there from an inpatient facility. No one could enter directly from the community.)

The point is that you can't just "do the math" in a cavalier way by simply comparing the costs per day for the halfway house program and the inpatient program and bank on collecting the entire difference. It could well be that the new level is financially viable, but that calculation is not as simple as it appears on the surface, and the savings are likely to be far less than the straightforward arithmetic would suggest.

Let's Talk Prevention

With this as a background, let's look at preventive care in general. Not smoking, managing stress, getting adequate nutrition, maintaining appropriate weight, and exercising regularly greatly enhance a person's health status. In general, the better one's overall health, the lower their healthcare costs.

There are increasing levels of preventive-orientated care:

■ *Screenings* – The Affordable Care Act (ACA) expanded the number of preventive services covered by health plans required to be part of all plans. Among the 21 levels of adult screenings now available under the ACA are cholesterol, colorectal cancer, type 2 diabetes, falls, hepatitis B, obesity, depression, and many others.[1]

■ *Relatively low-intensity interventional services* – These can be instrumental in staving off more serious conditions down the road and could include:
  - Free or highly subsidized care for minor physical or mental health issues to catch these problems before they get more serious
  - Adequate prenatal care to support the delivery of a healthy baby instead of one with significant health issues
  - Certain medications like low-dose aspirin for cardiovascular disease and colorectal cancer, statins for cardiac disease, hormone therapy for postmenopausal women, and vitamin D and calcium for bone health – Early administration of these medications can prevent future, more serious problems.[2]

■ *Addressing something called the social determinants of health* – These are environmental elements that typically adversely affect someone's health. Things like unsafe neighborhoods, food deserts, poor school systems, inadequate housing, poor air quality, and other factors are associated with reduced health status and quality of life.

How far we as a society go in addressing these issues is a prickly political question. As I mentioned, the ACA covers many types of screening. Some people think the government and private insurance companies should also pay for the type of low-level interventions listed above. Others go even further and suggest society is obligated to address the social determinants of care that contribute to health disparities. People of good will come down on all sides of the question of how much preventive care should be offered.

Although there is ample evidence for the clinical value of preventive care, not every intervention makes sense economically. It can take years for the clinical benefits of preventive care to take hold, and people frequently change insurance carriers before the savings can be reaped by the insurance company that paid for it. This means an insurer could spend a fairly considerable amount on preventive care for a patient who might switch to a different payer the next year, well before the health benefits blossom.

The following is reprinted from my blog posting at www. pearsonhti.com dated December 19, 2017 that addresses this issue:

The November 6, 2017 issue of *Modern Healthcare* featured an opinion piece entitled "What's behind America's epic fail on diabetes care" in which Editor Emeritus Merrill Goozner describes recent efforts around public awareness, prevention and treatment efforts, none of which seem to be having a significant impact. He also asks a question that prompted me to submit an idea that could potentially result in real improvement for this and other prevention-oriented issues. Here is my letter to the editor printed on December 4:

> In Merrill Goozner's article *What's behind America's epic fail on diabetes care* (November 6) he astutely asks, "In our fragmented insurance system where people are constantly changing plans or aging into Medicare, why spend money today when the benefits will accrue to some other payer down the road?" He's exactly right under the current system.
>
> However, here's an idea. We know that some preventive care is truly cost-effective if you look over a multi-year horizon. Although I'm not normally a fan of increased regulation, requiring all insurance

companies to cover those preventive services that are known to be not only clinically effective, but also cost-effective over time would eliminate the impact of insurance churn. If Insurance Company A pays for truly cost-effective preventive care for Patient 1 who subsequently moves to Insurance Company B, it is just as likely that Patient 2 might switch from Company B to Company A, thereby balancing the economic scales. At that point, it becomes a market share issue, introducing another element of competition where those insurance companies that achieve the highest level of patient care and satisfaction come out ahead through enrollee retention.

Of course, paying for additional preventive services would result in short-term cost increases for the overall system, but the benefits should balance out if only those preventive services that are cost-effective over the long term are covered.[3]

So, the idea is to identify which preventive services actually make a difference medically *and* economically when considering total cost to the healthcare system over a period of several years. Deciding what to cover would be tricky and controversial, but pinpointing and paying for clinically and financially effective services would be in the best interest both of patient care and fiscal responsibility.

Idea 2 – Revamp the Payment System to Create a Public/Private Hybrid Approach

Determining whether or not healthcare coverage is a basic human right is one of our most vexing health policy issues. Those who say "yes" feel that it's immoral to deny anyone care. How can we see human suffering and ignore it? Those on the other side highlight the economic challenges and implications – including likely rationing – of providing expanded care for all. They also point out that the rights enumerated in the United States Bill of Rights – life, liberty, and the pursuit of happiness – have no societal "economic cost" while providing care for others does.

In this contentious, polarized political climate, it's unlikely that either side will convince the other any time soon. But, if I may be so bold, there may be an acceptable compromise.

Before I present my idea, let's consider three primary drivers that brought healthcare coverage into the public's consciousness in recent decades.

1. Charges of hospital emergency rooms "dumping" patients in the 1980s. As I pointed out in the last chapter, some highly publicized cases where hospitals allegedly dismissed uninsured patients from EDs without properly stabilizing and treating them caused understandable public uproar and played a major role in passing the Emergency Medical Treatment and Active Labor Act of 1986 (EMTALA).
2. People being denied coverage or having extraordinarily high premiums because of pre-existing medical conditions
3. People literally being bankrupted by crushing medical bills triggered by catastrophic medical crises

Here's my proposal. What if we had a two-part hybrid system?

▪ Part 1 – A national public plan that provided emergency/ preventive/primary care and catastrophic care for everyone. It would be backed by a combination of increased employer taxes and redeployment of some existing funding for Medicare, Medicaid, and the Children's Health Insurance Program.

■ Part 2 – A reconfigured private insurance market that offered coverage to fill the gap between emergency/preventive/primary care and catastrophic care. This supplemental insurance would be paid for either by individuals who chose to purchase it or employers who wanted to provide extra coverage for their employees. Additionally, state Medicaid programs could help fill the gap for Medicaid patients if they so desired.

This approach would address all three problems listed above. It would:

■ Guarantee everyone coverage for life-threatening situations
■ Keep pre-existing conditions from freezing people out the insurance market for at least emergency/preventive/primary care and catastrophic care
■ Reduce the number of bankruptcies caused by catastrophic medical bills – The level where catastrophic coverage would kick in – $20,000, $50,000, or some other number – would be determined by the overall costs and finances of the program.

This solution has the added benefit of addressing the issue of coverage for adult children under their parents' health plans, which proved to be a wildly popular feature of the ACA. But my proposal goes one better because, unlike what happens under the ACA, adult children would not be disenrolled from the basic public plan when they turned 26.

Another benefit is that, since everyone would have access to preventive and primary care, this approach should offload unnecessary ED traffic. If this proposal was combined with my first suggestion about identifying cost-effective preventive approaches, it would also increase the likelihood of improved long-term health status, potentially resulting in lower overall societal costs.

Even though employers' taxes would rise, their total health-care spending probably would not. Their increased taxes would be offset by *decreased* insurance premiums since they would no longer have to pay for the emergency/preventive/primary and catastrophic care they pay for in their current policies.

Perhaps one of the most important aspects of this concept is that it maintains a place for private insurance companies, which are understandably dead set against a fully socialized program that would render them irrelevant. Any time the idea of a single payer health system gets put on the table, the private insurance market comes out in force to fight it tooth and nail. Why wouldn't they? Their very survival is at stake. Although moving to this hybrid concept would greatly disrupt the private payer market, payers would still play a significant role in the new system.

The "healthcare is a right" group should be pleased that everyone has guaranteed access to basic care, and those on the other side should see this as a more affordable option than all-out, expensive full coverage for everyone.

Some might complain that this concept would establish a two-tiered system since not everyone would have the supple-mental private coverage. But I would argue that in a free society, not everyone accesses the same products and services. That's why we have both Econo Lodge and Ritz-Carlton hotels. Furthermore, our current system does not adequately care for the needs of the "have nots," many of whom get almost no care at all. This change would at least be a good step toward more equity.[4]

I should point out that this plan would *not* involve expand-ing Medicare and it is certainly not a Medicare for All (M4A) plan. The existing Medicare program would stay pretty much as it is. Although – as I described in Chapter 1 – Medicare does not fully cover the cost of care it "orders," it works pretty well operationally, and politicians recognize that upsetting this program would be as wise as storming the gates of hell with a water pistol.

Idea 3 – Revamp the Payment System to Better Reflect Patient's Likelihood to Need Healthcare Services and to Better Incentivize Them

Quick quiz: Who has primary responsibility for healthcare cost containment?

a. Government
b. Hospitals
c. Physicians
d. Insurers
e. Patients

Trick question. The answer is "(f) All of the above." Since cost increases stem from many sources, any successful solution must address them all. Unfortunately, many approaches just focus on (a), (b), and (c) – government regulation or cutting providers' payments.

In 2003, former Speaker of the House of Representatives Newt Gingrich founded a think tank-type group called the Center for Health Transformation designed to examine the current healthcare system and suggest creative ways to revamp it to improve care while also saving money. I was privileged to serve on one of its committees and had a flash of inspiration during one of our meetings. This was my idea.

What if the industry developed a customized index that accounts for various factors that determine someone's expected level of health services consumption – sort of an individualized health status FICO® score? Financial FICO scores run information about a person's income, debt load, payment history, and other factors through an algorithm that generates a single number to rank-order individuals' likelihood to meet their credit obligations.[5]

Factors for the Health FICO (HFICO) would include age, gender, race, family history, biometrics, wellness behaviors, and potentially others. A few healthcare technology companies are starting to develop health FICO scores, primarily for wellness purposes and to provide additional insights for clinical care. But my idea goes two steps further.

The first involves using the HFICO for risk rating of patients for insurance premium purposes. The age-old challenge in determining premiums for any type of insurance is accurately predicting the likelihood that the individual being insured will indeed encounter the problem being insured against and, therefore, generate a claim and cost the insurer money. Current risk-rating approaches use various factors but are still somewhat crude. For example, the premium rates for people who buy individual insurance under the ACA are determined using only the following considerations:

■ Whether coverage is for an individual or a family
■ Their geographic area
■ Their age
■ Whether or not they use tobacco[6]

The age rating for adults can only vary by a factor of 3:1. For example, if a 21-year-old male's monthly premium for a particular plan is $250, a 64-year-old male's premium for the same plan can't exceed $750.[7]

The HFICO score would be far more granular and, as mentioned above, could potentially add:

■ Gender
■ Race
■ Family history
■ Biometrics
■ Wellness behaviors other than tobacco use

The HFICO score would be used to determine the premium amount for each individual based on all these elements. The *higher* the score, the lower their risk of needing healthcare services. Therefore, the insurance company would be assuming less risk, allowing it to charge lower premiums. Conversely, the lower the HFICO, the more likely that the individual would need care, and the insurance company would receive a higher premium to offset the added risk.

Many feel insurers "cherry-pick" and try to enroll only the healthiest people. Payers are, understandably, more interested in attracting enrollees who are less likely to require services than those with high expected care needs. Under the current, rather unsophisticated system, low-risk enrollees are typically more profitable. Some insurance companies sponsor enroll-ment meetings at places like health clubs so they can meet people who have demonstrated a certain level of commitment to staying healthy.

The idea behind the HFICO is to finely tune the premium attached to each individual based on factors known to affect average risk levels. This would theoretically make everyone equally attractive fiscally to payers. The premiums they would receive for enrollees with low HFICO scores would be actuari-ally set to, on average, make them as potentially profitable as enrollees with high scores, thus neutralizing the incentive to cherry-pick.

But there's a second way to potentially make a HFICO pro-gram even more effective. Besides theoretically "equalizing" the attractiveness of each potential enrollee to payers, it could also become a mechanism to draw in one of the largest "play-ers" in the escalating health cost equation: the patient.

In 2007, *The New England Journal of Medicine* included an article called "We Can Do Better – Improving the Health of the American People" by Steven A. Schroeder, MD. The author cites Centers for Disease Control and Prevention research that examines what it calls "Proportional Contribution to Premature Deaths." Put in plain English, this studies why do people die sooner than they "should." Examining potentially avoidable deaths can be used as a surrogate for determining health status.

As shown in Figure 3.1, the single most significant contribu-tor to someone's health status – with a 40% impact – is the

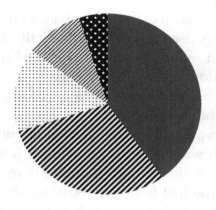

● Behaviorial Patterns (40%) ▨ Genetic Predisposition (30%) ⠿ Social Circumstances (15%)
▨ Health System (10%) ◑ Environmental Exposure (5%)

Figure 3.1   Proportional Contribution to Premature Deaths.

Source: New England Journal of Medicine 2007:1221-8.

lifestyle choices they make. At 30%, the second highest factor is someone's genetic predisposition.

If these statistics are valid, fully 70% of someone's health status is virtually untouched by current policies. Congress can't change my genetic makeup, and, to date, there have been few effective programs that significantly address lifestyle choices. As I mentioned previously, cost-cutting efforts typically turn to more regulation or cutting provider payments. Although we should pull all the levers – including those – if we can't do anything about the 30% hard-wired in our genes and we choose to ignore the 40% potentially addressable by changing people's behavior, we are trying to solve 100% of the health status and cost problem the back of the remaining 30%. How likely is that to succeed?

Here's how patient engagement would work. Just as my FICO score determines my credit-worthiness and, therefore, my cost of borrowing money, my HFICO score could be used to incentivize me through rewards like lower premiums or enhanced benefits. If I follow recommended improvement practices, I would receive actuarially based credits to offset my out-of-pocket expenses. These could take the form of significant premium reductions, greatly reduced copayments, or sizable contributions to an account from which out-of-pocket expenses could be reimbursed. Whatever form these incentives took must be *meaningful.*

I was once in a health plan that tried to entice people to get a "house call wellness visit" by offering a $15 gift card to one of the big box stores. Even though $15 might convince a few to spend the half hour necessary for the house call wellness visit, it isn't likely to convince too many people to implement whatever lifestyle changes they discuss during the wellness visit. On the other hand, something like a $60–$100 per month premium reduction or some other equally attractive bonus might do the trick and give enrollees real motivation to modify their habits.

This is extremely important! Under a HFICO plan, the only elements to include in determining patients' incentives must be factors *completely* under their control. When it comes to rewards, things like age, race, and family history would be strictly off limits. Although the fact that my father died of a heart attack at age 50 would be factored into my HFICO score, that would not be allowed to be considered when establishing my financial incentives.

Another thing, financial consequences should be presented as *rewards* not *penalties.* Back in 2011, the State of Arizona attempted to give Medicaid patients a reason to improve their lifestyles by imposing a $50 per year penalty on any enrollee who was diabetic and smoked and who also failed to follow a physician-supervised weight loss plan. The program correctly recognized that people's choices directly translate into utilization and therefore cost. But the initiative was immediately met with hostility and scorn and was labeled a "cruel and regressive fat tax" and dubbed "Arizona's flab tax."[8]

There were three things wrong with Arizona's approach:

1. Opponents to the plan complained recipients would be punished for things they couldn't necessarily completely control.[9] This allegation validates the point I just made about assuring that the HFICO must in no way penalize people for things they can't change.
2. Although Medicaid enrollees are by definition low income and would "feel" a $50 a year penalty, it may not be enough to motivate behavioral change. With cigarettes costing somewhere around $6 a pack, a pack-a-day smoker spends more than three times the annual penalty every month. Would the extra $4.17 a month hit ($50 a year divided by 12 months) be enough to convince any-one to lose weight? I doubt it.
3. The most serious mistake in my mind is that the pro-gram was presented as a negative rather than a positive. Instead of "taking something away" or punishing some-one, Arizona should have offered a positive incentive like offering no-cost dental coverage for complying with the changed behavior or some other benefit. The actuar-ies would have to rejigger the overall Medicaid program numbers to add the benefit while still arriving at the same total program cost, but that is entirely possible.

Initial reaction to my HFICO concept at the Center for Health Transformation committee meeting was positive, and I have had the chance to share it with several people since then. So far no one has identified a fatal flaw. In fact, one economics professor called it a brilliant idea.

However, there are several cautions:

■ One of the toughest aspects would be crafting the algo-rithm that determines the HFICO. All "artificial" indices involve arbitrary decisions. For example, how much weight should be given to smoking cessation vs. exercise vs. body fat metrics? And how much exercise would be necessary to qualify for the incentive? Should the thresholds be age-adjusted? No matter how much the designers try, some people will always come out on the wrong side of the methodology ultimately selected. Therefore, a great deal of research and discussion would be required to establish reasonable standards and algorithms. Furthermore, a process for regularly revising and updating the underlying methodology would necessary to take advantage of lessons learned as the program rolled out.

A hospital CEO friend of mine observed that the HFICO approach would parallel to the golf handicap system as a way to level the playing field so two very different golfers can play together. He commented, "It's taken a few hundred years for golf to figure out this system, and players are still arguing on the first tee at courses around the world every day." But the concept is valid: find a way to "equalize" the inputs to allow you to move forward in a fair way.

■ I fully realize how potentially inflammatory folding race and ethnicity into the HFICO equation could be. With the current hyper-sensitivity around racial issues, some might view including race as somehow discriminatory against minorities. In reality, it would actually be the opposite if done correctly. Taking into account things like social determinants of health – including difficulty in obtaining healthy food, living in unsafe neighborhoods, and having limited literacy – would *lower* the person's HFICO score. Whoever covered that person would get *higher* premium payments, making it more likely they would be actively courted as potential enrollees.

■ Having a single, very personal number like the HFICO could be considered an invasion of privacy. The same might be said about the financial FICO score. Of course, the highest levels of data security should be required for both the financial FICO and the HFICO scores.

Also, keep in mind that both numbers are generated by complex algorithms that are not generally available to the public. The unexpectedly low financial FICO score of a person who otherwise appears financially successful could be caused by several factors. If their FICO score was hacked, it would be impossible to determine if the lower score was due to a bankruptcy, over-extension of credit, poor payment history, or some other reason. Of course, the individual wouldn't want the FICO score disclosed at all, but just knowing someone has a low number doesn't provide much meaningful or specific information.

The same would be true of the HFICO. Since higher age would automatically lower the HFICO, part of a lower number for an older would be attributable to that. Also, an unfortunate family medical history would lower the score, and few people know much about their friends' and colleagues' family medical histories unless they choose to disclose them. So, knowing someone has a low HFICO does not necessarily reveal any specifics of their circumstances or behavior. And if there was major concern over confidentiality, the HFICO could potentially be brought under coverage of the Health Information Portability and Accountability Act (HIPAA), the federal program that requires strict guarding of protected health information.

■ Some might fear that a poor HFICO score could price people with individual (as opposed to employer-provided) coverage out of the insurance market. This issue could be addressed by placing a cap on total premium level paid by individuals not in group plans. Perhaps some of the current high-risk subsidy funds could be transferred over to the HFICO-based approach. This would protect individuals with very low HFICO scores from exorbitant premiums.

■ Another potential problem is the possibility of someone not receiving a job offer if the hiring company feared bringing in a high-risk individual would raise their group premium amounts. Health status is not supposed to be considered in employment situations today, and this would not change. Regulations could be tweaked to prohibit refusing employment based on someone's HFICO score. Discrimination can be tough to prove, but there is ample precedent for effective anti-discrimination policies based on other factors like age, gender, and religion.

By building in *meaningful* financial incentives for the individual *based only on lifestyle decisions completely within their control*, implementing a HFICO approach would be a great first step to crack the nut of the 40% of health status attributable to patients' health-related choices. And this approach could bring us closer to the quiz answer "(f) All of the above."

Final Thoughts

Most cost-control efforts amount to tweaking the existing system and usually take the form of provider payment cuts (think back to the *HealthLeaders* analysis I cited in Chapter 1 estimating hospital margins cuts of between 16% and 22% if M4A were implemented), some kind of price controls, or efforts to increase price transparency and competition. All these have their place, but to borrow a colloquial phrase, they amount to slapping lipstick on a pig. They don't address some underlying failings of our current system.

As disruptive as the ACA was, its biggest impact was largely just rearranging who pays for health insurance and the mechanism for how it's paid. Despite some modest preventive care elements and a few enhanced programmatic aspects sprinkled in, at its core it still preserves the fundamental insurance industry model. On the other hand, the three proposals in this chapter suggest reformulating our entire approach to health insurance by ushering in truly effective preventive care, by addressing a huge gap in our current coverage approach, and/or by encouraging patients' meaningful engagement in the care equation.

Everyone who has attempted to recalibrate this huge part of our national economy quickly concludes that it is a monumental, enormously complex task. I fully recognize this. To reiterate, *these are broad-based discussion concepts that need extensive additional thought and discussion.* And, although here may be ways to combine elements from each of these ideas, I am not saying they must all be implemented in tandem.

Much research would be required to fine-tune these ideas and develop detailed operating principles to make them really workable. Given the dysfunctionality of the current system, something must change, and I personally think we should at least introduce these concepts for public discourse. There's too much at stake to not try to bring about some needed, common-sense changes.

End Notes

1. https://www.healthcare.gov/preventive-care-adults/, accessed March 28, 2019.
2. https://www.uspreventiveservicestaskforce.org/BrowseRec/Index, accessed March 28, 2019.
3. This citation is from my December 19, 2017 blog posting at www.pearsonhti.com.
4. This section is adapted from my July 13, 2018 blog posting at www.pearsonhti.com.
5. https://www.fico.com/en/products/fico-score, accessed March 29, 2019.
6. Coventry Health Care, "The Affordable Care Act: Rating Factor limitations," http://coventryhealthcare.com/web/groups/public/@cvty_corporate_chc/documents/webcontent/c084481.pdf, 2013, accessed March 29, 2019.
7. ibid.
8. "Arizona's 'cruel and regressive' fat tax," *The Week*, April 2011, accessed April 5, 2019.
9. ibid.

Chapter 4

The Six Fronts of the Healthtech Revolution

We are in the midst of an unprecedented transformation in healthcare delivery. Thousands of new medical devices, scientific breakthroughs, analytical methodologies, health-related apps, and other innovations are introduced each year. Every successful new product or approach has the potential to either revolutionize the lives of a particular group of patients, help streamline operations, or introduce operational efficiencies that benefit everyone. Some can do two or even all three of these.

If we look back to care in the 1970s, we can see how much has changed. Among the incredible clinical advances of the last four decades are the following:

- Magnetic resonance imaging (MRI)
- Laparoscopic surgery
- Robotic surgery
- Teleradiology
- Cardiovascular implants
- Bionic limbs
- DNA sequencing

■ Genomics
■ Wearable technologies

These have changed the lives of millions of patients and they feed into a stream that continues to transform many aspects of the field. (Unfortunately, they won't address the underlying payment-related problems outlined in Chapter 1.) Later in this chapter, I will sketch out an exciting picture of what the future of care delivery might look like because of continuing health-tech breakthroughs.

This chapter covers a lot of territory. Here's what we will look at:

■ Why healthcare is behind other industries in adopting technology
■ Why this is changing now
■ The explosive growth in healthcare technology
■ Categorizing healthcare technology
■ The six fronts of the healthtech revolution

Why Healthcare Is Behind in Adopting Non-Clinical Technology

All the technology breakthroughs of the last four decades listed above are clinical, not business- or process-oriented. The healthcare field is universally recognized as being woefully behind almost every other industry in terms of its adoption of non-clinical technology. There at least two reasons:

1. *The complex, splintered nature of the healthcare field*
    Unlike manufacturing, retail, or hospitality industries, healthcare involves frequent, complicated interactions among various organizations, which are seldom aligned or integrated. All technology needs within the hospitality

industry, for example, are fairly straightforward. Hotels must process reservations, communicate with banks for payments, reach out to customers with pre- and post-stay communications, order supplies, handle human resources issues, and deal with many other transactions. However, many of these functions are pretty much self-contained with less need for real-time data exchange than in healthcare, where different players must interact every day.

Patient care requires trading data among physicians, hospitals, other clinicians, pharmacies, nursing homes, hospice programs, insurance companies, and others. Over the decades, each of these areas developed its own information systems with little recognition that someday in the future, they may need to communicate with each other.

Hospitals use the Electronic Health Records (EHRs) to collect detailed clinical information throughout an inpatient stay or outpatient encounter, but few EHRs were designed with the goal of transmitting data to, say, a nursing home's IT system. Making matters worse, there are many stand-alone IT systems and "data islands" even within a hospital itself. Historically, many hospital outpatient clinics, labs, imaging departments, pharmacies, billing offices, and other areas had their own IT systems, few of which followed universal data transfer protocols. Furthermore, various system use different code sets: ICD-10-CM diagnosis and condition codes, SNOMED Clinical Terms, Diagnosis-Related Groups (DRGs), Current Procedural Terminology (CPT), Healthcare Common Procedure Coding System (HCPCS), genomic classification sets, state-defined classifications required for reporting discharge disposition and other aspects of an inpatient stay, and many other classification systems. Not all these code sets have to interact, but ideally some should.

The reality that none of these was designed with the thought of eventually trading data with other internal systems is not a criticism of their designers' efforts as they defined the code sets. Rather, it reflects the fact that their primary objective was creating a robust classification system for use within their own domains, not setting the stage for future interoperability among various databases. Because most of them grew up independent of each other, interfaces, crosswalks, mapping, and other communications considerations are far more complicated than they would be had they be developed in tandem with each other.

There are also data challenges when trying to combine data even within the same functional area or when trying to track the same data in different databases. I saw this first-hand about 20 years ago when I led the data area at GHA. GHA is the keeper of the statewide discharge database that tracks every inpatient discharge from every hospital in Georgia. Another organization maintained a different health-related database, and we were discussing possibly combining them. But we quickly recognized the challenge involved.

One of the data fields we both collected was the patient's race, but as I recall, we had six categories but the other group had only five. Combining these retroactively is impossible since we had different definitions and delineation points. I don't remember the details, but let's say GHA had six categories:

- Asian
- Black or African American-American
- Hawaiian or other Pacific Islander
- Mixed race
- Native American
- White

If we decided to merge the efforts going forward, we would have to make a decision about which classification approach we would use in the future, GHA's or the other group's. That's a simple programming decision. However, there is no way to retrospectively combine the historical databases to use for meaningful analysis. If a mixed race record was in both databases and the other group didn't list mixed race as an option, that record would show up as mixed race in the GHA database but could end up in any one of the other five categories in the other data set. We can't know how they assigned it.

If we were *starting* with the historical GHA data set and wanted to develop a crosswalk between GHA's six categories and the other organization's five, what would we do with records in GHA's mixed race group? Should we consider them all White? All Black? Or something else? Would we just divide them out equally or proportionally into the other group's five categories? Any way we would do this would introduce inaccuracies and/or inconsistencies between the two data sets.

And the problem goes the other way too. If we tried to combine the historical data sets starting with the other organization's five categories and moving them to GHA's six, no records from the other database would be classified as mixed race in the GHA database. There's no way to tease out where a mixed race record ended up in the other database since that detail was lost when the record was entered into one of the other group's five categories. Once a record is assigned to one of its five buckets, backing out mixed race records is impossible.

This is a small example of the many complexities we faced as we considered how to combine databases. We ultimately abandoned the effort. Our failed exercise illustrates the difficulty of cross-walking historical data when various data sets were developed in isolation from each other. And healthcare is filled with such databases.

People who fail to grasp these complexities sometimes simplistically criticize the healthcare industry about our inability to exchange data. There is an analogy that has "made the rounds" for more than a decade. It goes like this.

The speaker says, "I was in Madrid last month and I was able to use an ATM there to withdraw money from my bank account back in Atlanta. If I can get money from halfway around the world, why can't I get my medical record across the street from my doctor's office to the hospital?"

Here's the problem with this analogy. The speaker assumes the impediment to data transfer is *geography*. Atlanta and Madrid are pretty far apart. But the problem isn't distance. It's the transaction complexity and the structure and definitions of the databases you are accessing.

I myself have used ATMs in Madrid to get Euros. Once I'm authenticated, I simply push a button on the screen to request a certain amount and then my money appears. All the banking system has to do is verify that I have enough in my account back in Atlanta to cover the request and then I get my money. There are only three steps involved: converting my request for so many Euros to dollars, verifying that I have enough dollars to cover the request, and then subtracting the dollar amount from my account. That's about as simple as it gets.

By contrast, trying to exchange healthcare data is infinitely more complicated. There are all kinds of potential issues: data security requirements, technical interfaces, data compatibility, data definitions, data mapping, data integrity, and data latency. Add to this the fact that not every provider in the entire stream of my care is necessarily even connected to all the other elements. For example, I may be admitted to Hospital A but may have a specialist at Hospital B which uses a different EHR that cannot trade data with Hospital A. So, Hospital A will not be able to electronically collect my specialist's physician notes. Nor will my specialist be able to access Hospital A's discharge summary. And my home health provider may have limited IT capabilities and be unable to connect with any outside organizations at all. This example makes it clear that when I'm dealing with communications within the healthcare world, I am trying to do a whole lot more than get a few Euros from an ATM in Spain.

A more apt comparison would be if I could use the ATM to do the following: update my federal and state income tax payroll withholding amounts, check the balance in the 401(k) plan at my independent investment brokerage, check my mortgage's escrow account balance with a commercial lender not affiliated with my bank, pay my water utility bill, and transfer money to one of my kids' accounts at their local credit union in California. This begins to approximate the complexity of getting my medical record across the street.

So, yes, there is a good reason I can withdraw cash in Spain but not get all my medical information across the street.

2. *The expense*

Technology is not cheap. Developers and entrepreneurs typically invest years designing their new products and devices. The Food and Drug Administration (FDA) approval process is lengthy and can be very expensive. Not every device or pharmaceutical product has to go through this step, but if they do, the medical device and pharmaceutical companies have to recuperate considerable overhead costs. Consequently, clinically oriented products usually carry hefty price tags. Given the financial challenges I outlined in Chapter 1, health systems have to carefully weigh each of their expenditures. Funding for patient-care technology is in competition with nonclinical technology – and a whole lot of other things – and sometimes the scales are tilted toward clinical tech applications.

Why Are Things Changing Now?

Despite the impediments listed above, we have witnessed in recent years an encouraging uptick in healthcare's adoption of non-clinical technology. Many healthcare accelerators and incubators have popped up all over the country, and numerous new companies have developed gangbuster products. There are several reasons for this impressive growth:

- The rise of the Internet in the late 1990s – The Internet's transformational impact on the business world hasn't been lost on healthcare technology developers. If vast improvements happened in general commerce, they can happen in healthcare too.

  Perhaps the Internet's most important impact is the shift in mindset and expectations. We have learned that it is possible to conduct almost any kind of transaction electronically from almost anywhere in the world. Whole industry groups – like telephone directory publishers, travel agencies, map-making companies, toy stores, record shops, and book stores – have been decimated by the Internet. When was the last time you reserved a flight or hotel room through a travel agent? The public expects – no, demands – to conduct more and more business online, and we get annoyed if we go to a site advertising any type of consumer product and it doesn't allow an immediate online purchase. Although healthcare is notoriously behind other industries, it is catching up, and more and more retail-type transactions like booking appointments and paying bills are becoming the norm.

- The explosion of smartphones and tablets – *Media Tech Reviews* reports that there were 224.3 million smartphone users in the United States in 2018 and the number is expected to grow to 270.7 by 2022.[1] Statista states that 53.8% of the US population owned a tablet in 2018.[2] As in the case with the Internet, these users expect instant communication with every important organization they deal with, including their doctors and health systems. This greatly ups the demand for communications technologies.

■ The care environment migrating toward population health management, value-based purchasing, and bundled payments – In order to support the new demands create by these significant changes in the payment and delivery environment, provider and patients alike need immediate access to relevant health data. It is virtually impossible to maximize quality, coordinate care, reduce costs, manage resources, comply with regulatory requirements, and operate under the new financial realities without tapping into the emerging technologies that were not around even five years ago. This dynamic has spawned hundreds of phone and tablet apps that track patients' progress and alert caregivers when intervention might be needed.

■ Cloud storage and Software as a Service (SaaS) hosting – These breakthroughs have made it far easier for healthcare organizations to conveniently store data and ensure that each user within the organization has the very latest version of each application.

■ The availability of more robust Internet bandwidth – The fact that 5G technology offers download speeds 10 to 100 times faster than 4G is encouraging some healthcare organizations like Rush University System for Health to become a "5G-enabled hospital."[3]

Explosive Growth

These forces are coalescing to create a climate of unprecedented growth for healthtech, and all indicators point to this upward trajectory continuing and even accelerating. Consider these statistics and factoids:

■ The total digital health market is projected to grow from the 2016 level of $179.6 billion to $536.6 billion in 2025.[4]

- The market for precision medicine alone (which is explained later in this chapter) is expected to exceed $96.6 billion by 2024.[5]
- Although venture capital (VC) investments in healthtech have flattened a bit in recent years, the projected level of 2017 VC investments was three times what it was in 2012.[6] The top three digital health areas receiving VC funding in 2016 were genomics and sequencing, analytics and Big Data, and wearables and biosensing.[7]
- There has been a dramatic shift in the amount of VC going into digital health vs. more "traditional medtech" (devices, etc.). In 2011, traditional medtech received 2.68 times more Series A funding than did digital health. By 2016, the relative proportions had flipped and digital health got 1.75 more than traditional medtech.[8]
- There are currently at least 325,000 mobile health apps.[9]
- An estimated 245 million wearable devices will be sold in 2019, making it a $25 billion industry.[10] The advertising spending alone for wearables is projected to reach $68.7 million in 2019.[11]
- According to Liquid State, "Mobile has become the default technology for patient engagement."[12]
- Blockchain technology is widely anticipated to hit the healthcare market in a big way. LDJ Capital Chairman David Drake recently commented, "The healthcare industry is booming with innovations like the blockchain-powered technologies for the past few years. I think the trend for coming years will be healthtech protocols paired with blockchain tech and crypto . . . ."[13]
- Seeing the growing impact of mHealth, several large health systems have developed their own healthtech incubators, are partnering with start-ups, and/or are establishing venture funds.

Research 2 Guidance (R2G) is a German-based organization that supports businesses that develop digital health products through market research, competitor insights, and strategy advice. R2G facilitates partnerships "between best-in-class innovators and established healthcare companies and help(s) them to align their service offerings and business models."[14] One of its hallmark publications is *mHealth Developer Economics: Connectivity in Digital Health* billed as "the largest research program on mHealth app publishing." Highlights from the November 2018 version of the report give glimpses into the current and future state of the healthcare app world and predict that integration and the expanded use of sensors will continue.

■ Forty-nine percent of mHealth app publishers are currently integrating EHRs into their mobile apps.

■ Rather than merely being repositories of health data, future EHRs will incorporate Artificial Intelligence (AI) which will offer care recommendations to clinicians. EHRs will also transmit appropriate data to public health reporting systems.

■ Moving forward, medical devices will be the most important category (at 65%) for sensor integration, while wearable devices (at 52%) will also be relevant integration points.

■ Built-in sensors will be accessible in various types of devices:
  – Smartphones and tablets – for use as accelerometers and for taking heart rate measures and will also be installed in phone cameras
  – Wearables – such as bracelets, helmets
  – Plugged-in or wirelessly connected devices – such as blood glucose meters, thermometers, and blood pressure meters
  – In-body implantable sensors – used to detect glucose levels for diabetes control
  – Intimate contact items – such as stick-on tattoo sensors[15]

In January 2018, Amazon, Berkshire Hathaway, and JPMorgan Chase created a huge stir in the healthcare community by announcing the formation of a not-for-profit entity (subsequently dubbed Haven) with the mission of taking on "the hungry tapeworm" of soaring healthcare costs. Technology will play a big role in this initiative. Although its first target group is the three organizations' one million employees, any significant breakthroughs could clearly serve as models for other companies and could potentially end up benefiting all Americans. The formation of Haven was one of the most significant healthcare stories of 2018. *The New York Times* reported that the initial announcement of Haven's formation "landed like a thunderclap – sending stocks for insurers and other major health companies tumbling."[16]

Partially as a response to Haven, Apple announced it's developing its own tech-enabled clinics for Apple employees. This is a logical extension of Apple's health-related focus that began with the 2014 introduction of its HealthKit, an Application Programming Interface (API) for developers of health-related apps. Since then, the company has launched or used several different platforms to enable connecting health data across various apps and for use in clinical research.[17]

As I was putting the final touches on this book, speculation was growing that the Amazon/Berkshire Hathaway/JPMorgan Chase and Apple initiatives might join forces. Having Apple link up with Haven would close two gaps by Apple's being able to provide the following:

■ The ability to continuously monitor biometric data
■ A data aggregation platform for health information which could form the basis of new services[18]

Who knows where all this will lead? But anytime you hear the words "Amazon," "Apple," and "technology" in the same conversation, it's a safe bet something big will likely result.

And it even gets wilder. *Automobile* magazine recently ran a story called "The Big Data Boom" featuring incredible tech-driven automotive breakthroughs and predicting the connected car will change the industry. Self-driving cars are generating a lot of buzz these days, and according to this article, a fully developed autonomous vehicle is expected to generate 100 gigabytes of data *every second*! In the future sensors will collect data from engines, transmissions, brakes, and even windshield wipers and be able to use the resulting data combined with other data sources for traffic control purposes, to predict the location of black ice, to offer location-based special offers (like a free cup of coffee at Dunkin' Donuts), to find a parking spot, and even to support law enforcement if officials can overcome likely privacy concerns and have the ability, say, to access the cameras of all the vehicles in a particular area that just suffered a terrorist attack.

None of this pertains directly to healthcare, but this story goes on to report there are medical applications for other car-based sensors. One company is working on what it calls an Active Wellness chair that will measure heart rates and respiration to be used by a system designed to help alleviate driver drowsiness and stress. Ford has developed a steering wheel that tracks pulse rate and other vital signs, and, as the author says, "it's not difficult to imagine how valuable biomedical data would be to a driver's doctor, health insurer, or a pharmaceutical company."[19]

Motor Trend magazine reports on an Israeli company with technology that accesses information from a car's onboard technology and sensors active during an accident to predict the likely severity of passenger injuries. This data is transmitted to first responders so they have a better idea of what to expect upon arrival. And if the projected injuries are serious enough, a medevac unit can be immediately dispatched even before the ambulance arrives with the emergency medical technicians. This can save precious minutes and potentially many lives.[20]

Wild indeed!

Categorizing Healthcare Technology

Usually, when I tell people that I help technology companies with their strategies for selling into the healthcare world they say, "Oh, so you work with EHRs." Well, no, not really. Most EHR companies have been around long enough to have pretty much developed their strategies, while many of my clients are earlier in their growth cycles and are still developing their understanding of the field and their strategies.

I've had this conversation enough times to make me to want to figure out why people assume that I work mostly with EHR companies. I think I know why. Because of federal mandates and funding for EHRs) through the Medicare Access and CHIP Reauthorization Act (MACRA) and the 21st Century Cure Act, EHRs have been the most visible technology in recent years. However, healthtech includes a whole lot more than EHRs: everything from mobile phone apps to the Internet of Things (IoT) to implantable devices to Artificial Intelligence (AI) and all other kinds of things in between.

Whenever I approach a complicated subject, I find it helpful to look for patterns and themes so I can create a framework to categorize disorganized and potentially confusing material. This led me to think of healthcare tech in two very broad buckets:

1. Traditional technology
2. Everything else – specifically emerging, disruptive, and transformational technology

Allow me to elaborate.

There are three main services within my "traditional" category:

1. IT infrastructure
2. Complying with the Health Information Portability and Accountability Act (HIPAA) concerning protection of Personally Identifiable Information (PII)
3. EHRs

This might seem like an odd grouping. It's easy to recognize IT infrastructure as traditional technology. Even the smallest physician practice must have some sort of computer capability, and that means they have an IT infrastructure.

But why would I consider the other two traditional? After all, HIPAA is not even a technology product. It's a federal law that governs the safeguarding the privacy of patients' health information. (Other countries have corresponding laws concerning PII protection.) Creating a secure IT infrastructure is an obvious competent of every HIPAA compliance plan, so the CIO typically plays a central role on the HIPAA team. And to most people, the CIO equals technology. Therefore, HIPAA is often seen largely as a technology issue.

Regarding EHRs, just like IT infrastructure and HIPAA compliance, they have essentially become a cost of doing business for anyone in healthcare. *Modern Healthcare* recognized this in a 2017 article entitled "Á disruptor becomes the norm" where they called EHRs "a ubiquitous and necessary part of both the provider and the patient experience."[21] I don't suggest that EHRs are fully mature. They have a long way to go and will continue to evolve. My point is that the healthcare ecosystem has already recognized EHRs as part of the new reality and, in that sense, they are no longer revolutionary.

Interestingly, there may soon be a fourth category labeled "traditional" and considered to be expected. And that is telemedicine, defined as physician consults conducted via technology. Telemedicine may be reaching the point of becoming an expectation rather than a novelty. *Modern Healthcare*'s March 25, 2019 cover story was called "Use it or lose them" and describes how some patients may begin to migrate away from providers without telemedicine capabilities.[22]

So, IT infrastructure, HIPAA compliance, and EHRs (and perhaps telemedicine) are woven into the fabric of today's healthcare delivery world. Most of their impact on healthcare has already been baked into the system. Even though EHRs continue to be tweaked, the many positive changes they offer are already factored in.

This is like what sometimes happens to the stock market when the Federal Reserve raises interest rates after leaving them alone for a couple of years. The markets often react negatively when interest rates increase, but sometimes they don't. When they don't, expert analysts explain that the markets had been expecting a rate increase for many months and maybe were even a bit surprised that it hadn't happened sooner. So, when rates did increase, they weren't surprised and had already considered that move into their expectations. As a result, the markets pretty much yawn.

It's the same with these three aspects of technology. The bulk of their impact has already been absorbed into the delivery system. Another way of saying this is that you can't operate without all three of them. None of them is a "marketing talking point." Just like no hospital touts in its advertisements, "Come to our hospital because we have elevators," neither do they say, "Come to our hospital because we have EHRs."

So that's traditional technology.

I call the second major category, "emerging, disruptive, transformational technology." This is where all the exciting innovation is happening but it's a little hard to precisely define. Different people apply the following terms to this grouping: telemedicine, telehealth, digital health, mHealth, mobile health, virtual health, and maybe even a few other terms.

Regardless of what you call it, here is a partial list of emerging, transformational technology applications:

- Smartphone peripheral plug-ins for measuring blood pressure, takings electrocardiogram (EKGs), etc.
- Big Data
- AI
- Predictive analytics
- Precision medicine/personalized medicine

- Wearable technologies
- 3-D printing
- Expansion of genomics and DNA sequencing into routine care decisions

Unlike IT infrastructure, HIPAA compliance, and EHRs, many of these *are* the objects of marketing campaigns.

You can see how varied the new offerings are. Smartphone peripheral plug-ins have almost nothing in common with DNA sequencing, yet they are both part of this revolution. To get my arms around these wildly varying elements, I decided to look for organizing principles to better understand the overall lay of the land. In this case, I subdivided the group of emerging, disruptive, transformational technology into six categories. Hence, the title of this chapter.

The Six Fronts of the Healthtech Revolution

Let's look at the six along with examples of each. In some cases, the technology has already hit the market and in others it is still developing and evolving.[23]

1. Physical items representing clinical breakthroughs – Direct patient care items used to diagnose or treat clinical conditions. There are three categories:
   - Diagnostic equipment – such as MRI technology, teleradiology, and some wearables (like Apple Watch 4's recent approval for certain EKGs). Many medical imaging devices are already being miniaturized, and hand-held ultrasound devices are now on the market. In the near future, nanosensors will become embedded into a patient's bloodstream to constantly monitor for cancer, autoimmune attacks on vital tissues, or artery wall cracks which can be precursors of strokes and heart attacks.[24]

- Interventional tools – such as equipment for robotic surgery and laparoscopic surgery
- Devices and implantables – such as 3-D printing, cardiovascular implants, the artificial heart, stents, and bionic limbs.

2. Mobile tools in the care delivery process – Most of the following information appears in an article entitled "The future of Medicine is in your smartphone," by futurist Eric Topol, MD, a cardiologist and director of the Scripps Translational Science Institute. His article describes smartphones' many uses in the arsenal of care delivery.

- App-based telehealth visits between providers and patients – These can be for initial inquiries about newly manifesting medical problems or for virtual house call visits. App-based physician visits are becoming more common and both Deloitte and PWC predict that virtual visits will soon be the norm, replacing in-person office visits.[25]
- Smartphones as a cost-containment tool – Topol reports that in some cities, patients can use a mobile app to request a physician house call during which the physician can not only do standard consultation but can perform low-level procedures such as stitching up a wound. This avoids what otherwise would have been an expensive trip to the ED.
- Plug-in smartphone peripheral devices – These make it possible to screen for problems like ear infections, thus avoiding a trip to the doctor's office or urgent care center. Future developments will include the ability to conduct routine lab tests for blood electrolytes; kidney, liver, and thyroid activity; and breath, sweat, and urine analyses. Besides being far more convenient than institution-based testing, these tests should be considerably cheaper.[26]
- Sensors – Topol also predicts that eventually wristwatch sensors could become the equivalent of having

an intensive care unit on your wrist. "As a result, except for ICUs, operating rooms and emergency rooms, hospitals of the future are likely to be room- less data surveillance centers for remote patient monitoring."[27]

– The Internet of Things (IoT) – Topol references necklaces that monitor heart function and check fluid levels in a patient's lungs, contact lenses that track glucose levels and eye pressure, and head- bands that monitor brain waves. In the future, he says, we may see socks and shoes that can analyze a person's gait to tell Parkinson's patients whether their medication is working or inform caregivers when an older person is at increased fall risk caused by unsteadiness.

– Sensors to monitor environmental conditions – Smartphone sensors will be able to monitor exposure to radiation, air pollution, and pesticides in food, all of which have an impact on people's health.[28]

Topol sums these possibilities up like this:

> This is heady stuff – but this vision of medicine raises some serious and reasonable concerns. Before these tools enter widespread use, they must all be validated through clinical trials and shown to not only preserve health but to do so while lowering costs. Without such validation, the whole promise of digital medicine will be for naught.[29]

3. Enhanced information-based care – Taking data from various sources to design tailored care plans for each indi- vidual and determine which treatment approaches will likely yield the best results clinically and economically and which best match the patient's preferences and cir- cumstances. Although there is some overlap between the

following categories, enhanced information-based care can generally be subdivided as follows:

– Clinical: precision medicine – As opposed to a "one-size-fits-all" approach where prevention and treatment strategies are developed for the "average person," precision medicine factors in differences between individuals.[30] It's really a merger of the Human Genome Project (which identified all the approximately 20,500 genes in human DNA and determined the sequences of the 3 billion chemical base pairs that make up human DNA[31]), population health (which looks at the health status of large groups of people), evidence-based medicine (which identifies the treatment approaches most likely to result in good outcomes based on credible scientific research and evidence), and predictive analytics (which takes known information and projects trends and outcomes into the future).

– Clinical: predictive analytics – Rather than merely looking backward at a patient's medical history, predictive analytics combines historical data with other relevant information to calculate the likelihood of future outcomes. Outbound patient progress alerts help clinicians and management staff track the patient's progress. This allows them to modify their care plans as needed.

The online publication *Health IT Analytics* lists ten ways Predictive Analytics can be used in healthcare:

1. Risk scoring for chronic diseases and population health
2. Avoiding 30-day hospital readmissions
3. Getting ahead of patient deterioration
4. Forestalling patient no-shows
5. Preventing suicide and patient self-harm
6. Predicting patient utilization patterns
7. Managing the supply chain
8. Ensuring strong data security

9. Developing precision medicine and new therapies
10. Bolstering patient engagement and satisfaction[32]

Each of these is a universe unto itself with great potential to move the ball down the field when it comes to improving outcomes and control costs.

– Clinical: reduction in variation of care through evidence-based medicine – Evidence-based medicine seeks to bring greater uniformity to care through supporting those treatment protocols that have been shown to be most effective for most people. This may seem in opposition to precision medicine where care is tailored to the individual, but evidence-based medicine's real target is *unnecessary* variation in clinical practice patterns that are not grounded in evidence of the effectiveness of various treatment protocols. *Modern Healthcare* reports that clinical variation "is a significant contributor to healthcare's multibillion-dollar overuse problem" and cites a 2012 *JAMA* study that concludes spending could be reduced by at least 20% without affecting outcomes if care consolidated around best practices.[33] The British medical journal *BMJ* defines evidence-based medicine as "the conscientious, explicit, and judicious use of current best evidence in making decisions about the care of individual patients" which integrates a clinician's "individual clinical expertise with the best available external clinical evidence from systematic research."[34] Evidence-based medicine often leads to automated clinical protocols as a starting point for physicians to consider as they develop care plans for patients with a particular problem or disease. Combining evidence-based medicine with precision medicine – which tailors the final course of treatment to the individual based on the various factors mentioned in the previous bullet – results in fine-tuned care plans likely to yield favorable and more cost-effective outcomes.

- Care coordination – This can help pre- and post-discharge care and can also factor in a patient's life circumstances and preferences beyond just the clinical concerns. Examples include:
  - Chronic care apps that provide daily feedback about patients' vital signs and other circumstances to physicians
  - Patient-scheduling apps and software to remind patients of appointments and allow easy rescheduling if necessary
  - Social support aspects of Big Data such as psychographic/demographic data that indicates the patient's preferred method of communication and lifestyle preferences
  - Post-acute patient placement based on a patient's insurance, certain clinical criteria, bed availability, and patient preference

4. Communications – This category is subdivided as follows:
  - As a front door to care or an information source for patients – Examples include:
    - Online physician directories to assist patients in identifying providers
    - Triage apps to help patients determine severity of medical problems and the most appropriate care setting
    - Apps that help patients determine cost of prescriptions, lab tests, physician visits, scans, and other items so they can find the most affordable suppliers[35]
  - Communication between providers and patients for patient education and to monitor patient progress and trigger early intervention if necessary – As I explained in Chapter 1, there is a movement toward bundled payments, value-based payment, and accountable care

organizations all of which encourage more coordinated care and interventions in the most appropriate and cost-effective settings. I am thoroughly convinced that these efforts cannot ultimately succeed without effective deployment of mobile technology, which can be used in the following ways:

- Communicating via apps and email – Examples include reminders to use sunscreen; instructions to pregnant women about what to do at various stages of pregnancy; and contextualized messages reminding diabetes patients to improve their activity levels, taking into account the weather, diabetes patients' location, their activity levels, and their motivation.[36]
- Providers being able to direct patients to appropriate and trusted websites for clinical information
- Automated post-discharge information and personalized instructions delivered on laptops or mobile devices that reinforce patient follow-up actions at the appropriate intervals
- Some wearable technologies that provide biometric data and subjective information, allowing the clinician to track patient adherence and progress
- Behavioral health patient engagement apps and telemedicine consults
- "Telesitter" services capable of monitoring several at-risk patients at the same time
- Smart pill boxes that enable clinical personnel to track a patient's medication adherence
- Communication among providers
    - EHRs that can be accessed by various clinicians involved in treating the same patient
    - Teleradiology that allows remote consultations among physicians

5. Clinical research – 21st-century mobile technology is having an impact on research. Here are two examples:
   – The proliferation of iPhones and the apps built into Apple's ResearchKit have made recruiting clinical research participants easier. ResearchKit helps find participants and collect their data and also provides an open source framework facilitating researchers' app development. These apps can also gather more data resulting in more robust analyses.[37]
   – Apps themselves are also the subject of research – The University of Michigan and Apple have teamed up to determine if the data collected through the Apple Watch can be combined with other data to better assess patient's health, wellness, and risk for disease.[38]
6. Business functions – This category can also be subdivided.
   – Clinical applications
     ■ Lean process improvement – Data-driven multidisciplinary teams that meet to seek improved outcome measures. One example is an ED workflow study to enhance quality, efficiency, and throughput.
     ■ Automating clinical tasks, thereby allowing caregivers to focus on things only they can do. For example, one app attempts to alert physicians about the availability of certain prescriptions as well as determine if the patients' health plan covers that particular drug. If this verification is done before the patient leaves the physician's office and an availability or coverage problem is discovered, the clinician can immediately seek a substitute drug. Without this capability, if the patient goes to the pharmacy and discovers the problem, they have to recontact the physician's office, and the physician must review the

patient's chart to refresh their memory and then order a substitute. This is not good use of the physician's time.

- Non-clinical applications – These are standard business functions that every organization has:
  - Market analyses
  - Operating room, lab, and therapy session scheduling
  - Billing and administrative processes
  - Staff scheduling and other human resources functions
  - Wayfinding apps to help patients navigate health system campuses
  - Optimization of facilities functions such as utility consumption, maintenance tasks, etc.
  - Device warranty management

This list of the six major categories is both overwhelming and incredibly exciting. As these capabilities continue to roll out into the marketplace, millions of patients will benefit. Collectively, products in these areas are changing how care is delivered, and I firmly believe that many aspects of the healthcare system of 2030 will bear little resemblance to what we have today because of these exciting innovations. And that's truly a reason to be optimistic. If you work in the healthcare technology realm, congratulations. This is a great place to be!

End Notes

1. "How Many Cell Phone Subscribers in the US 2018," http://www.mediatechreviews.com/how-many-cell-phone-subscribers-the-us/, accessed April 5, 2019.
2. "Tablet Penetration in the United States from 2011 to 2020," https://www.statista.com/statistics/208033/forecast-of-the-tablet-penetration-in-the-us-up-to-2014/, accessed April 5, 2019.

3. Jessica Kim Cohen, "Rush University goes all in," *Modern Healthcare*, May 13, 2019, pp. 26-28.

4. www.healthstandards.com/blog/2017/10/25-digital-health-trends-2025/, accessed April 23, 2019.

5. "Precision Medicine Market Statistics and Research Analysis Released in latest report," https://www.marketwatch.com/press-release/precision-medicine-market-statistics-and-research-analysis-released-in-latest-report-2019-04-26, accessed April 27, 2019.

6. Sean Lightbown, "Here are 4 key trends in VC healthtech investments," https://pitchbook.com/news/articles/4-trends-in-vc-healthtech-investment, accessed April 24, 2019.

7. "On the digital health frontier," *Modern Healthcare*, April 10, 2017, page 29.

8. Deloitte, *Out of the valley of death*, 2017, page 9, https://www2.deloitte.com/content/dam/Deloitte/us/Documents/life-sciences-health-care/us-lshc-medtech-innovation.pdf, accessed April 26, 2019.

9. https://research2guidance.com/325000-mobile-health-apps-available-in-2017/, accessed April 23, 2019.

10. CCS Insights, "Wearables Market to Be Worth $25 Billion by 2019," https://www.ccsinsight.com/press/company-news/2332-wearables-market-to-be-worth-25-billion-by-2019-reveals-ccs-insight/, accessed April 24, 2019.

11. Jessica Wade, "Wearable Technology Statistics and Trends 2018," https://www.smartinsights.com/digital-marketing-strategy/wearables-statistics-2017/, accessed April 24, 2019.

12. https://liquid-state.com/digital-health-app-trends-2018/

13. "What are the investment trends in the healthtech industry for 2019? Answers in this Hong Kong event," https://www.prlog.org/12750042-what-are-the-investment-trends-in-the-healthtech-industry-for-2019-answers-in-this-hong-kong-event.html, accessed April 24, 2019

14. https://research2guidance.com/about-research2guidance/, accessed April 23, 2019

15. *mHealth Developer Economics: Connectivity in Digital Health*, Research 2 Guidance, November 2018, pages 12–14.

16. Nick Wingfield, Katie Thomas and Reed Abelson, "Amazon, Berkshire Hathaway and JPMorgan Team Up to Try to Disrupt Health Care," *The New York Times*, January 30, 2018,

https://www.nytimes.com/2018/01/30/technology/amazon-berkshire-hathaway-jpmorgan-health-care.html, accessed April 24, 2019.

17. Roman Luzgin, "Healthcare Will Catalyze Apple's Growth," https://seekingalpha.com/article/4155362-healthcare-will-catalyze-apples-growth, March 11, 2018, accessed April 23, 2019.

18. James Thorne, "Should Apple Join Amazon's Health Venture? Analysts make the case for collaboration between tech giants," https://www.geekwire.com/2019/apple-join-amazons-healthcare-venture/, April 19, 2019, accessed April 24, 2019.

19. Doug Newcomb, "The Big Data Boom," *Automobile*, October 17, 2017, https://www.automobilemag.com/news/the-big-data-boom/, accessed April 26, 2019.

20. Frank Markus, "Medi-Cars: Taking 'onboard diagnostics' to a new level," *Motor Trend* April 2019, page 27.

21. "A disruptor becomes the norm," *Modern Healthcare*, April 24, 2017, page 29.

22. "Use it or lose them," *Modern Healthcare*, March 25, 2019, pages 18–20.

23. Some of the specific technology examples that follow were included in *Modern Healthcare*'s, fortieth anniversary issue published July 11, 2016 that lists the industry's top milestones of the previous forty years.

24. Eric Topol, "The future of Medicine is in your smart-phone," *Wall Street Journal*, January 9, 2015, https://www.wsj.com/articles/the-future-of-medicine-is-in-your-smartphone-1420828632, accessed April 28, 2019.

25. ibid.

26. ibid.

27. ibid.

28. ibid.

29. ibid.

30. "Help Me Understand Genetics: Precision Medicine," Lister Hill National Center for Biomedical Communication, U.S. National Library of Medicine, https://ghr.nlm.nih.gov/primer/precisionmedicine/precisionvspersonalized, April 16, 2019, accessed April 27, 2019, page 3.

31. Human Genome Project Information Archive, 1990-2003, https://web.ornl.gov/sci/techresources/Human_Genome/index.shtml, accessed April 27, 2019.

32. Jennifer Bresnick, "10 High-Value Use Cases for Predictive Analytics in Healthcare," *Health IT Analytics*, https://healthitanalytics.com/news/10-high-value-use-cases-for-predictive-analytics-in-healthcare, September 4, 2018, accessed April 28, 2019.

33. Jessica Kim Cohen, "Using AI to reduce clinical variation," *Modern Healthcare, March 11, 2019, page 30.*

34. From *BMJ* 1996; 312:71-72, cited in "Evidence-Based Medicine Definitions," NYU School of Medicine Frederick L. Ehrman Medical Library, https://library.med.nyu.edu/library/instruction/handouts/pdf/ebmdefinitions.pdf, accessed April 27, 2019.

35. Topol, "The Future of Medicine Is in Your Smartphone."

36. Karen Wahner, "How Mobile Health Is Changing Care Delivery," *leadership*, Fall 2014, page 24.

37. "Top 10 Digital Health Use Cases for 2018," https://www.progress.com/solutions/health-cloud/resources/top-10-digital-use-cases-for-2018, accessed April 27, 2019.

38. "University of Michigan, Apple team up on study," *Modern Healthcare*, March 25, 2019, page 5.

Chapter 5

Timing Pitfalls

Timing is everything.

One thing I appreciate about entrepreneurs is that many of them see opportunities and are able to anticipate future needs and, as hockey star Wayne Gretzky once famously said he skated "to where the puck is going to be." Having a good sense of developing needs and being able to arrive there ahead of others is admirable.

The danger for some innovators, though, is getting there *too* early, before the market is ready. Musicians, artists, and authors are among those most adversely affected by being underappreciated in their times or early in their careers, only to have their genius recognized down the road. Perhaps you will be encouraged by the story of Max Lucado. With well over 100 titles to his credit, he is an international best-selling author and one of the most successful writers of inspirational books of all time. However, his career as a published author got off to a rocky start. His first manuscript was rejected over and over – ultimately 14 times – before one publisher finally took him on. In his case, he understood the reader market better than the "experts" did, and it took time for him to find the one publisher who "got it." Having unrecognized genius can be frustrating, but sometimes it just takes perseverance and patience before you achieve success.

Unfortunately, this phenomenon can plague healthtech innovators as well. I'm aware of some worthwhile products that ultimately failed only to see someone else come along later with substantially the same concept and succeed because either the market or the technology had finally caught with the concept. I wish I could advise you on how to get around this problem, but if the market isn't ready, it just isn't ready and there's not much you can do about it.

There are, however, several pitfalls related to timing that I can help with, so please read about these problems and possible solutions in this chapter.

1. Launching Either Too Early or Too Late

Developers and entrepreneurs spend months or even years preparing their products for market introduction. A danger they face is misjudging when to launch. They must heed the old saying, "You only have one chance to make a first impression," but some may obsess over this too much and, therefore, delay their product's introduction longer than necessary. This can lead to either losing the "first-to-market" advantage – giving competitors some daylight – or to missed sales, which could hamstring a cash-starved company.

On the other hand, in an attempt to beat the rest of the market, some vendors make the opposite mistake of launching prematurely, with sometimes devastating results. Do you remember Apple's disastrous 2012 launch of its new Maps app? It worked perfectly, unless you didn't want to have to find a baseball stadium on the top of a mountain or were confused by aerial-view interstate maps that resembled overcooked spaghetti. Once a product gets cast as inferior, it can take years to recover. Some never do.

Recommendation:

■ *If you are introducing a groundbreaking service or product, seek the sweet spot where your minimally viable product performs all its essential functions adequately yet still gives you a head start in the market. Waiting until every "nice-to-have" is in place can unduly delay your launch. The concept here is to not let the perfect get in the way of the good. As you release version 1.0 – which will have all the essential features – you can simultaneously start talking about the enhancements in the works for version 2.0.*

A product that does exactly what it purports to do – even if it's not particularly fancy – establishes your credibility and starts the cash flow so vital to continued development. When early adopters like what they see, they will likely talk your product up among their peers.

There is less pressure to launch prematurely if you are entering a commoditized market. Since you are not the first one offering such a product, you don't run the risk of someone encroaching on your new approach, so delaying a bit probably won't prove fatal. However, you must still evaluate your cash flow needs. All companies must find just the right balance between hitting the market too early and waiting too long.

2. Failing to Get a Serious Hearing Because You are a Start-Up

This problem plagues tech start-ups in all fields, not just healthcare. Over coffee, a friend with an exciting new company in the communications/sales arena relayed his tale of woe over being rejected outright by a large corporation before he even was able to meet with them in person. "Our policy is to only work with established companies," he was told. This company was more upfront about their policy than some. I've had some healthtech clients lament over the fact that a healthcare organization they were targeting lost interest once they found out the tech company was a very early stage company with no active customers.

This reluctance is understandable. The healthcare environment is incredibly complex, both in terms of how its organized and how a bewildering array of technical pieces must fit together. Working with an unproven company can be risky, and issues with an installation or with how the product operates can cause problems to cascade to other parts of the healthcare organization.

However, this leaves the start-up in a lurch. It's the same dilemma early careerist face. They can't get a job without experience, and they can't get experience without a job. Start-ups desperately need at least a few clients they can point to. Additionally, every start-up needs an infusion of cash, and unless they have a stable source of capital, not having paying clients early on can be the death-knell.

When Oracle launched in 1979, they pursued the interesting strategy of calling their initial version Oracle 2 – there was no version 1 – to minimize the impression they were a brand-new company.

Recommendation: There is nothing you can do to hide the fact that you don't yet have any clients, but there are three schools of thought about whether or not to charge your very first users.

1. *Just as someone embarking on a new career must often complete an unpaid internship, you may need to seek one or two free pilots to prove the value and effectiveness of your product. Any pilot requires a certain degree of accommodations by the host as it adapts operationally, so there is a cost to them, even if it is not monetary. Also, the pilot host is taking on a degree of reputational risk as they trust an unproven product that could fail. Some companies that decide to offer a free pilot to one or two organizations feel that charging anything at all creates yet another hurdle in the approval process.*

2. *Another approach is to offer a greatly reduced price for the first few users. This at least gets the cash flow started and may be necessary if you are very tight on finances and/or if the installation process would require significant out-of-pocket costs for you. This approach also makes sure the client has some financial "skin in the game."*

3. *Other start-ups charge full price right out of the gate. This approach reflects the old adage that something you get for free is worth every penny you spent. Charging full price can be effective if your product is relatively affordable (as opposed to involving a multimillion-dollar investment).*

There are several factors to consider in determining your initial pricing option: your financial condition, how expensive your product is perceived to be, and the "prestige" of the potential pilot site. Remember, the overriding goal is to get a referenceable user or two.

3. Launching a Product Before the Overall Healthcare System Has Caught Up with Its Financial Policies

By definition, disruptive technology upsets the status quo. A new healthtech product is worthless if no providers buy it, and no one will buy it if there is no way to pay for it. The healthcare world is notoriously slow in responding to changes in the environment.

There are three financial problems some vendors face relative to this issue:

1. A new clinical technology does not fit within the existing payment codes. No code means a procedure can't be billed. And without a way to bill, no one will adopt the innovation. This problem most typically affects medical devices.

2. Even if an adequate code exists, payers must agree to pay for the service. Telemedicine is the most prominent recent victim of this problem. There are many reasons to employ this technology, among them convenience of patient access, an ability to tap into specialty care otherwise unavailable, and a chance for providers to reach into remote markets. However, insurance companies were slow to pay for this type of remote intervention, and that hampered the sector's growth. Fortunately, the tide has begun to turn in the last few years regarding payment for telemedicine.

3. Even if a new device greatly improves clinical outcomes, it will face strong headwinds if it increases costs for patients paid under any kind of prospective payment system like Diagnosis-Related Groups (DRGs), which pay a flat fee for a given type of inpatient admission. DRG payment rates are based on historic costs for that service. If a new device costs the provider $1,000, unless it replaces an existing approach that costs at least $1,000, the net impact is increased cost to the hospital. Until the payers factor the net increase of cost into their DRG payment, the additional expense comes from the hospital's bottom line.

Recommendations:

■ *Addressing the first problem listed above – First and foremost, be aware of the need for an appropriate billing code. Don't finalize your sales and revenue projections until you understand whether there a billing code for your device and, if not, when you can expect one.*

■ *Addressing the second issue – If there are appropriate codes but payers don't yet recognize the service, approach some of the major payers in your market to open a dialogue about how to go about getting them to consider your new approach.*

■ *Addressing the third point – Your objective is to get providers to incorporate your new technology into their*

*standard treatment protocols. Make sure you understand
the payment dynamics surrounding the current treatment
modalities. There are three possible scenarios regarding
introducing a new device:*

1. *It can replace and is less costly than an existing
   device – This is the dream scenario. As long as your
   technology is demonstrably clinically or operationally
   equal to or better than the one you are trying to upend,
   it's easy to make the case that they should switch.*

2. *It can replace an existing technology but is more
   expensive – You must recognize that this will result in a
   net negative financial impact for any cases paid under
   a DRG. At that point you must stress non-financial
   benefits. These might include superior outcomes which
   could potentially shorten length of stay or contribute
   to the hospital's readmissions reduction efforts, added
   convenience for clinicians, or greater patient comfort.
   Just be very conservative in your projections about cutting length of stay or readmissions. Don't over-promise
   results that can't be realized. See Chapter 12 that dis-
   cusses Return on Investment (ROI) issues for ideas
   about how to develop believable ROI projections.*

3. *It supports enhanced outcomes but does not replace
   another approach and, therefore, results in a direct
   financial loss for DRG patients. This situation is tougher
   than option 2 immediately above. The suggestions
   offered there also apply here, and you must be even
   more conservative in your ROI numbers. Adding a
   costly new device without replacing an existing one
   can put significant stress on the hospital's cost structure.
   In order to justify the new expenditure, you might be
   tempted to be more aggressive with potential savings
   through reduced length of stay or readmissions. As
   indicated above, it's important to heed the advice in the
   ROI chapter.*

Chapter 6

Credibility Pitfalls

Credibility is one of the most important factors in any business relationship. There are at least two aspects to credibility: how much you know and how trustworthy you are. Even if you are a wonderful person, if you don't really understand my business or don't have the qualifications to carry out what I've asked you to do, I'm not willing to work with you. One of my very best friends is a great guy who is a highly effective sales executive in the commercial fitness equipment field. But there's no way I'm going to let his do my root canal. Similarly, if someone has demonstrated that they cut corners ethically or don't always follow through with their promises, I will certainly think twice before agreeing to partner with them.

This chapter presents 13 credibility-related pitfalls and how to minimize their impact.

4. Tipping Your Hand as a Healthcare "Outsider"

The healthcare world has one of the highest densities of well-educated people of any industry. All clinical people have earned their credentials through years and years of education and practical experience. Physicians, for example, typically have a four-year undergraduate degree and a four-year medical school degree. This is usually followed by post-graduate training programs that can last from three to seven years. After all this, many pursue certification by the medical boards in their respective specialty areas: surgery, cardiology, family medicine, etc. Earning and maintaining these designations requires ongoing education and passing rigorous exams.

Physician assistants (PAs), nurse practitioners (NPs), licensed practical nurses (LPNs), certified registered nurse anesthetists (CRNAs), physical therapists (PTs), radiation technologists (RTs), and other professionals have their own demanding educational and certification requirements. Hospitals and healthcare organizations also employ many highly trained and experienced experts in non-clinical areas. This group includes senior executives, statisticians, government relations officers, and many others.

This rarified environment can lead people in healthcare organizations to be justifiably proud of their accomplishments and knowledge bases. Although most individuals in the healthcare world are gracious, you will occasionally find someone with a condescending attitude toward those who have not invested in their education as they have.

Some vendors from outside the healthcare industry underestimate the gulf that exists between industry insiders and "everyone else" and incorrectly conclude that their expertise as a business leader or technology expert grants them equal footing with their sales target. It's easy to act a bit too casually in their interactions with these people. Not a good idea.

Recommendations:

- *You can't – nor should you try to – pretend that you're "one of us" if you're not. Your resume and background clearly demonstrate the degree of your healthcare experience, or lack thereof.*

■ *Get thoroughly familiar with the operational principles and clinical dynamics of the area that your product falls into. If it changes the workflow in a given department, it's important for you to demonstrate that you know both how the existing process works and how practices will change if they adopt your product.*

■ *Make sure to use credible examples for any case studies or application examples you might present. In my role as executive vice president at the Georgia Hospital Association (GHA), I often had vendors seeking the association's endorsement come through my office. In the early days of the Internet, I had one salesman bluster his way into my office and announce that he was proud to be a healthcare outsider since he could look at the industry with fresh eyes and "bring efficiency into hospitals." He had one of the first Internet-based hospital supply management software products and wanted to demonstrate it. He offered to show how he could get a really good price on some medical supplies. "What should I get a price for," he asked, "band-aids?" As soon as I heard the word "band-aids," I knew he didn't know the first thing about hospital purchasing practices. That term is never used in serious clinical settings. His approach reminded me of the old saying, "Remain quiet and be thought a fool, or speak and remove all doubt." Having a poor example like he had is not necessarily a fatal mistake, but it won't certainly bolster your credibility.*

■ *Learn the relevant vocabulary and how to pronounce unfamiliar terms. Nothing identifies an outsider quicker than misusing, misspelling, or mispronouncing a term that everyone in the industry uses. Learn the difference between a Medical Assistant (MA), a Licensed Practical Nurse (LPN), and a Registered Nurse (RN), and learn their various roles. Another common mistake outsiders make is the misspelling HIPAA, the acronym for the Health*

Insurance Portability and Accountability Act. Because of the word "HIPAA"'s resemblance to the name of that large, gray zoo animal, many non-healthcare people inadvertently spell it HIPPA. I have heard more than one healthcare person mutter under their breath that that's the kiss of death when they see that.

5. Violating an "Unspoken Rule" or Protocol of the Industry

Industry outsiders don't necessarily know the "rules of the road" that everyone within that sector observes. As with the previous pitfall, these aren't necessarily deal-killers, but why place unnecessary roadblocks in your way?

This pitfall could be considered an extension of the previous item. One non-negotiable expectation is that physicians will be treated with utmost respect and be referred to as "Doctor" instead of "Fred." The protocol around executive staff varies from institution to institution. In some organizations, the top executives are called "Mr." or "Ms." while in other hospitals, first names are fine. I did a summer administrative residency between my two years of graduate school at an academic medical center with an *extremely* formal executive team. No one ever considered calling the CEO anything but "Mr. Black." One Sunday afternoon, my wife and I were furniture shopping and we ran into Mr. Black with his family. He was dressed in a $700 navy blue wool suit with a dark tie, perfectly knotted. He immediately apologized for being dressed so informally on a Sunday. He was informal?!? Compared to him, I was a slob. I wanted to dive behind a sofa so he wouldn't see that I was wearing jeans. He remained "Mr. Black" to me.

Another unspoken rule is that outsiders should be careful not to be too critical of the healthcare field. Everyone who works within it is thoroughly aware of all our shortcomings, and we talk freely about them among ourselves. Although many of us don't mind admitting our shortcoming to "outsiders," we typically only go so far in doing so. Healthcare is an extremely complex environment, and those who are not part of the industry don't always catch the nuances of why we do things the way we do and come to conclusions and make judgments that aren't exactly wrong but aren't completely right either. I once had a vendor lecture me on how poorly run hospitals are. Although he had some valid points, I found myself getting a bit defensive because some of his comments revealed he really didn't understand or appreciate why we do some things the way we do.

It's one thing for people to be self-critical and another for others to make disparaging remarks about you. Several years ago, I saw a great example of this. Our city of Marietta, Georgia, has a great little theater right on the downtown square. For many years, they hosted a play called *Smoke on the Mountain* that looks at life in a tiny, very conservative 1940s church in the Tennessee mountains. The play pokes fun at many of the typical traditions and practices of that type of church. But it's done lovingly from an "insider's" perspective and it quite funny. As a Christian, I greatly enjoyed seeing the wit of "one of us" who's not afraid to point out some of the funny and silly things we do.

On the other hand, I was at a professional meeting in Jackson Hole, Wyoming, several years ago and we had a free evening, so our group decided to go to a play at a small theater that dates back to the late 1800s. It ended up being a different comedy that also poked fun at religious people. Although a lot of the barbs were justified, the tone was a little off. There was just something about the dialog that revealed the playwright didn't really understand or appreciate the motivations of the churchgoers he was lampooning. It wasn't particularly offensive, but it was just "off" enough that this play didn't come across as well as the other one had or as particularly funny.

This is analogous to what can happen when non-healthcare people get too pointed in their critiques of the industry. I'm the first to admit that our industry is far from perfect, but I get a bit protective when an "outsider" starts taking swipes before they really understand the culture.

On another note, I recently had a slightly uncomfortable experience with breaking one of the rules of another industry. After spending 30 years in the hospital field, I launched my consulting business where I advise developers and entrepreneurs with their strategies regarding how to approach the healthcare market. Another target client base of mine is the investor community since they evaluate newer companies, trying to decide if they should fund them or not.

Right after starting my new company, a professional friend gave me the list of several organizations that might benefit from my experience. One of them was an association that hosts monthly breakfast gatherings for local investors. Interestingly, their meetings are in the exact same meeting room in the Buckhead Maggiano's that the Georgia Association of Healthcare Executives (GAHE) – a group I've been associated with for decades – meets in. GAHE goes out of its way to invite newcomers, hoping to expand our involvement, and first-time attendees are given special recognition and a round of applause. I am very familiar with and comfortable with the meeting room where I have consumed way too many calories over the years.

On the appointed day, I showed up at the investors' meeting and was politely greeted. As the meeting progressed, I slowly realized that newcomers really aren't supposed to just show up without having been specifically invited by an existing member as a "sponsor." The building didn't cave in on me, but my minor faux pas created a bit of a barrier between me and the other attendees, resulting in a mild level of discomfort.

The reason this is such a great example is that both the GAHE group and investors' group meet in the very same room, and I was transferring my behavior from GAHE to the new group, not knowing they operate differently.

Here's one final example. Physicians, business executives, and technology developers live in separate worlds. Although every profession should adhere to the highest ethical standards, values important to one group may not be so key for others.

I asked a very good friend of mine who is a just-retired OB/GYN physician to review part of this book's manuscript. As we were discussing his reactions, he told me he saw one phrase he didn't like. I wondered if I had misused some kind of medical term, and I was surprised to learn the words he didn't like were "disruptive technology." That phrase has become an accepted buzzword within both the technology and the business worlds. Everyone is all about *trying* to disrupt the old ways of doing things, interject innovation, and reformulate processes to create more contemporary and streamlined approaches. So, disruption is good.

That's not how my physician friend saw it. "When I hear you talk about disruption," he said, "it sounds like you're trying to mess up my day." This example is technically not a violation of any protocols, but it does show that word choices don't always accomplish what we think they will.

Recommendations:

▪ *The default should always be to refer to a physician as, for example, Dr. Campbell, until and unless they invite you to call them by their first name. On more than one occasion, I have seen younger salespeople, in an attempt to appear friendly, jump immediately to calling physicians by their first name. Maybe they're trying to create a relaxed restaurant environment, as in "Hi! I'm Bobby, and I'll be your server tonight." Bad idea. It's never a problem to be too formal with a physician, but doing the opposite can set you back. Even as someone with decades of experience in the hospital field, when I first interact with a physician (some of whom are younger than I am), I use their formal title unless they suggest otherwise. My unofficial rule is that if I ever get to the point with that physician of being a friend they would go out to a social lunch with, then I flip to a first name basis.*

■ *Regarding non-physician staff, take your cues from others in the organization. If the CFO calls the CEO "Ms. Roberts," do the same.*

■ *If you don't come from the healthcare world, it's OK to acknowledge some of our shortcomings. But do so with a sense of respect.*

■ *Try to spend time with some of your more experienced colleagues and ask them for any helpful insights. Probe around for any sensitivities you may need to know about, and fine-tune your vocabulary to match your target group's preferences before you get in front of them.*

■ *If you inadvertently breach a minor protocol, learn from the experience but don't obsess over it. The field is not so unforgiving that you will be excommunicated over a minor infraction.*

6. Showing Naïveté by Asking to See the Hospital's Strategic Plan So You Can See Where You Can Help Them

Most sales people try to build bridges to potential clients by showing how they can address the client's need. That's a great approach. However, occasionally, a vendor asks to see an organization's strategic plan so they can demonstrate how their services can address their objectives. Asking something like that clearly labels you as an outsider. Most executives feel that any company that provides them services should be in tune with them to the point that they have a good handle on what they need.

Physicians and healthcare executives are surveyed on a regular basis, and information about their needs is readily available online and in industry publications. The top felt needs inevitably make their way into every strategic plan. Many executives expect their partners to understand their needs and don't feel compelled to educate sales people on things they should already know.

Recommendation:

- *Rather than asking to see a healthcare organization's strategic plan or asking open-ended questions like, "What's your greatest need?" a better approach is to go into the meeting armed with industry-specific information and ask targeted questions. For example, if you are offering a new analytic tool that helps physicians address their cost structure, you can start the conversation with something like, "According to a survey by (name of the survey company), physicians' biggest frustration on the cost side is their inability to manage personnel costs because of variable patient volume. Would you say that's a big problem for you?" This demonstrates that you have done your homework and are attuned to one of their important pain points. This paves the way for a meaningful discussion.*

7. Showing Naïveté by Expecting a Hospital to Become a Developmental Partner

One of the exciting aspects of breakthrough technology is its ability to create new solutions to chronic problems. A big challenge, though, is designing your approach to hit the center of the bullseye. Enlisting the involvement of potential customers in the design and implementation phases goes a long way toward accomplishing this. However, finding a partner can be tricky. Hospital resources are greatly stressed, and few organizations have available bandwidth to redeploy people to help with a new project *unless* it is one of their obvious areas of major concern. Be careful about requesting their involvement in a vague area or with a fairly undeveloped concept.

I myself violated this principle not too long after starting my consulting business. Some fellow consultants and I banded together around a concept for an analytical approach to fixing throughput problems in hospitals' Emergency Departments (EDs). Two of us had good relationships with a local health system's innovation department director, so we approached him about helping define a specific problem and then developing an appropriate solution. Even though we had a robust team with the right skillsets and understood the generic issues surrounding ED throughput, our problem was that we didn't know enough about this system's particular ED challenges to propose a specific approach that would immediately help them out. Not surprisingly, we never even got to first base with them. They were too swamped with other priorities to take on a vague project to solve a problem they may or may not have had. The fact that two of us had some degree of personal relationships with this department head demonstrates that, although relationships are important, they're not enough to carry the day if you have a bad idea.

Recommendations:

■ *It's entirely possible and highly desirable to partner with a healthcare provider organization in the development of a new product. You can maximize your chances of success by approaching a potential partner with a very specific and fairly well-developed proposal that you know attacks one of their important problems. The closer to beta testing you can be, the less development effort they will have to make, and the more likely it is that they will agree to work with you. The best partnership candidates are organizations with which you already have a good working relationship. That will help you be very specific in putting forth an idea that you know will target one of their identified problem areas.*

■ *If you are fortunate enough to find a healthcare organi-*
zation willing to join in the development effort, be aware
that if they decide to jump in, they are likely to ask for an
equity stake in the resulting product.

8. Implying a Stronger Level of Support or Endorsement from a Client or Reference

Every time a vendor meets with a potential client, they understandably want to create the most positive impression possible.
Providing credible user references always helps and is standard
practice. Before you list an existing client as a satisfied user,
though, common sense dictates that they will, indeed, say
good things about you. And it's always a good idea and only
polite to ask their permission to include them on your list.

Start-ups have the additional problem of having few or no
existing clients. Since I work with a lot of these companies, I
hear how they describe their relationships with their potential
customers. In an attempt to maximize their perceived attractiveness, some of them are tempted to exaggerate the positive
comments they are receiving. Sometimes in my conversation
with start-ups who drop the names of hospitals or physicians
considering their products, I push back a little to find out if
their targets are truly as positive or invested as they imply. If
their support is not quite as strong as the vendor suggests and
another potential customer checks into their reactions, your
reputation will be tarnished, something you should avoid at all
costs. Don't do anything to damage your reputation.

Recommendation:

■ *Be positive yet completely honest about the feedback you are*
getting from clients or potential clients. It's fine to mention
that a particular healthcare organization had a positive
reaction to your product and is considering purchasing it.
However, don't overstate the degree of their support. The

healthcare community is a small one, and an executive at one organization could very well pick up the phone to ask their friend at another one to verify that they really liked the product as much as you say they did.

9. Offering a Clinical Product with Minimal or No Demonstrated Clinical Validity or Having Only Anecdotal Support

Physicians are trained to adopt evidence-based treatments, so they are not about to embrace any diagnostic tool, medical device, or service without assurances of its clinical effectiveness. The gold standard of medical research is a double-blinded clinical study where patients are divided into two groups, one which gets the experimental intervention and the other which gets an alternative approach. In order to minimize the chance of bias, neither the patient nor the researcher/clinician knows which group gets which treatment in a double-blinded study. This type of study is most common in pharmaceutical research.

Double-blinded, peer-reviewed studies are very expensive and time-consuming. Conducting these can be problematic for start-ups, few of which have the resources or timetables to undertake such extensive studies.

Typical research project measurements include the differences between the two groups in post-intervention outcomes like recovery time, time to return to full activity, and patient satisfaction. The experimental and the control groups are compared to determine whether the intervention's differences are statistically significant with a known probability of error.

Technology-related products run the gamut from medical devices and pharmaceuticals to medical apps to interventions that involve information collection and care coordination. The first group requires the Food and Drug Administration (FDA) approval, a whole world of its own. Care coordination or information sharing approaches don't demand the same level of scrutiny, but being able to demonstrate effectiveness is still vital.

Another research consideration is where study results are reported. Each medical area has its own specialty society and, typically, its own journal. Most journals have editorial committees composed of physicians from that specialty who review and approve all articles. There is a definite "pecking order" of medical journals, and the more prestigious the publication, the better. These journals can be influential references because they regularly include studies of how changing pre- or post-discharge care – often supported by new technologies – affect patient outcomes. If you can have an organization use your product and get it written up in a credible journal, you are well on your way toward market success.

Mobile apps targeted for consumers are particular objects of clinicians' skepticism. Spyros Kitsiou, a University of Illinois at Chicago assistant professor in biomedical and health information sciences, indicates that very few consumer-facing apps have been formally evaluated and calls for greater regulation and oversight of these apps.[1]

Recommendation:

- *Lacking quantifiable clinical credibility can be a tough problem to overcome. If you don't have the research, you don't have it. But you can still point to whatever clinical support for your product you have. Perhaps you have a study underway or have a beta installation. In those cases, you can point to preliminary results, even if they are anecdotal. Expect extended discussions with physicians about the clinical effectiveness of your approach. A key is remaining very humble about the level of clinical evidence you can point to. In other words, understand that anecdotes are seldom convincing. But they are not nothing either.*

10. Offering a Clinical Product without Credible Clinicians as Part of the Organization or Advisory Board

This relates to the previous pitfall. Clinicians demand evidence that your offering is good for patients. More than once, I have seen a physician get into a somewhat heated discussion with a non-clinical executive or a salesperson over a decision that has an impact on patient care. If the doctor is in a bad mood or is somewhat lacking in social graces, they might blurt out, "Where did you go to medical school?" This can be very disarming and is dropped as the ultimate conversation-stopper.

Recommendation:

- *If your product is, indeed, clinical, expect and prepare for a challenge to its clinical validity. You do not personally have to have direct clinical experience, but it is vital that you be able to point to a highly credible source within your organization who does. This can be a physician medical director or physician members of an advisory board when they have actually had input into the product development. At some point, it may be desirable to fly your clinical representative in to meet face-to-face with the healthcare organization's medical staff. By all means, act with confidence concerning your product and what it can do, but be very careful about over-stating its capabilities. Doing so just invites the "Where did you go to medical school?" conversation. Never make claims about clinical results that you can't back up with solid research.*

11. Not Understanding the Difference between Association and Causality

It's easy to confuse association and causality. Here's a simple example. Statistics show people in the Southeastern United States tend to have higher rates of poverty, diabetes, stroke, and obesity, some of which are partially associated with cultural practices. These problems are all *associated*. However, not all of them are *causally* linked.

There is a strong relationship between obesity and diabetes to the point where it's pretty safe to say that obesity can cause, or at least is a major contributor to, diabetes. Also, since lower income individuals often have greater difficulty in purchasing healthy food and sometimes revert to less healthy choices, we can safely assert that poverty and obesity are also connected. However, it would be stretch to say poverty *causes* diabetes. Not every poor person has diabetes, and there are factors other than poverty that contribute to whether or not someone develops diabetes.

Also, notice that all these problems are associated with living in the Southeast. Even though there is a link between living in the Southeast and suffering a stroke, living in the Southeast doesn't *require* someone to have a stroke. You can't say that someone who moves from Chicago to Birmingham is guaranteed to have a stroke. That reminds me of the old joke about the guy who heard that 80% of car accidents happen within 10 miles of home so he moved 15 miles away so he wouldn't have a wreck.

If you are trying to make the case that adopting your product or program will improve outcomes, it's important to communicate that you understand the difference between causality and association. A simple example that expresses the difference between the two is a smoking cessation program with several elements, each of which could be implemented independently:

- A smartphone app that allows smokers to track the number of cigarettes they smoke, what activities they were doing right before they smoked, and other factors
- Out-bound emails sent directly from their physician – not using the app – twice a week reminding them of the benefits of not smoking

- Pairing up participants as "buddies" so they can turn to someone for support when tempted to smoke
- Once-a-month in-person group meetings to create a support community

Let's suppose that at the end of a study that incorporates all four of these elements, 40% of the people in the study cut their smoking in half and another 45% stopped altogether. The app development company would certainly like to claim that using the app *caused* the decrease. But that would an overstatement.

Confusion over association vs. causality can come into play in a few ways in this example. The most obvious is attributing any success strictly to the phone app. It may have played a role – perhaps even a primary role – but since there are three other elements, we can't say with any certainty that the program worked *because of* the app. It was only one element. The case would be far stronger if there were a control group – an equal number of smokers who took all the same steps as the app users did *minus* using the app. Then differences in outcomes could be attributed to the app. Also the issue goes beyond controls. There are certain accepted research protocols for measuring the validity, reliability, and significance of a study. Without incorporating certain accepted research principles, scientific research will most likely be deemed invalid.

Another confounding variable from this example is the motivation level of the study participants. How patients were selected to use the app could add "noise" to the study results. If they volunteered, they obviously have a certain level of motivation. However, if there is no control group, you really can't say the app *caused* the reduction. First of all, since the smokers stepped up to be in the program, they had to have a certain desire to stop smoking in the first place. Maybe they had tried unsuccessfully to quite a few times and, for whatever reason, they determined to finally do it this time. Because of their motivation, they might have succeeded with or without the app. Clearly, the app was associated with the success, but there is not enough evidence to claim that results were caused by or attributable to the app.

Recommendations:

- ▪ *Keep in mind that physicians are trained scientists. They are well aware of valid experimental design and will immediately detect any softness in your presentation if you claim your product caused the favorable result when it may not have.*
- ▪ *If you plan to present any results of a study, be sure to run your conclusions by a qualified statistician, researcher, or physician in advance and ask them what language you can legitimately use as you present your findings.*

12. Acting with Questionable Ethics

This one is a no-brainer and should apply to every aspect of your life. However, there is a specific consideration in business settings. The healthcare world is surprisingly small, for two reasons.

- ▪ There are many subgroups within healthcare: physicians, nurses, executives, physical therapist, pharmacists, lab technicians, supply chain managers, food services directors, and many, many more. Most of these groups have regional and national meetings, so they typically know their peers all across the country. And they talk to each other.
- ▪ People tend to move around. In the 1980s while I was in planning department of a Midwestern hospital, I worked with a consultant who assisted us with our market strategy. We hit it off, but after we both moved on, we lost touch with each other for many years. I moved to Atlanta in 1995, and my old friend called me 12 years

ago because he was applying for the CFO position at one of the GHA's largest member health systems. He wanted my thoughts. As it turns out, he got the position and has thrived there. In his new role, he could have damaged my reputation if he didn't trust me. If I had acted unethically all those years ago up in the Midwest, my bad behavior could have harmed me many years and several states away.

Here's an example of how unethical behavior can backfire on you. In the early 1990s, I worked at a regional hospital association in the Midwest, and we operated a medical paging business to help physicians and hospitals. (This was obviously long before the days of smartphones and tablets.) Due to technology changes and the evolution of the overall paging industry, we decided to contract with an outside vendor to take over the operation we had managed in-house for years.

After going through a Request for Proposal (RFP) process, we selected an organization we thought offered the best combination of technology, service, and financial terms. This company sent a very lengthy contract filled with lots of technical jargon and technology infrastructure terms well over my head. Apart from the terminology I didn't understand, the agreement looked pretty good, but I sent it to our internal technical staff to get their assessment. They came back and told me the contract was filled with ticking time bombs because of what they were proposing from a technology standpoint. Our staff said there was no way we should sign that agreement.

The company's representative came to a meeting with me expecting a friendly conversation where we would discuss some minor points of the contract, but instead I essentially threw him out of my office and told him we don't do business with people we can't trust.

Here's another example. A close professional health system CEO colleague – I'll call him Kurt – related the following story.

The vendor rep of a company that offers a high-end end, very expensive technology, succeeded in getting the medical staff at Kurt's main competitor to buy his product. This salesperson then went to Kurt's medical staff to get them all excited about his product so they would pressure Kurt's hospital to buy it too. This pressure created problems with Kurt's finance committee and board. Here's Kurt's summary:

> Ultimately we saw no alternative but to proceed, even though this was not budgeted ... I felt the rep was sleazy and underhanded and would have loved to have told him to never darken our door again. He knew he had the upper hand as he had the only product on the market and had drummed up interest with our competitor.

As far as I know, Kurt did not invite this sales rep to Thanksgiving dinner that year.

Here's one final example. Recently, a healthcare C-Suite executive complained that he had been burned more than once after signing an agreement by a vendor who subsequently revealed that there were additional training or implementation costs that hadn't been included in the project proposal. Those should have been clearly communicated very early in the sales process, and this executive felt he was intentionally kept in the dark. Needless to say, he did not have good things to say about this company.

Recommendation:

- ■ *Keep your nose clean and always act with 100% integrity in all you professional and personal dealings. People in the healthcare field know each other and talk all the time. One rock-solid mantra in the professional world is that people like to do business with people they know, like, and trust. You do not want them to roll their eyes in disgust whenever your name comes up.*

13. Falsely Claiming to be the Only Company That Offers a Particular Product, Service, or Feature

For 24 years, part of my job working for two different hospital associations was serving as a primary gatekeeper for companies seeking the associations' endorsements. Over those 24 years, I heard hundreds of sales pitches from wannabe vendor partners. Of course, every company tries to stand out from its competitors, and I soon discovered that many of them claimed to have unique capabilities. Sometimes this was true, and sometimes it was not.

In the day of Google and other search engines, people can enter a few key words and instantly discover how valid those claims of uniqueness are. If they are false, it tells me one of two things. Either:

1. The vendor representative is so ignorant about the market that they don't even know who their competitors are or what products they offer. If this is the case, I'm not impressed by their commitment to their product or company; or
2. The vendor knows the claim is exaggerated. If this is the case, they have taught me that I can't trust their word.

Recommendations:

■ *Preserve your credibility above everything else by knowing your competitors and by providing accurate information about your product and your position in the marketplace. If you claim to be the leading company in a particular category, make sure you have some legitimate statistics to support that claim. For example, "We are the largest supplier of imaging equipment based on ..." And then tell them the basis of that claim: total number of machines in the field/total revenue/number of client locations or whatever*

*metric you are using. As I said, people like to do business
with people they know, like, and trust. Make sure you don't
mess up this last one.*

14. Jumping on the Bandwagon of the Latest Healthcare Fad and Making Non-Credible Claims about What Your Product Can Do

Tapping into timely issues is always a good idea. It shows you
understand the current industry stress points and have a valuable product to address the problem.

However, in their enthusiasm, vendors occasionally stretch
their logic beyond credulity in claiming to solve an important
issue. Let me give you an example. One of the latest "hot"
healthcare issues relates to readmissions of Medicare and,
increasingly, some privately insured patients within 30 days of
their discharge from the hospital. In order to encourage high-
quality care, the Medicare program penalizes hospitals if they
exceed the expected number of readmissions in some high-
volume Diagnosis-Related Groups (DRGs). Clearly, no hospital
wants to be dinged.

Everyone involved in the hospital sector knows this, and
many consultants and product developers have jumped in to
help hospitals with their readmissions avoidance efforts. Many
vendors now explain that using their product or service will
help hospitals avoid unnecessary readmissions, thereby helping offset the cost of their product. This is a great marketing
strategy.

However, some of the marketing claims seem to push
the limits of believability. In order to have a true impact on
an otherwise avoidable readmission, a product would have
to make a true difference in patient care to the point that
someone who was destined for readmission now can stay
out of the hospitals because of the intervention. Since many

readmissions result from poorly coordinated post-discharge care, a communication-related program that tracks patients' recovery progress at home can legitimately claim to potentially help the readmissions problem.

In order to not single out some of the more dubious claims I have seen, let me fabricate an obviously preposterous example. A food services contractor that provides a hospital's meals would have a difficult time making a credible claim that they could help avoid readmissions based on the superior nutritional value of their food. A patient is typically in the hospital only a few days, and they obviously get fed. In order to claim they help keep patients from being readmitted within 30 days of discharge, the new food services vendor would have to make the case that its food is so much more nutritious than the hospital's current food that a patient who would have deteriorated after being discharged because of the poor quality of the food *while in the hospital for a few days* will now be healthier. This is a ridiculous claim that no one would believe, and the vendor would be written off as naïve and ridiculous.

Recommendation:

■ *By all means, be aware of the current important issues of the day, and if your product can legitimately help with them, make that a key part of your sales appeal. But keep in mind that you may be hurting your case if you exaggerate your ability to truly address the problem under discussion.*

15. Not Having "Hometown Clients"

During my 19 years as the "front door" for vendors wanting to be designated a preferred vendor by GHA, I heard many of them complain about their poor traction in the state because they lacked existing local customers. Some hospital leaders shy away from being the first one to jump in with a new approach. Even if a vendor can claim some fairly impressive customers in other parts of the country, some local leaders may still be reluctant. This might stem from the legitimate recognition that the operating climate varies a bit from state to state because of local regulations or politics. Some requirements in Georgia might be slightly different than those in New York. But I heard this complaint over and over and even involving products that would seem to immune from local differences.

Erlanger Medical Center is located in Chattanooga just a few miles north of the Georgia/Tennessee border. A good hiker could easily walk to Georgia from the hospital in about an hour or so. I used to joke that even if Erlanger were using a particular product, that might not impress hospitals in Georgia because Erlanger is in a different state, so they don't count.

This phenomenon is becoming less relevant as hospitals merge and work more with other organizations, but it can still exist.

Recommendation:

- *There is little you can do to counter this trend. As frustrating as it is, it can be a reality, so don't be surprised if you encounter it.*

16. Not Fully Appreciating the Lack of "Uniformity" of Patient Inputs and, Therefore, Overestimating the Potential Impact of Your Solution

A common criticism of healthcare is that both the outcomes and the cost of care vary enormously from provider to provider. Undoubtedly, some hospitals and physicians do a better job than others, but some of the variation is beyond their control.

One major variable is a patient's condition upon entering the healthcare system. About 30 years ago, in an attempt to help patients determine which cardiologists to consider using, the State of New York began publishing the mortality rates for each New York cardiologist by name. One of the unintended consequences was that patients with complicated problems started having trouble finding a doctor who would take them on. The reason? Patients with the most severe conditions tend to die at a higher rate than those with fewer problems. As a result, physicians treating the sickest patients had among the worst mortality rates in the states, leading some patients – and the media – to conclude they were bad doctors. Consequently, these high-end physicians started refusing to treat the most severe cases so their numbers would improve.

Another sticking point relates to the degree of patient compliance in the medical process. A physician can provide the best care available anywhere, but if a patient only half-heartedly follows instructions, the final outcomes may not be great and the provider might be "blamed."

These two problems greatly frustrate care providers.

Recommendations:

- *Evaluate your descriptions of your product's impact on patient care. You will enhance your credibility with potential customers if you demonstrate you appreciate the challenges with the patient part of the care delivery equation. Rather than claiming to help patients in general, you should pinpoint the characteristics of patients most likely to benefit from your approach. Besides allowing you to discuss credibly the possible impact of your product, this helps the healthcare system or physician evaluate how large the relevant patient population is and, therefore, the potential impact of your product.*
- *If possible, point to successes other physicians or hospitals have had using your product with their various patient subgroups.*

- *If you are especially confident in your product, consider offering some kind of performance guarantee with explicit definitions and clear definitions of their responsibilities.*

End Note

1. Joseph Conn, "Mobile medical apps gain support, but many lack clinical evidence," *Modern Healthcare*, November 30, 2015, page 22.

Chapter 7

Product Design Pitfalls

The first "P" in the seven "P's" of marketing is Price. (The others are Place or Distribution, Positioning, Promotion, Packaging, Pricing, and People.) But it all starts with the product. If yours suffers from a fatal flaw, it is destined for the reject pile.

This chapter advises on how to avoid some potentially success-killing product design pitfalls.

17. Answering a Question No One Is Asking

Right after I launched my consulting company, I met an entrepreneur at a conference who was trying to figure out how to introduce what he considered a sure-fire offering. (I am substantially modifying the details of this example to avoid embarrassing him.)

His company had deep clinical expertise and had just completed an infectious disease project for the World Health Organization for which he had created a rudimentary screening device to detect a certain disease with reasonable accuracy and at a relatively low cost. Since he owned the underlying research rights, he saw a possible opportunity to extend his methodology to develop a commercially viable product for the private market in the developed world.

He envisioned selling the more sophisticated version to infectious disease doctors who sometimes treat tourists from the burgeoning "adventure travel" market. He saw this as an attractive client base since there had been a noticeable uptick in people returning from overseas with this particular disease. His product's demonstrably better results convinced him that it would succeed. Consequently, he asked his team to spend another year-and-a-half developing a sophisticated stand-alone device that would detect the targeted disease with about 96% accuracy.

When we met, he was trying to figure out where to start with his marketing. The first thing I asked was how many physicians he thought would be potential users. He wasn't sure but he thought it was a big number. I then asked how unsatisfied they were with the existing approach. Again, he wasn't positive, but he knew his product was better. Next, I asked what the physicians thought of the price he was considering. He indicated that the few of them with whom he had informally talked mentioned the price range he was thinking about seemed a bit high.

When I saw him a year later, I asked about his progress. He was a bit dejected. It turned out that the market for his product was far smaller than he had imagined. Even though the prevalence of the particular disease was growing, the consequences of getting false-positive test results from the existing diagnostic technique were rather low so no one seemed particularly alarmed. Furthermore, patients were spread across the country to the degree that the average infectious disease physician only saw a handful of patients with that problem each year, and they didn't feel the extra accuracy justified the heavy price tag.

His problem was his utter failure to do any kind of market research. He neglected to determine whether there was even a need and, if so, if it was large enough to warrant developing what turned out to be a fairly expensive product to address it. A technology without a viable market falls into the category of an interesting science project.

And just because there may be a need, that doesn't guarantee that physicians will be willing to buy it if it's cost prohibitive. Very basic stuff!

Recommendation:

- *Do your market research! Don't commit massive resources to a product until you know there is a legitimate market and that your approach fits within the range of what the industry will accept and actually buy.*

18. Developing a Product without Adequate Input from Potential Users

Every sector can benefit by having "industry outsiders" step in with fresh eyes to suggest new and better ways of doing things. They can bring an unvarnished perspective to processes and problems and possibly cross-pollinate solutions into healthcare from other fields. The downside is that those not familiar with healthcare may not sufficiently understand the nuances and non-negotiables of the new sector and, therefore, propose solutions that violate certain "must-haves" of the industry's philosophy or work flow.

During World War II, "Loose lips sink ships" was a popular phase that showed up on many patriotic posters. The idea was that if stateside family members of military personnel fighting on the front lines openly talked about what their loved ones were doing overseas, enemy agents might be tipped off about military secrets, resulting in ambushed ships and lost lives.

Entrepreneurs are understandably protective of their great concepts, especially if their idea could be easily "borrowed" by others. This creates lips that may be too tight.

Products with few barriers to entry are especially susceptible to being hijacked. The good news is that heeding the warning to put your lips together allows you to keep your product under wraps until just the right time. The bad news is that this sequestration could cut you off from critical information vital to successful product development. This can be especially dangerous if you have minimal direct experience in the healthcare arena. A very secretive process can result in a product plagued by a fatal design flaw because it doesn't match providers' workflow or preferences. Or it could be answering a question no one is asking, as illustrated by the previous pitfall.

I recall a conversation with a vendor about 10 years ago when she was looking for a pilot site for a product that promised to streamline the billing and collections process. Although I thought she had some very good ideas, implementing her approach would violate one or two very fundamental "can't be changed" aspects of the interplay between hospital billing offices and the insurance industry. Admittedly, the existing process was somewhat irrational, but I had spent enough time in that sub-universe to know that it would be easier to shift the earth's axis tilt from 23-½ degrees than to bring about the changes she proposed, and I told her so. Her response: "Well, they just need to get over it. This is the 21st century." Nice thought, but it ain't going to happen. As far as I know, she never did get her pilot site. She apparently failed to heed my advice and that of others who told her the same thing. This example illustrates the danger of ignoring sound advice from industry-insiders.

Recommendations:

- *Let me repeat: Do your market research! Don't commit massive resources to a product until you know there is a legitimate market and that your approach fits within the acceptable range of what the industry will accept and actually buy.*
- *By all means, seek new ways to streamline and even up-end the status quo. But make sure you have got a "reality check" from actual users as to your approach's viability. And get that input early in the process. As you are designing your product, seek advice from people who actually work in the exact area that would be affected and ask*

for honest feedback about what works and what doesn't. You may have a spectacular solution – in concept – to a recognized problem, but it's worthless if no one is willing to use it because of a miscalculation. You may sometimes run into the situation where the leader of a particular area loves your product, but the end users who report to them may not share their enthusiasm. The customer and the end user may not always be the same.

▪ *If you have a revolutionary approach, carefully evaluate the risk of letting potential competitors learn about it vs. the risk of missing a key requirement that compromises the viability of your product. You should seek industry insiders to serve as sounding boards, and consider asking them to sign a Non-Disclosure Agreement (NDA). Doing so would help protect your intellectual capital, but it could also scare some potentially valuable advisors away. Recognize that people can be wary of signing overly restrictive NDAs. Some of them I've been asked to sign go well beyond protecting documents, drawings, spreadsheets, prototypes, etc. and seem to cover even concepts, random comments, and speculation. Those are way too off-putting. My attorney tells me that, ironically, that type of NDA could unravel because it is so constraining as to be deemed unreasonable. Depending on the extent of the involvement you are asking from your advisors and your relationship with them, you might also need to design a compensation arrangement to attract and retain valued advisors.*

19. Receiving Inadequate Input from Your Advisory Board

This one surprised me. As I was talking to a potential client, explaining how my company could help him, he mentioned his advisory board and listed some of its members' impressive credentials. Having had similar conversations with other companies, I was prepared to hear him say he saw no need to work with me. With such a strong group, I figured he had all the input he needed. To my surprise, he said that despite the advice he was receiving, he felt he had to get additional feedback. Here was his explanation.

> I have known the members of my advisory board for several years and, in some cases, we are personal friends. I have utmost respect for their professional judgment, but I sometimes wonder if they are telling me what they think I want to hear rather than what I really need to hear.

I found this fascinating. As an analytical thinker, I immediately move toward both strengths and potential problems of an idea. And as someone with a good sense of what I know (and what I don't know), I'm usually not reluctant to openly (yet tactfully) share my thoughts. I often preface my comments by labeling them "devil's advocate" observations, I tell my clients I'm the Reality Guy. By that, I mean I sometimes tell them things they may not like hearing but need to know. It's best to get this type of feedback from someone who is on their side and as early on as possible in order to make whatever midcourse corrections are necessary.

That is what an advisory board is supposed to do. But apparently it doesn't always happen, perhaps because:

■ As indicated above, the board may not want to hurt the developer's feelings.
■ Sometimes advisory boards are only loosely involved with the company. A colleague recently told me she has been on the advisory board of a particular start-up for three years, but the board only met one time for a 30-minute phone call. It's hard for someone with such a minimal relationship with the company to engage and

do serious thinking about what it does. The message the company is sending is that they are more interested in being able to list your credentials than truly tap into your expertise.

■ The company CEO's personality might create a climate where it's obvious they are more interested in confirmation of their ideas than in getting honest input. About eight years ago, I served on such a board. The CEO was the classic Type A personality and treated the advisory board like employees, and not particularly bright ones at that. Whenever someone would make a suggestion that challenged one of the CEO's pretty fundamental assumptions, I could see he struggled to not appear offended. He was only partially successful. After a few such incidents, I decided to exit the advisory group.

Recommendations:

■ *Select the members of your advisory board carefully, making sure they have the required skillset to provide you with complete and informed advice.*

■ *Engage the advisory board in creating their own purpose statement in which the team collectively agrees on why they exist and the roles they will play. It need not be lengthy. This document then becomes the touchpoint for confirming that the advisory board is fulfilling its purpose.*

■ *Think through your posture toward your advisory board.*

 – *Be sure you communicate repeatedly that you want their candid input.*

 – *Don't make unreasonable demands on their time, but don't make the opposite mistake of failing to engage them in a meaningful way.*

 – *Consider your reactions to ideas that might seem somewhat contrarian. Sending the message that you are looking for "yes men and women" may rob you of their valuable insights.*

■ *Make sure you don't discourage people from joining your advisory board. I was once asked to sign an advisory board agreement that, if interpreted a certain way, could have made me personally liable for the company's actions and decisions. Although I was happy to lend my expertise to the organization, I was not willing to put myself in potential legal jeopardy, nor was I willing to engage my $425-an-hour attorney to review and modify the agreement's language.*

■ *If you have the financial means, consider offering a monetary compensation arrangement to give them more skin in the game.*

20. Getting Resistance from Providers Because Your Product May Be Too Complicated for Elderly or Non-Tech-Savvy Users

The technology breakthroughs of the past 20 years have been astounding. Millennials have never known a world without laptops, the Internet, and smartphones. The good news is that every industry, including healthcare, is marching forward boldly to tap into the awesome potential of these and other technologies. In my work with healthcare start-ups, I'm regularly exposed to capabilities that were only dreamed of a few decades ago. Many of the breakthroughs are developed by extremely bright entrepreneurs at the early ends of their careers.

As positive as these developments are, there can be a pretty big downside if developers don't recognize that not everyone shares their enthusiasm for and comfort with emerging technologies. Parents are often astounded that even toddlers intuitively understand tablets and other electronic devices. Many people over 40 consider that an acquired skill that is akin to learning a foreign language.

I recently participated in a conference call hosted by a wonderful not-for-profit organization I have actively supported for many years. The president was explaining their decision to migrate one of their smaller-circulation publications to an electronic-only version. This publication is designed to push out timely information that requires quick action, and the time lags in creating and distributing it often rendered their calls to action "old news." Furthermore, the production costs exceeded the associated revenue by nearly $100,000 per year. So, they concluded moving to electronic distribution would both increase the timeliness of the document and provide a significant cost savings.

After his announcement, the president invited questions and comments. The first few callers were very positive, but one gentleman weighed in with the concern that some older readers might be left behind. He explained that his elderly mother had just complained loudly that her bank, insurance companies, and other business partners keep pressuring her to move to electronic communication only. She seldom turns on her desktop computer, and, when she does, she has trouble reading the screen.

Recognizing the almost-universal adoption of cell phones, many developers design their new health products strictly for that platform. Doing so eliminates the need for the end user to invest in a dedicated device since almost everyone already owns a smartphone. The problem, though, is that many elderly patients have trouble navigating on four-inch screens with no physical buttons. Besides lacking physical dexterity, they may also have trouble reading the small screen print.

Some technology companies recognize this general discomfort some seniors have with technology and have developed dedicated, stand-alone devices with very clear and large buttons to simplify operations for older patients. This addresses the accessibility problem but creates two new barriers: your need to invest in the device's design and production, and the purchaser's need to purchase a single-purpose device.

Recommendations:

- *Carefully evaluate the pros and cons of creating an application designed for use on a dedicated device that is easy-to-use for the end user vs. one that uses smartphones or tablets. Choosing the former will add to your capital outlay but could increase usage among people who may be wary of technology as long as it is immediately intuitive. Going the smartphone/tablet route will keep costs down for both you and the end user but may discourage some potential buyers from using it because of their limited physical dexterity.*
- *Think through the characteristics of your intended users. Rarely are they all of the same skills, age, and interests. Have each of these user categories weigh in on their need and your product. It's better to invest the time discovering this earlier in the process rather than when you are trying to determine why sales are not materializing.*
- *Assess every aspect of your product pretending you are afraid of technology. What is confusing? What is intimidating? What assumptions are you making concerning the user's level of sophistication? Are the icons and font sizes large enough to be read by someone with fading vision? Is there an easy-to-access help icon?*
- *Find someone totally unfamiliar with your product and ask them these same questions.*
- *If your app requires the user to read detailed charts or conduct data entry, consider encouraging them to use a tablet or laptop instead of a phone. Some people may not have a tablet, but if they do have to purchase one, at least they can use it for other purposes.*

Chapter 8

Market Misreading Pitfalls

Once you have designed your product that appeals to the broader market and is one the market is, ideally, even eager for, you must understand just who it is you're selling to. Some products are extremely niche and apply to very narrow markets, but most are applicable in many different types of organizations and even many different sectors. Just because you have a great product and may understand one segment of your market pretty well, you may be missing opportunities in other parts of the market.

With only two pitfalls, this chapter is tied with the external political pitfalls chapter as the shortest one in the book, but don't underestimate the ability of these two to ruin sales opportunities.

21. Failing to Recognize That the Healthcare Field Is Not Monolithic

Newcomers to healthcare appropriately view it in big buckets: hospitals, physicians, insurance companies, nursing homes, etc. But they are making a mistake if they don't subdivide the market by other factors.

All hospitals are not alike. A 400-bed suburban community hospital and a 25-bed rural Critical Access Hospital face many of the same challenges: clinical, financial, demographic, regulatory, staffing, and many others. However, these issues manifest themselves very differently to each. For example, when it comes to physician relations, large suburban community hospitals may have the challenge of physicians splitting their admissions among two or more hospitals while rural hospitals may have trouble getting any physicians in the first place. Similarly, various physician subgroups – primary care physicians, specialists, employed physicians, independent practitioners – face different clinical, operational, and financial challenges. One size definitely does not fit all.

Newcomers to healthcare may not adequately differentiate among these various subpopulations and, therefore, fail to tailor their operational implementation processes, pricing schedules, and messaging to each group. The result is missed opportunity if they don't appeal to each market segment in terms it can relate to.

Recommendations:

- ■ *Be sure to understand the needs and dynamics of the different sectors of your market. You should develop policies, processes, and pricing tailored to each segment of your market. Everyone who works within the healthcare universe understands the varied circumstances faced by the different subgroups. A large academic medical center understands that it will have to pay far more than a small rural hospital for the same service, so don't be afraid to develop differential pricing. The key is to mentally step into each group's world to the point that you understand their needs and can respond accordingly.*
- ■ *See Pitfall 60 for advice on developing a pricing schedule that can achieve maximum penetration among different-sized hospitals.*

22. Misusing "Guerilla Marketing" due to Misreading the Organizational Climate

Guerilla marketing involves using unconventional tactics to bring attention to your product or service. The term was inspired by guerilla warfare in conflicts like the Vietnam War where a small band of combatants ambush or surprise the enemy (typically a larger, less agile army). Some people use the other spelling – "gorilla marketing" – probably as a way to invoke the brute force of gorillas.

This one is tricky, and I will share two stories with completely opposite outcomes. First, I will give one example of where this approach failed miserably and then I will highlight one where it worked flawlessly.

Over the years, part of my job responsibilities at two different organizations included overseeing their sales-related functions. Once we had an opening for the manager of one of those companies, and I had a delightful interview with a highly qualified applicant. He had a strong background and presented very well. He even had some experience with sales to physician groups. I remember telling my boss that I thought I had found the right person.

However, two days later, our receptionist buzzed me to tell me I had just received a package from this applicant. When I opened it, I discovered a dozen beautiful strawberries covered in different types of chocolates with our company's logo infused into the chocolate. I was taken aback. I had never had anyone do something like that before, and, although I felt it was thoughtful and creative, it came across as pretty cheesy.

I asked a few others in the office what they thought – and in the process "had to" offer them one of the strawberries. Everyone agreed with me that this gesture really wasn't appropriate in an organization like ours and showed poor judgment on his part. He lost the job over this. (I have since shared this story with a few other professional healthcare colleagues, and they all had the same reaction we did – his action was a bit over the top.)

Having relayed this story, let me give you an example that had the opposite effect. One of my clients told me about a time when she tried several times to get in to see a department head in a healthcare organization she was targeting. He was new to the position, but my client had met with his predecessor and knew the department's administrative assistant. After trying for the third time to set a meeting with the new department head, his assistant mentioned off-handedly that he was in the middle of a week-long culinary tour of Napa Valley.

This triggered a creative thought for my client, and when the department head returned to the office, he discovered a bottle of fine, 28-year-old balsamic vinegar from my client awaiting him. As a fan of fine foods herself, she knew the department head would appreciate the gift. As it turns out, that did the trick, and she was able to penetrate the veil and eventually made the sale.

Recommendation:

■ *I'm not sure what to tell you. These anecdotes demonstrate that guerilla tactics can either be spectacularly successful or blow up in your face. My advice would be to carefully think through how this approach might come across and, if possible, get some insights from others in the organization as to how such an approach might be received. When in doubt, don't do it!*

Chapter 9

Data Pitfalls

This is one of my favorite chapters in the book. I cut my teeth professionally on healthcare data and truly enjoy seeing how relevant and reliable data can be used to generate key insights into healthcare delivery. However, just like every other area of healthcare, there can be treacherous seas to navigate when it comes to acquiring, analyzing, and presenting data and in helping prospective customers understand the great potential of your data-related product to support their effort to achieve their goals.

23. Having Someone Challenge the Quality and Integrity of Your Data, the Relevance of Various Data Sources Brought into a Big Data Project, or the Validity of an Index Number You Create

These can be significant issue for any data-related project. There are five types of healthcare projects that involve data:

1. Non-clinical projects – Examples include studies of patient origin, Emergency Department (ED) throughput, where patients are discharged to, and others. Although data

accuracy is important for any data project, minor data discrepancies are not fatal for this type of study.

2. Clinically oriented projects using non-clinical data – Administrative data like the UB-04 medical claims billing set or the MedPAR data set can be used to draw important insights about clinical care, but it is not complete enough to offer definitive conclusions. This data can be used to study admission patterns, length of stay, and clinical classification of patients. However, without either supplementing the data with more clinically robust information or performing sophisticated adjustments to account for patient severity and other factors, this data is not appropriate for drawing medically valid conclusions about providers' medical or economic performance. Physicians typically bristle over unsophisticated studies based solely on this type of data.

3. Big Data projects – Big Data is routinely used in many industries, and healthcare is beginning to incorporate it more and more. By definition, Big Data combines data from various sources, and someone has to determine the relevance and appropriateness of the combinations. A related concept is the Data Lake, a large, semi-structured repository of various types of often-raw data that the owners hope to use for a variety of reports, analytics, and machine learning.

4. Projects that create any kind of index – Years ago, I headed up one such effort relative to hospital financial efficiency. The charges listed on a patient's hospital bill come from an internal data set called the Charge Master file. There are reasons charges are set as they are, but they are largely meaningless to most patients since very few actually pay charges.

In an attempt to help a local healthcare business coalition compare hospital pricing, several years ago, I led an initiative to create a new way to look at hospitals' economic efficiency. We attempted to identify and assign a weight to several fiscal and performance indicators to come up with a single, final number that would accurately determine financial efficiency and allow hospitals to be compared. Among the factors we discussed were the hospital's clinical mix, overall payer mix, severity index, and several other measures.

After hours of discussion over several meetings, we finally abandoned the effort because we determined that any weighting approach we came up with would be arbitrary and based primarily on our opinions. Should payer mix count more than patient severity? Who knows? Even economists and statisticians who spend years analyzing data can't agree on optimal composite measures. How could we have come up with a meaningful and acceptable index number?

5. Well-executed analyses using rich clinical data appropriately collected and cleansed.

Recommendations:

■ *You should be very humble when discussing projects or products that draw on data from any of the first four categories. There are three important considerations that limit the validity and applicability of such studies:*

  – *The data collection process – How complete and accurate the data is. Generally, UB-04 data is fairly complete since it spins out of the hospital's system using automated processes. Other studies that involve manual collection might be subject to different types of errors. For example, bad data could creep into a study of discharge disposition from manually collected data on a particular unit if the weekend staff is not fully trained in the study's objectives and data collection techniques. If definitions are not crystal clear, some might interpret them differently, and some may feel overwhelmed by their workload and not spend the time needed to provide accurate or complete responses.*

- *The degree of data cleansing applied – All data sets are subject to errors. Generally, vendors using UB-04 data apply numerous algorithms to ferret out problem records such as men giving birth, patients being discharged before they were admitted, or patients older than 125. Furthermore, if you are involved in a multi-year study, you can compare results of this year's data set to those of previous years to look for major changes. Most analyses such as payer mix, patient origin by zip code, market share by region, and others stay pretty stable from period to period. Significant changes from one year to another could signal underlying data issues.*

- *The logic behind your Big Data project or any effort to create synthetic indices or draw conclusions – You must be prepared to defend your thought process. For example, does someone's traffic violation record shed any light on their likelihood to develop cancer? Maybe yes, but probably not. Do you have any external, statistically valid verification for the analytical framework you are proposing?*

■ *Be sure you communicate to any potential critics that you understand these limitations. Present your analyses as* starting points for discussion. *With thousands of potential analytical points to examine, a healthcare organization could spend thousands of hours studying every possible factor for a quality improvement program. However, these studies can identify the specific areas that appear to be outliers and* that warrant additional research. *No one should be hired or fired based on any of these starting point analyses.*

■ *You should also keep in mind sample size for each cell in your analysis. Clinicians are most likely to accept statistically significant results, but these require a large sample size. Few hospital departments generate enough data to allow for statistically significant results. You should always*

*be mindful of how many cases are being compared for
each group. If you are studying outcomes of a particular
procedure by physician, you don't want to suggest comparing a physician with two cases to one with three cases.
Results will be highly unreliable, and the physicians will
not be pleased.*

■ *Be prepared for pushback. Even with thoughtfully developed projects with defensible logic, some clinicians or
executives may object to the results if they come out looking
bad. It's human nature to try to defend your performance,
and since no analytical approach is perfect, every analysis
is subject to challenge. Following the guidelines presented
here will allow you to develop thoughtful responses to the
criticisms.*

24. Having the "Age" of Your Data Challenged

This is related to the previous pitfall. Perhaps the most common complaint of any data project is that it's using old
data. The dream of any analytical project is real-time data.
Unfortunately, for a number of reasons, this is virtually impossible to get.

About eight years ago, I led a team to create a project that
allowed hospitals to compare, within the limits allowed by
antitrust laws, their payments from individual managed care
companies by individual product lines. One of the first challenges was defining what data we would use and how to
collect it.

There were many antitrust parameters we had to operate within, one of which was that data had to be at least
three months old. We elected to have two six-month reporting periods a year for this project. Because of how hospital
payments from managed care organizations work, it can take
months for a claim to settle. For example, if a patient is discharged on January 1, it can take a few weeks for the full bill

to be assembled from the various departments that provided care. Insurance companies are supposed to finish processing a so-called clean claim within a few weeks. However, a large percentage of claims have issues of either missing or incorrect data, so the payer returns the claim for correction. This back-and-forth can take several weeks or even months. The hospitals participating in our project strongly wanted to consider only "complete" claims, and as a result they directed us to allow a total of six months for the claim to fully settle.

After the hospitals submitted their data, it took about three months for us to cleanse the data, verify its accuracy, and upload it into the analytical software we developed.

So, this is what it looked like when you add all the timelines together:

- Reporting period: January 1–June 30, Year 1
- Because some patients in the reporting period were discharged on June 30, the six-month allowance for all claims to be finalized is not over until December 31, Year 1
- Processing time: January 1–March 31, Year 2

This means there is a nine-month lag between the most recent discharges (June 30 of Year 1) and a lag of 15 months for the oldest discharges (January 1 of Year 1). Clearly, this is much longer than anyone would like, but the nature of the process required that much time.

Several hospitals complained about the age of the data, so about a year into the project we pushed hard at one of our users' group meetings to get them to agree to reducing the claim settlement time from six months to four. Try as we might, they insisted on keeping it at six for fear that some of the more complex claims would still be in flux.

As an aside, we tried to convince them that even if there were a few unresolved claims, it probably would not affect the results very much. We were never able to quantify the number of claims unlikely to close within four months, but it had to be a very small percentage. And since the project was designed to help hospitals understand how adequate or not their payments from managed care plans were, the center of gravity of the analysis was on the more "standard" cases, not the outliers that were represented by the cases that required the extra two months. Furthermore, even if the data would have been slightly distorted by the omission of the most severe cases, I made the case that the data across all hospitals would probably be pretty much "equally distorted." In other words, if 1% of cases – the most complicated ones – were missing from Hospital A's data, the total payments Hospital A received from a particular health plan might be understated by, perhaps, 2%. But the same would most likely be true for Hospital B. Its 1% missing data would probably also result in a 2% understatement. So, the overall comparison among the hospitals would not be materially affected. I thought my explanation was brilliant, but apparently no one else did, and the group insisted on keeping the window at six months.

Recommendations:

- *There is no way to hide the fact that data in many comparison projects is older than everyone would like. Acknowledge this as a problem, but walk through the mechanics of why that is the case. To the extent that their own institution "contributes" to the delay because of the steps they have to follow, explore whether or not they can speed up the process themselves at all. As in the managed care data project case, it's probably not likely they can materially improve the turnaround. Explaining this dynamic doesn't solve the problem, but it at least helps them understand that the timelines are dictated by circumstances beyond everyone's control. Furthermore, it shows that you are aware of and understand this reality.*
- *Very tactfully point out that, although your project may use old data, there's no better alternative. So, they have a choice: settle for a less-than-perfect project or use nothing.*

> ■ *You may want to consider using a daily claims feed,
> which is what payers receive to get closer to real-time infor-
> mation. However, recognize that this set is highly unedited,
> and data integrity could be a real issue.*

25. Lacking Local and/or Regional Peer Data for Benchmarking

By definition, benchmarking projects involve comparing one hos-pital's or physician's results to those of external reference points, either other individual providers or composite averages. So, whenever someone suggests that type of project, the first question everyone asks is, "What other organizations are part of this?"

The need for relevant participation pools is crucial for two types of projects:

1. Those that track real-time availability of a particular level of care, such as rehab facilities. These projects allow hospital discharge planners to see immediately who has availability and who doesn't. Ideally, every relevant pro-vider in the market should participate to allow immediate, accurate information. I will further address this type of project in Pitfall 67
2. Data projects where you are comparing results among relevant peer groups

As we developed the comparative managed care payment product described in the previous pitfall, the most common question we got was, "Who else is doing this?" It was the classic "chicken and egg" scenario. Everyone tends to stand around the edges of a circle and say, "I'll do it if you do too." Other hospitals reply "No, I'll do it if you commit first." At some point, nothing happens unless a few are willing to step up and commit.

We hit on the strategy of soliciting conditional commitments – asking a hospital to agree with a provision to "uncommit" if we failed to achieve critical mass by a specified date. We developed a one-page non-binding Letter of Intent asking the hospital to give us permission to publicly announce their intention to participate with the understanding that we would evaluate commitment level at the particular date which was about six months out. If we had sufficient participation, we would move forward. If not, everyone could walk away. No harm, no foul.

The strategy worked perfectly, and we successfully launched the program right on schedule.

Here's another important aspect of peer grouping. The main objective of our managed care project was to allow hospitals to compare the level of their payments from managed care plans to an aggregated, blinded grouping of other hospitals. Of course, everyone was most interested in what was going on in their local market, but we also wanted to allow them to compare themselves to other similar hospitals in other markets, so we let them select their own peer groups as long as they complied with our strict guidelines for peer group selection. This meant a hospital could choose all the hospitals in its particular market, or it could select similar size hospitals in other markets. This allowed a large teaching hospital in Atlanta to create a peer group consisting of other large teaching hospitals from the total participant pool.

Recommendations:

- *If your product requires broad participation of different institutions, follow the non-binding Letter of Intent strategy.*
- *If you are operating in different geographical markets, consider allowing multiple peer groupings hospitals can select.*

26. Getting Trapped by the "Alarm Fatigue Syndrome"

Data is good. More data is better. At least that's what some people think. Although there is some truth to that position, at some point, too much leads to overload and inaction. There is a difference between the volume and the value of data, and more data doesn't automatically lead to better patient or operational outcomes.

In an interview published in the April 30, 2018 issue of *Modern Healthcare*, Allscripts CEO Paul Black discussed data that is not properly managed, harmonized, and de-duplicated. His comments referred to assimilating Big Data feeds that incorporate information from several sources, but his remarks apply to all of healthcare data. "It's like reading the *New York Times, Wall Street Journal*, and C-Span all at once," he said.[1] Without an interpretive framework, data is just noise.

Anyone who has spent any time in either an inpatient or ED setting has heard numerous alarms happily chirping in the background and being ignored by virtually everyone. Many electronic gizmos that are part of patient care these days sport alarms to alert caregivers when some kind of threshold is exceeded. And these thresholds are exceeded regularly. By many devices. And they are sometimes ignored. If everything becomes urgent, nothing is urgent.

When medication management software for physicians first hit the market, there were so many low-threshold alerts about dosing and potential interactions that many physicians learned to click right through them and essentially ignore most of them, defeating the alerts' purposes. In some cases, they missed truly important warnings, resulting in patient harm. This has also been a problem with Clinical Decision Support software and Electronic Health Records in general.

Patients may think it's wonderful that their primary care physician can access the steady stream of heart rate and other biometric data from their wearable fitness monitors, but no physician has the time – or desire – to sort through tons of undifferentiated data. Even getting a condensed daily feed of summary data can be overwhelming unless there is an analytical overlay to alert the clinician when action is required. The best apps provide clear alert systems (e.g., color-coding patients as green, yellow, or red) so someone from the physician's staff can quickly identify the patients who require immediate attention.

Recommendations:

- *Be very careful about the volume of alerts and flags your product offers. Too many marginally important ones will result in clinicians ignoring all of them, even the ones that are truly critical.*
- *If you are a vendor offering a product that greatly increases data flow to physicians or hospitals, be sure to solicit input from relevant clinicians concerning the types of information that are truly helpful.*
- *You must include an analytical framework that provides immediately identifiable intervention thresholds.*
- *Incorporate the ability to conveniently modify alert thresholds so clinicians can customize notifications to match their preferences.*
- *Develop mechanisms that guide clinicians toward suitable corrective steps so they can immediately recognize the issue and easily intervene. Remember that beyond being valid, data must also be useful and actionable.*
- *As you present your product, make sure you communicate that you understand the difference between volume of data and value of data that has been curated and analyzed.*

27. Not Recognizing Hurdles in Getting Permissions to Access the Healthcare Organization's Data

Some data-related initiatives such as Big Data projects or highly focused studies that need detailed data sets not available in normal output files require accessing internal data. Because of growing concerns about data security, healthcare organizations are increasingly reluctant to make any data available to third parties. The more outside organizations with their data, the greater their exposure. Hence, they are increasingly cautious about being drawn into such initiatives.

Recommendations:

- *As you approach a healthcare organization about possibly joining your program, make sure your contacts know you understand their sensitivity about making data available and fully support their decision-making process.*
- *You* must *present a strong description of your data-handling and security policies and processes.*
- *Recognize that most healthcare facilities will require a lengthy documentation and validation process before granting any access to their data. Not only does this require additional time, but you may also have to modify your security standards to satisfy their requirements.*

Bonus Material – The "Art" of Interpreting Data

Using "art" and "interpreting data" in the same sentence may seem as sensible as comparing an octopus to a bicycle. Isn't data supposed to be objective? So how and where does the "art" part come in.

Years ago when I worked in the planning department of a Midwestern hospital, I became a huge fan of healthcare data using the revolutionary-for-the-time Market Planner and

Physician Practice Planner software developed by the original Sachs Group. It combined various data sets and use rates to create precise projections of future inpatient, outpatient, and physician services need five years into the future.

Despite the software's mathematically driven underpinnings, interpreting and applying the data required a light hand. I followed these five principles:

1. Recognize data and methodology limitations – Although we used the best available data, it still had some degree of error, especially when it came to showing the number of physicians already in the market due to fairly incomplete data. Also, since the model employed patient use rates from all of a 20-county area, it assumed behavior in my market would mirror that of the whole region. That's probably a good assumption, but it does introduce some fuzz.

2. Rather than talk in terms of absolute need, indicate the *direction* of the need. Some medical specialties were predicted to have a future surplus of physicians while others indicated the need for more. In other words, the analysis pointed to either an excess or a deficit.

3. Coupled with this, emphasize the *magnitude* of the need. Is the need slight or significant?

4. Next, look at the *context* of the overall market. Can physicians from other specialties provide the same services for a specialty with an indicated deficit? There may be a deficit of internists, but extra family practitioners can address much of that need.

5. Finally, when reporting, rather than treating results with mathematical certainty, use terms like "*the model suggests a market need*" or "*there does not appear* to be a need for additional cardiologists." This shows an appropriate recognition that, although the results are reasonable, they are not bulletproof. I have seen more than one belligerent physician or healthcare organization executive make it

their personal mission to undercut the results of a modeling projection they didn't like. Using more "humble" language helps soften some of the criticism.

So, here's an example of how to apply all this. If an analysis of a particular market shows the need for 4.2 pediatricians, I would explain that the initial analysis *suggests* a need for pediatricians, and *apparently* it is pretty strong. However, before I send the physician recruiters to get four more pediatricians, I would crosscheck the supply of family physicians and internists. If those specialties have excess capacity, it is likely that some of the need for pediatricians already is and will continue to be filled by the complementary specialties. And four might be overly aggressive. I would be more comfortable recommending one or two. Besides, the reality is that finding four more pediatricians would be very tough. The action point would be starting the recruitment process in hopes of attracting one or two more pediatricians.

So, the art of interpreting data involves a degree of humility over the limitations of the data and modeling approaches plus a nimble hand when finalizing recommendations. You can't eliminate all criticism from people who don't like the message, but don't give them additional ammunition with which to shoot the messenger.

End Note

1. Rachel Z. Arndt, "EHR systems evolving with the times (and needs), *Modern Healthcare*, April 30, 2018, page 16.

Chapter 10

Technology Pitfalls

If the last chapter was my favorite, this one is the one I was most nervous about. Although I thoroughly understand how important IT is and how effective IT management supports an organization's objectives, I am not an IT guy myself. My nervousness stems from the very technical nature of the subject and the fact that it is ever-changing. I'm thankful for the several CIOs and other IT experts who reviewed this chapter and suggested additions and corrections that assure the advice is sound.

⇛ 28. Introducing System Security and/or Privacy Vulnerabilities
Top 10

Anything that potentially compromises a healthcare organization's IT network or data security raises all kinds of red flags. Providers thoroughly understand the absolute need for iron-clad security and the negative impact if their healthcare network (hardware, software, medical devices, etc.) or organizational/patient data are compromised. Of particular concern is patient data that is designated Protected Health Information (PHI) and which falls under Health Insurance Portability and Accountability Act (HIPAA) and other related laws and regulations. Healthcare trade publications regularly report on massive data breaches, sometimes involving hundreds of thousands of records, and providers know all about the financial and reputational damage these lapses create.

Healthcare organizations' concerns are heightened whenever someone pitches a service that involves storing or accessing PHI offshore. Data handling requirements can vary wildly from country to country, and providers get understandably nervous at the prospect of their data taking an overseas trip. For many providers, proposing a project involving the international transfer of data is a non-starter.

Recommendations:

■ Do not underestimate providers' obsession with security as it related to PHI and HIPAA! *They won't give you a second look if they suspect your security processes are in any way sloppy or subpar. Go the extra mile when it comes to establishing your data security standards, policies, and procedures.*

■ *Provide thorough documentation of your security protocols, results of your penetration testing, and examples of how your organization handles PHI.*

■ *Where needed, share with prospective clients your plan and the tools you use to ensure that application and hardware security updates and patches are up-to-date.*

■ *Stress your eagerness to work with the facility's security staff or other vendors to make sure they are completely comfortable with your approach.*

■ *Avoid at all costs using offshore data storage.*

29. Failing to Offer a Product That Is State-of-the Art Technologically

Although they do not necessarily want to be on the "bleeding edge" of technology, most physicians and healthcare organizations want state-of-the-art products or services. They tend to look favorably on organizations that offer innovative yet stable technologies and which can demonstrate a sustainable growth pattern.

At the other end of the innovation curve are "dead end" products. Major acquisitions or upgrades can be disruptive, and few organizations want to have to repeat the installation or updating process by buying a soon-to-be-obsolete technology. Therefore, they often write off vendors with products built on older technology platforms.

Smaller vendors may not have the resources to constantly update their product lines. This can be especially problematic when the IT field experiences a wholesale technology change or when operating systems are no longer supported by the manufacturer. Larger vendors can often afford to rewrite and upgrade their more popular programs to take advantage of the latest platform, but this may not the case for smaller ones.

Years ago, I had the chance to buy into a partnership that was considering buying the assets of a healthcare claims processing company. When I went to see what the company actually had to sell, I was shocked to see green-bar paper printers and ancient computer monitors that were hard-wired to a giant CPU with minimal computing power. The equipment looked like leftovers from a bad 1960s sci-fi movie. Since the hardware was so antiquated, I concluded the company's only real asset was its list of current clients, so I (wisely) passed on the purchase offer. This was an extreme case of a company with non-viable assets. Other companies may have a product that is one or two generations behind the leaders. They will certainly not be perceived a market leader, but they can still be successful with certain clients and with the right approach.

If you offer services that are not central to the organization's core mission but are still serviceable, you may be just fine. Examples include a pneumatic tube system for transporting certain supplies; a facilities tracking system that records building maintenance, repairs, painting schedules, and the like; telecom systems; and customized systems for research.

Recommendation:

■ *Recognize that most healthcare organizations want the latest and greatest. But if your product is more of a "workhorse" product like the organization's copiers, its supply chain software program, or a bed-tracking program, something less than market leadership may be just fine. Even if it doesn't have to be incredibly innovative, it must still be robust and dependable. Also, keep in mind that if your offering is perceived as delivering less than the latest capabilities, you must make concessions – like very favorable pricing or enhanced servicing beyond what others offer – to be successful. If you're not cutting edge, you can't hide the fact, but that maybe OK for certain products.*

30. Offering a Product or Service That Taxes an Organization's Infrastructure, Thereby Introducing the Need for Additional Capital Requirements and/or Delays

Many smaller healthcare organizations have patched-together IT systems and little-to-no onsite technical support. Some high-end data projects like implementing an EHR can place significant demands on their technological capabilities. Decentralized radiology Picture Archiving and Communication System (PACS) technology is particularly challenging, especially if data is stored locally or if the system is formatted in a way that makes it dependent on particular hardware.

If your product would require your target healthcare organization to conduct hardware upgrades, the worst-case scenario is that it decides to pass on your project. However, if you are fortunate, it may agree to move forward, but the upgrade will add cost and extend the implementation timeline.

Recommendations:

- ▪ *Consider offering a less technologically demanding version of your product that might create fewer technology interface issues.*
- ▪ *Build the possibility of a delay to upgrade infrastructure into your projected timelines.*
- ▪ *If your product or service requires specific infrastructure upgrades or add-ons that many clients may not have, consider partnering with a vendor that can provide these additional requirements at a discounted rate as part of a more "full service" solution.*

31. Offering a Product That Does Not Interface with Other Technologies Such as Existing Systems or Devices

While some technologies are designed to run in a stand-alone mode, in today's world most healthcare organizations want technologies that are fully integrated in a secure manner. Some technology products tackle a very tightly defined clinical or operational issue without addressing larger related issues. So, if a healthcare organization implements the solution, although it may be solving a particular narrow problem, it may have to continue following the old process for the larger picture, which has not been addressed.

A related problem is designing an IT application with functionality that should interface with other internal healthcare organization technologies but doesn't because of the underlying interoperability problems. Some programs such as post-encounter tracking apps work best when data from visits is automatically dumped into the app. The need for these interfaces creates an expensive challenge for the app developer who must create separate bridges for each of the major EHRs. And if a particular hospital uses a non-supported EHR, this lack of bridging ability may mean they are not a viable target client. Without automatic data transfer, the healthcare organization would be forced into manual data entry, which will kill most projects.

Integrated systems are generally best for operations, but standalones have the advantage of fewer security concerns since they are not linked into any other applications. However, this is becoming less and less of an advantage as most healthcare organizations expect any application to have strong security while being open to interoperability with other relevant systems.

Recommendations:

- ■ *Determine early on the extent to which your product should interface with other operational processes and technologies within the healthcare organization. It's easier to properly design or configure your product right from the start rather than having to do multiple retrofits.*
- ■ *Where appropriate, seek ways to integrate your technology into healthcare organizations' typical systems and infrastructure configurations, but anticipate the security concerns this raises and address them in your offering.*
- ■ *Recognize that integrating your technology into other systems can be quite costly and time-consuming. Since healthcare organizations use various EHRs and other data systems, multiple bridges or interfaces may have to be developed. And keep in mind that some vendors are highly non-cooperative when it comes to assisting other vendors to interface with their programs.*
- ■ *Wherever possible, offer both the option to automatically integrate or not. Obviously, a non-integrated approach can minimize the effectiveness of an app if the data is not automatically available. The alternative is to move ahead with a process that requires additional staff time for manual data transfer.*

Chapter 11

Communications Pitfalls

You can have a world-class product and a great understanding of the market, but if you are unable to clearly communicate with your target clients, your success will be limited at best. The fact that this chapter highlights 13 pitfalls demonstrates how many ways there are to get it wrong. Don't let any of these sideline you.

32. Offending the "Mission" Aspect of Healthcare

Healthcare delivery enjoys a very long history rooted in service and sacrifice, going back centuries. As a matter of fact, while others in ancient Rome were fleeing urban areas because of the deadly plagues, early Christians developed a reputation for compassion because of their willingness to stay behind to take care of the sick and dying, even at their own peril. Over the centuries, the church established many hospitals, and since then many not-for-profit mission-driven healthcare organizations and for-profit companies have joined them as part of the contemporary American healthcare landscape. All of these institutions are dedicated to addressing patient needs and providing high-quality care.

Anyone relating to the healthcare sector would do well to keep the altruistic aspects of healthcare delivery front and center. This is especially important with religiously sponsored organizations.

Let me tell you about an unfortunate incident from early in my career. I was working in the planning department of a Midwestern hospital. As a Christian, I always try to live out my faith, sometimes more successfully than others. Apparently, some of my motivation shined through enough that after working at this hospital for about a year, I was invited to serve on its Mission Effectiveness Committee. I had become a good professional friend of Sister Suzanne, the nun who led the group. The committee was charged with ensuring that the sponsoring order's values were integrated into the hospital's operating policies and procedures.

One of my major projects during my second year at the hospital was leading its planning efforts around the geriatrics service line. We considered a number of aspects including the demographic trends of our service area, the number of seniors we were currently serving, and the number of physicians and other clinicians who specialized in caring for older patients.

As I was preparing my slides to present our plan summary to the committee that oversaw the geriatrics service area, I included bullets listing our findings followed by a concise recommendation. As it turned out, I selected an unfortunate term – "The Bottom Line" – for my summary conclusion for each slide. What I was saying was, "As we consider the various aspects of the demographic changes our market is experiencing, as identified in the bullet points, here's what it all adds up to." What Sister Suzanne heard was, "All we care about is *the bottom line* of how much money we will make." That was not at all what I was saying, but that's what she heard. And that's what mattered in this situation. It took a couple of one-on-one meetings with Sister Suzanne to recover from this incident, but I finally got back on good terms with her.

This was an extreme and rare example, but it still serves as a cautionary tale.

Recommendation:

■ *Be sure to assess the climate of any provider organization
and the key individuals with whom you will be dealing.
Many organizations expect a no-nonsense, hard-hitting
approach, and being direct is appreciated. In other cases,
as in my experience with Sister Suzanne, you need a
much gentler hand to not offend the "mission aspect."
Do your best to discern the most appropriate approach
and be ready to modify it on the fly if necessary.*

⇒ Top 10 33. Not Being Able to "Break Through the Clutter" and Even Get a Hearing

Since this pitfall represents one of the toughest challenges
you will face, it may be the most significant one in the entire
book. Getting on a senior executive's schedule or even getting
them to pay attention to your emails is extremely difficult.

Schedules

All healthcare leaders are extremely busy. It's not unusual for
senior executives to have to attend early morning physician
meetings, work all day in the office, and then attend an evening professional or community meeting. Then, executives
with operational responsibility often have evening or weekend
on-call responsibilities on a regular basis. The more complex
the environment, the more demanding the schedule.

Let me give you an example of how hard it can be to set
a meeting with some C-suite people. I am the treasurer of the
Georgia Health Information Network (GaHIN), the statewide
health information exchange. I also chair GaHIN's Financial
Sustainability Committee. When GaHIN was just getting started,
as Financial Sustainability Committee chair, I had to interface with the Technology Committee chair. The Technology
Committee would investigate the technical viability of various

products and approaches and decide which ones to pursue. Then the Financial Sustainability Committee was charged with handling the business relationship with the vendors.

The Technology Committee was chaired by the CIO of one of the area's biggest health systems. She and I are friends, and she fully supported the relationship between our committees. Despite a personal relationship with her and an agreed-upon mission, I had great difficulty getting in to see her. Her assistant would explain that she had back-to-back meetings and that her first available time might be two weeks out. And this was for a meeting with someone she knew well and for a purpose she fully supported.

With a schedule like that, how likely do you think it would have been for an unknown vendor to get in for a "cold call"? And unannounced drop-in visits are not necessarily a good idea either. Many executives feel that just showing up is presumptuous and might guarantee that future meeting requests will be ignored.

Emails

Like most people, healthcare executives get hundreds of emails a day, most of which they ignore. One of my professional colleagues has worked both sides of the vendor equation. For several years he led a state hospital association's services company helping their endorsed vendors in their visibility and promotional efforts. Later he worked as a hospital CEO. So, he knows what vendors want and what CEOs are up against. As CEO, he was constantly bombarded with emails of every kind. Out of frustration, he finally asked his assistant to track how many emails he got each day and was amazed to learn that the average daily count during one week was 360. Yours might have been one of them.

A few years ago, I heard a hospital CIO explain what his day was like. When he got to the part about emails, he flashed on the screen a few of the many, many emails he gets.

Interestingly, almost every one began with some variation of "I hope you're doing well." He commented that, if he ever sees that as the first line in the email's body (assuming he even opened it in the first place), he immediately hits "delete." I had never detected this pattern, but after his presentation, I started noticing that he was right. Many unsolicited sales-oriented emails I receive actually do start that way.

Another thing he pointed out was that many vendors try to get into his office by saying, "I only want ten minutes of your time." He said that comes across as pushy, and it's never just ten minutes. One respected CEO I know used to have his assistant interrupt his "only ten minutes meetings" at the ten-minute mark to remind him of another obligation.

Using Leverage

This same CEO recently listed three factors that would make him more likely to agree to a vendor meeting:

1. If the vendor company offered a broad array of products or services and the CEO was trying to leverage the hospital's position to receive concessions as one of the company's major clients – He found, though, that some of the mega-companies are so siloed that, despite being under a single corporate umbrella, it was tough to get them to think across their entire product line and offer significant discounts.
2. If a potential purchase represented a major expenditure – Such a meeting would allow for detailed discussions and information gathering so he could evaluate this product in the context of potentially competing ones.
3. Upon the request of someone he respected such as a peer executive, another senior manager, an influential physician leader, a department manager, or even an existing vendor with whom he had a good relationship – In some cases, a timely referral from a peer or colleague can even interrupt a vendor selection process close to landing and

result in the healthcare organization selecting the last-minute candidate.

Recommendations: As I said, this is a tough obstacle to overcome, but here are some of suggestions. As you read through the following recommendations, you will see that many of them are based on having or enhancing some kind of relationship with the person in the organization. Some sales executives have very high sales goals that involves a lot of "hit and run" type contacts. That strategy involves a set of dynamics different from what is presented in some of the following bullet points:

- *See if you can tap into one of the three dynamics mentioned above.*
- *Be extremely respectful of healthcare leaders' calendar and time. A physician friend mentioned that she was surprised at the number of times she would agree to a vendor appointment only to have the person neither show up nor call ahead to cancel. How likely is she to accept a future meeting request?*
- *If you are fortunate enough to get on their calendars, be friendly but direct and professional, and be sure to stick within your allotted time to make sure you aren't "blackballed" from future meetings. In fact, you might consider only using one-half to two-thirds of your scheduled time to allow for a late start or an interruption. If you wrap up early, you can use the remaining time for relationship building.*
- *It's always a good idea to verify at the beginning of the meeting how much time you have and find out if anyone will be leaving early. Keep in mind how much time you have and continually refocus the conversation to the main points if you start running out of time. Some attendees will arrive late, or the cordial portion of your meeting may run longer than expected, and you do not want to be rushing the most critical parts of your pitch if key participants have to leave the meeting early.*

■ *If you have limited time, stick to your "elevator pitch," and highlight one or two aspects that may warrant additional discussion. At the end of the time, ask if the executive would like to continue the conversation, and then suggest that there might be someone better suited for the next meeting. One healthcare organization CEO commented this approach shows courtesy to the executive and gives him an out. If a graceful exit is what the healthcare organization leader was looking for, a follow-up meeting is likely to be a waste of time anyway. Another CEO automatically brings another manager with her into her "ten-minute meetings" so when she leaves, the follow-up person is already engaged. If you request a ten-minute meeting, you might suggest the senior executive include someone else who can serve as the future contact point if they are interested. During the meeting, you can ask the senior executive if and how they would like to remain involved.*

■ *Become a recognized and valued member of the local healthcare community. Get involved with pertinent professional organizations – like Health Information Management Systems Society (HIMSS), the American College of Healthcare Executives (ACHE), Healthcare Financial Management Association (HFMA), or other relevant group – by serving on committees and boards. It's a great way to get to know key leaders in your market and to become a known, helpful, and trusted entity. If you cover a wide territory, it's impossible to be personally invested in dozens of markets across the country. No one expects you to be 100% vested in a dozen different geographic markets, but you can be involved to the extent possible in your own city. If you are personally contributing to local groups' efforts, your reputation will precede you. Your goal should be that whenever your name comes up, people nod their heads and say, "Yeah, he's a great guy." Despite its national presence, the healthcare world is amazingly small. You want your strong reputation to go out in front of you.*

Also, if your organization operates out of various locations, another strategy is to encourage your local reps to engage to the extent possible. This will greatly enhance your corporate image.

■ *Pursue your company's "official" recognition status from a state hospital association or other respected group. Those organizations have formal vetting processes, and being designated a preferred vendor may lead to some degree of preferential consideration. It can be a differentiator, and it may encourage your target to take your call, but don't expect this designation to cause doors to fly open before you.*

■ *Seek other ways to connect with senior leaders. Perhaps they serve on the local Chamber of Commerce or participate in Kiwanis or some other service organizations. Also, check out LinkedIn or other social media platforms. If you see a common connection with a colleague you know well, you can reach out to them to see if they would be comfortable making a professional introduction. You might even be able to relate to a common "off-line" activity. I mention under the "Personal Interests" part of my resume the fact that I am a professional blues harmonica player. Someone in Chicago who saw my resume reached out to me one time and told me to think about taking a job in his city because of the great blues scene there. The blues harp reference proved to be a good conversation starter.*

■ *Try to have a reason why a senior executive should pay attention to you. One of the benefits that Georgia Hospital Association's (GHA) vendor partners receive when they are endorsed by the association is the opportunity to occasionally send out promotional material through the GHA publications. When I led that area, I found that some vendors would want to send out the same tired material time after time. I admonished them to come up with something new: a new product launch, an updated version of their software, a major study they just released, or anything else to grab the hospitals' attention. Manufacturers of toiletries and other consumer goods recognize the need to offer something new to the point that they will sometimes even announce in bold letters, "New Packaging." One detergent manufacturer recently went so far as to slap a sticker on its bottle bragging about the "New Look, Coming Soon." Even though neither the detergent nor the packaging had changed, they were trumpeting their* plan *to change something. I'm not sure I care about that at all, but this tactic shows that the advertising world sees the value of putting something new out there.*

■ *Consider whether you are violating the "I hope you're doing well" principle. I don't know that this opening line is universally frowned upon, but there may be enough people who dislike it that you should consider whether or not it's a good fit for you.*

■ *When it comes to email communication, what's in the "From" box often determines whether or not the recipient opens it. People always read emails from others who are important in their world. There's nothing you can do if you don't happen to be in that inner circle. However, recognize that the second most important lever for getting an email read is the subject line. I maintain two different blogs, and I spend almost as much emotional energy writing my subject line as I do in selecting my topic in the first place. I can't tell you how many blogs I get with some variation of "This Week's Blog." Unless you are the Queen of England, someone of equal stature, or the most brilliant person in my field, I'm pretty unlikely to stop what I'm doing to read an email entitled "This Week's Blog." Tell me what it's about. Lure me in with an intriguing title. Arouse my curiosity. "This Week's Blog" doesn't do it.*

■ *Similarly, you must keep your email communication as crisp and brief as possible. One CEO friend commented that she gets tired of reading very long emails to find the relevant points, and (as she put it) "an 'apology for the length of the email' in the subject line or introductory line is a dead give-away" that it will require a lot of effort to read.*

■ *Because of the "cluttered inbox syndrome," some people are revisiting the "old school" concept of writing personal letters. This can be more cumbersome and expensive than sending an email, but a carefully crafted personalized letter – not a sales pitch form letter – can help you get your prospect's attention.*

34. Failing to Do the Research on Your Competitors' Products to the Point Where You Can Credibly Show the Superiority of Your Product

I may be one of the few people on the planet who enjoys buying a new car. We tend to drive our vehicles into the ground, so I only get to enjoy my hobby every eight or ten years. Part of the fun is researching the available models to find just the perfect blend of style, performance, and value. When I go into a dealership, I am pretty familiar with their offerings and most of my preferred vehicle's features. Nevertheless, I do have a few questions about some of the finer details.

About eight years ago when I was on one of my car-buying expeditions, I went to test-drive one of the cars I was strongly considering. The sales guy was friendly, but I was surprised that he couldn't answer some pretty basic questions. Although I didn't necessarily expect him to have memorized how many square feet the trunk had, in the course of the conversation, I quickly realized that he had only a passing acquaintance with the cars he was selling. I mean, isn't that his job?

I thought, "How can I as a potential customer know far more than the salesman about what he is selling?" When I walked into the dealership, there wasn't another customer in sight, and he was sitting at his desk drinking coffee and reading *Sports Illustrated*. Why wasn't he brushing up on all the details of his cars and those of his competitors?

This principle carries over into healthcare. Anyone in a sales role should be thoroughly informed about their products and also know enough about competitors' offerings to show how their own product is superior to their competitor's. Unfortunately, during my 24 years of meeting with vendors, I found a surprising number who didn't know their offerings as well as they should have.

Recommendation:

- *If you're a vendor, you should know your products inside-out and also be prepared to discuss what your competitors offer. Just be careful not to exaggerate your superiority or bad-mouth the competition. Your potential customers expect you to be professional and positive about your products, but be careful to not undercut your credibility by overstating your advantages or understating those of your competitors. This could come back to haunt you.*

35. Focusing on "Features" Rather Than on How Your Product Solves a Customer's Problems

This is as basic as it comes. Sales professionals are constantly reminded to demonstrate how their product *solves a problem* they know the potential customer has. Of course, the customer wants to see that your software screens are attractive and easy-to-read, but what they really want to know is that you can help them address whatever pressing need they are facing.

One rural hospital CEO recently told me of an unpleasant encounter he had with a signage company salesperson who took a "features" approach. Rather than investigate his hospital or even the healthcare field in general, he showed up, talked about how great his company was, and presented a boiler-plate proposal that included nothing specific about his hospital. Instead, he should have researched this CEO's institution, explained his prior experience with similar organizations, asked some relevant questions, offered a tailored proposal, and then asked him how he could refine the proposal to even better match the hospital's needs. The vendor's message should have been, "I've worked with a number of other rural hospitals, and based on my experience and after hearing what your needs are, I think this approach will give you what you want. Here are my initial thoughts about the look and feel your new signs should carry. Does that seem on track to you? How can we make it even better?" This type of discussion would have made all the difference to the CEO.

Recommendations:

- *It's natural to tout your product's superiority, but don't forget that, instead of stressing what your product is, you should stress what it does and what problem it solves.*
- *Don't forget to ask a lot of questions to make sure you really grasp the issue and can provide an appropriately targeted proposal.*

36. Having an Inadequate Web Page That Fails to Let Potential Clients Understand What You Really Do

Nowadays your website is your front door. The first place most people go when they hear about a particular company is their website. Most are quite good, but some that I see could stand improvement.

Disclaimer: Although I have extensive communications experience, I am *not* a communications consultant or a social media expert. Nevertheless, here are some of my observations.

The websites of early-on companies tend to fall into one of three categories:

1. They provide a solid overview of the company and what they do – This is what you want.
2. They look very impressive, but on further examination, it turns out there is less to the company than the website implies – In my opinion, this is not bad. You want to project as professional and "big" an image as possible. As long as you don't cross the line of misrepresentation, putting your best foot forward is fine.
3. They fail to communicate the basics of what the company is really about – When I visit a website, I want to know what the company does, who the leaders are, and how to get in touch with the company. Some sites don't provide this. There can be two reasons:
   - The company is still a bit squishy and hasn't completely formulated what it does
   - The leadership is trying to guard their proprietary information and is reluctant to share too much

   I will address these two issues in the rest of my comments about this pitfall.

I believe most healthcare people are sympathetic toward and supportive of innovative entrepreneurs. They recognize their potential to upset the apple cart in a good way and understand that start-ups are start-ups.

If you engage in a serious discussion with a physician or executive, they will quickly be able to figure out that you're a small, early-stage company, but that is not necessarily the kiss of death. Despite what I mentioned in Pitfall 2 about some organizations ultimately declining to work with an untested company, you shouldn't let that possibility inhibit your preliminary conversations with them. You are who you are, and you can sometimes muscle through an organization's reluctance to work with smaller companies. And depending on what you offer, you will find some healthcare organizations actually prefer to work with a smaller company to get more personalized attention.

The issue of protecting your intellectual property is a bit more complex. A longtime friend who is a former hospital CEO-turned-consultant recently mentioned an unforeseen problem created by inadequate web pages. He was asked by a friend to become an adviser for a new tech-related product. The technology they are using has been around for many years and is already widely used. The entrepreneur claims on his website that his approach is far better than the existing one but offers no details or evidence.

Wanting to be helpful and so he could provide a meaningful critique, my friend agreed to meet with the product's manufacturer and dig into the details. The manufacturer, though, presented him with a very restrictive, ten-page Non-Disclosure Agreement (NDA) with a ten-year shelf life. Here's my friend's evaluation:

> After reading it, I've concluded that most sales targets will have to sign a similar NDA just to engage in a discussion that differentiates it from older solutions. I think the lack of pertinent information on the website combined with an overly ambitious NDA is a potential "non-starter." If the solution is that good and the "secret sauce" so secret, it should be protected with patents, or be patent pending, in my opinion. If they can't get a patent, then I ask if the solution really all that different.

He also pointed out that many healthcare organization boards are very reluctant to allow anyone in the organization to assume the kind of legal liability typical in most NDAs. His comments parallel my remarks under Pitfall 18 about the dangers of overly restrictive NDAs and their impact on potential advisors.

Recommendations:

- ■ *Review your website to make sure you adequately communicate the basics of who you are, what you do, and how to reach you. One of my pet peeves is a web page that doesn't list the organization's physical address and phone number. There have been times I am on the way to visit with a local company and I need the street address for my GPS. Similarly, there are times I have a very basic question that could be answered by a simple phone call. But I can't find their contact information anywhere. I recognize the value of having inquirers complete a form to submit their contact information to you, but that means a delay in them being able to talk to you. You should make it as easy as possible for potential clients to reach you on their timetable, not yours.*

  As long as we're on the topic of phone calls, let me also express my frustration over people not including their cell number in their email signature lines. More than once, I have been on my way to a local meeting when Atlanta traffic unexpectedly kicks in and I have to let the person I'm meeting with know an accident has slowed me down. I may not have them in my smartphone contacts yet, and when I find their email, it turns out they haven't included their mobile number in their signature line. You should make it as easy as possible for people to reach you!

- ■ *Even if you are still in your developmental stages, try to be as detailed and specific as you can be on your website.*

- ■ *Consider the possible interaction between the level of detail on your website and the need for restrictiveness in your NDA. Don't be so vague on your web page and so overly protective of your product that you back potential clients into an NDA corner.*

37. Cluttering Your Presentation and Marketing Material with So Many Product Features, Some of Which Are Not That Important, That Your True Differentiators Get Buried

Vendors are understandably excited about their products and sometimes stress the "glitzier" aspects of the software. Although the flashing lights and pretty colors may be fun, focusing too much on them may cause the potential client to lose sight of what the product actually does and why they should care.

Many of the vendors who visited me at GHA would come in with great-looking brochures touting all the features of their products. This isn't a real example, but some of their lists would include things like this:

- Has state-of-the-art graphics
- Is user-friendly
- Is Software as a Service (SaaS)-delivered
- Features cloud-based storage
- Is the only product with database X, a proprietary resource developed by former U.S. Department of Health and Human Services (HHS) employees
- Is offered by a company with a seven-year track record
- Was selected as top software product in its class
- Is customizable
- Allows comparisons with other facilities

First of all, these are features and don't explain how the product will help me. (Refer to Pitfall 35.) They are all wonderful features, but every other vendor in the marketplace can say many of the same things. After all, how many software products are *not* SaaS-delivered, cloud-based, and customizable? The last bullet about facilitating comparisons among facilities shows what the software does and is very important. The two other items on the list that really stand out to me are its proprietary database developed by credible people and the fact that it was selected as top in its class. These three items should be shouted from the housetops. Unfortunately, the jumbled approach that mixes in less relevant information is far more common than you would expect.

Recommendation:

■ *Lead with the two or three product capabilities (i.e., what only you can do for the client) or features that truly differentiate you from the others, especially if you are operating in a commoditized market. Give your prospect a reason to buy your product instead of someone else's. After you have clearly made your pitch for how your product can help them like no one else's, you can list, in almost a matter-of-fact way, some other capabilities or features that are good but not game-changers. You want them to walk away with a clear understanding of the two or three reasons why you can help them better than anyone else can.*

38. Failing to "Layer" Your Message and Tailor It to Various Audiences

No one understands your product better than you do, especially if you are an entrepreneur who spent months or even years turning your brainchild into a product. One of my first clients was a very talented lady who had spent 15 years as a data analyst with a large healthcare company. Her experience led her to a novel way to analyze data for a particular outpatient area, so she quit her job and spent about six months developing her product. I immediately saw the value and was pleased to be able to jump in to help her with her market strategy. I rarely accompany my clients on sales calls, but because I thought her approach was so good, I agreed to help her find a hospital beta test site.

She obviously knew every nuance of her product and was very enthusiastic about what it could do. Her problem was that she was so familiar with it that she felt compelled to explain every single detail about every decision tree branch in the software. As a result, potential beta site executives glazed over within about ten minutes and got lost in the minutia. She also failed to recognize that clinicians would care about certain aspects of her approach, executives would focus in on others, and IT people would want to discuss yet a third area. She completely missed this point and got into the IT weeds with the hospital CEO.

At the beginning of the meetings with potential beta users, I provided a two-minute intro including why we were there and a very high-level discussion of what her product did. I then turned it over to her. And, despite my repeated prior advice, she proceeded to over-explain absolutely everything and get into programming-type explanations that had little to do with patient care or anything else the CEO cared about.

Recommendations:

■ *As with the previous pitfall about cluttering your explanations with too many features, it's important to focus on the problem your product solves and two or three main reasons potential customers should use your product. This is the primary point you should reinforce several times, perhaps wording it slightly differently each time. Media relations experts advise their clients to decide in advance of a TV interview what message they want to get across to the public and then keep coming back to it several times in the course of an interview. If you watch politicians, you often see them* not *really answering the question they are asked but using it as a springboard to get their predefined message out. I'm* not *suggesting you act deceptively, but you should steer the discussion toward your main points to the extent possible.*

- *Think layers. Start with a very brief product overview (i.e., the "elevator pitch"). Then feature your product's unique capabilities and how it will address their issues. Follow that with a high-level product description, and then finally dive into whichever area of detail they are most interested in.*
- *Tailor your presentation to your audience. Clinicians are not likely to care about the technical challenges you had to overcome in combining databases. However, the IT staff might. Of course, your overarching message – that is, what problem you are solving – will still be the same, but your focus will vary depending on your audience.*
- *If you are presenting to a group that includes clinicians, executives, and technical people and you start getting bogged down in technical minutia, you can suggest a separate meeting with the tech people to answer their questions to their satisfaction.*

39. Being So Concerned to Not Oversell Your Product That You Undersell It

I have a theory that people tend to listen to the wrong advice. Let me explain. I am wary of "hard sell" approaches and have seen that most healthcare executives and clinicians are as well. Neither they nor I tend to respond well when we start feeling like we're being "sold to."

As a result, I routinely advise my clients to avoid oversimplification and high pressure techniques.

Apparently, I'm fairly convincing because one of my clients took my "soft sell" advice to the *n*th degree and ended up underselling and almost de-marketing her product. I happened to sit in on one of her presentations and saw that she was so worried that she would come across as pushy that she qualified every statement to the point that I began to wonder if she even believed in her product herself. Her natural desire for credibility and absolute accuracy led her to overdo the caveats and appear wishy-washy about what she did. In this case, she should have thought through how her personality fit in with my "generic advice" about not being pushy and not taking it to the extreme she did.

Recommendations:

■ *Keep in mind the resistance most executives and clinicians have to hard-sell techniques. Pitches that include "this offer expires on ____" seldom succeed with them.*

■ *As you develop your presentation materials, factor in your demeanor and natural inclinations and don't swing too far the other way. Your goal is to come across as respectful, enthusiastic, and confident, but not brash.*

40. Presenting a Totally Unfocused Message

Companies, of course, want to cast a wide net to try to reach as many potential clients as possible. Sometimes in that process, though, they end up presenting themselves as being able to do so many things that they totally confuse potential clients who can't quite figure out what they actually do.

A few months ago, I was talking to an Austin-based potential client of mine whose website included dozens of seemingly unrelated healthcare services: facilities management, compliance with human resources regulations, the Health Insurance Portability and Accountability Act (HIPAA) services, nurse education, and several other topics. Each major category had numerous sub-bullets elaborating on their offerings. The vendor's physical brochure was an 11" × 17" sheet folded in half and was filled with close to 50 separate products and services.

Beyond being cluttered and confusing because of the dozens of things they offered, it was a mess visually – very dense text with few headlines to separate the material. My rule of thumb is that I should be able to hold the document about five feet away and, based on how it is laid out, see the major sections. This helps guide the reader through the material. This particular brochure was a pretty solid mass of gray.

The combination of their online description and their brochure was such a jumble of unrelated items that left me with two impressions:

1. I really don't understand what this company's core business is.
2. If they really do cover all these things, they must have hundreds on their staff to be able to competently offer so much.

As I poked around further, I discovered that the company is actually very small – only five employees. But they had loose affiliations and contractual relationships with many other organizations, which allowed them to legitimately claim a broad range of services. As a small consulting company myself, I understand the value in partnerships to supplement the central services my company can provide, but this particular company was little more than a contracting shell with not a whole lot at its heart.

Once I finally got to the bottom of what they actually did, I was not impressed. Their basic competency was actually fairly limited, and I wasn't sure I could really trust them because I felt they were bordering on misrepresentation by trying to project the image of a huge multi-faceted organization.

Recommendation:
- *Present your company in as positive a way as possible, but don't clutter your message to the point that potential clients are thoroughly confused by your real offerings or question your integrity. Reverse the roles. How would you feel if you found out that a potential business partner hid the*

fact that, rather than having a strong in-house staff team, they outsourced 95% of what they claimed to do and were not particularly transparent about that?

41. Being Unable to "Break Through" and Convince the Healthcare Organization It Truly Needs Your Product

Every entrepreneur's dream scenario is securing a meeting with a senior healthcare organization executive, presenting their product, and having the executive place an order on the spot. I'm sure this happens, but only as often as the Chicago Cubs win the World Series.

A more likely version is either that the vendor gets a ho-hum response or that the executives does have some interest but then must engage others in the healthcare organization, thus ushering you into a black hole. Buying something in a hospital is typically a team sport where multiple individuals and departments have to suit up.

Whether it's the person who is directly over the area most likely to use your product or someone else on the "extended team," one of the hardest sells is someone who fails to see why they need your product. There can be three reasons for their resistance:

1. Maybe your product really doesn't fit, either because that particular healthcare organization is not the right target or because there is an underlying design flaw. Of course, not every organization will be a good match for every product. If that's the case, you can use the meeting as a learning opportunity for future presentations. Ideally, the problem should not be a basic design flaw. If you followed the advice given in Pitfalls 18 and 19, you should have gotten adequate real-life input so that you designed your product to truly meet real needs.

Recommendation: If you suspect your product is deficient, respectfully ask for candid feedback and ask what it would take to make your product saleable. You may need to go back to the drawing board and tweak your product. It may not require a wholesale makeover. Perhaps just adding one element, data source or capability is all that's required.

2. Maybe the roadblock individual lacks vision and is a "heads-down, I just want to do my job"-type person. This is a tough one. One executive who has served as interim and full-time CFO and interim CEO at numerous hospitals is a fun-loving, no-nonsense guy who seldom minces his words. However, he tells the story about how he learned to persuade people in a very gentle way. He literally spent one of his college summers as the proverbial door-to-door vacuum cleaner salesman. Think about his challenge. If he got in the door in the first place – which in and of itself is a huge accomplishment – he had to convince the lady of the house that she needed his product without insulting her. If she thinks her current vacuum is doing the job, why does she need his? But if he implies her house is filthy, he's out the door.

   Recommendation: Your goal is to get the "heads-down" person to lift their head up long enough to see that your product may be able to help them to accomplish their goals, but not in such a way that you imply they're not performing adequately. Your task is made easier if you can legitimately explain you are applying a new approach to their operational area. The lady considering buying a new vacuum cleaner won't think you're calling her a slob if you have the first turbo-charged, supersonic machine with three times the suction of conventional cleaners. Similarly, if your product introduces a new technology or approach, that provides a natural explanation for why the facility is still doing things the old way.

3. Maybe you have not adequately tied your product to a strategically important initiative for the healthcare organization.

   Recommendation: As I mentioned in Pitfalls 35 and 37, you should always focus on how your product solves the organization's problems and the two or three capabilities that truly differentiate your product from others. Reinforce how it addresses a strategically important priority. Your sales target may think you are offering a commodity and, therefore, fail to see why it might be worth making the switch from their current approach. This can be especially true for the "heads-down" person.

42. Including Your Pricing on Your Website or in Written Material

Sales executives who believe their products are quite attractive sometimes try to make the purchasing process as simple as possible by providing in their publicly facing material full details of their product, including pricing. This is almost always a bad idea unless you are offering a straightforward, completely commoditized product and your sales appeal is almost strictly your pricing.

One vendor I met at a conference had a very nice but somewhat unusual software product that tracked supervisors' comments about their employee and other HR functions I hadn't seen elsewhere. The problem was that it takes about ten minutes to fully explain his software. His website included a fairly thorough description of the product, including details of the four variations available. It also had pricing for each of the options. He may have been inspired by the chart on the back of some tax preparation software boxes that includes a checklist of what each version (standard, deluxe, professional, etc.) includes, but his product had several unique, potentially confusing features that would not be obvious to uninitiated users. After he explained his product to me in full detail, I was able to understand most of the variations, but I knew that someone who stumbled onto his web page would probably miss most of the details.

If you have an elaborate or potentially confusing offering, your goal is to *engage* potential clients in a conversation so you can assess their level of understanding and correct any misconceptions they may have. They probably don't fully appreciate the value of your product, and listing prices removes one of the reasons they may have to contact you.

I, myself, made the mistake of publishing prices when I first launched my consulting business. I had developed an offering called the Healthcare Marketing Tune-Up Program with three elements:

1. A review of the company's products in light of the "7 Ps of Marketing"
   - Product
   - Place (distribution methods)
   - Positioning
   - Promotion
   - Packaging
   - Price
   - People
2. Suggestions for avoiding the relevant pitfalls I had identified. These pitfalls are what eventually made it into this book
3. A summary Strengths/Weaknesses/Opportunities/Threats analysis

My objective was to offer a clearly defined "product" that potential clients could easily understand. With thousands of start-ups, I thought a straightforward description of my offering, including its affordable price, would essentially "sell itself." I was wrong. Even though my description was quite complete and there were few comparable products, I found it necessary to discuss what I do in some detail for potential clients to be able to understand it. Very few people "got it" from just the written description. I had to engage them in a fairly detailed conversation.

Publishing my prices undermined the goal of engagement. Potential customers had no reason to reach out unless they took the initiative to seek answers to their question or wanted to engage me. I should have set up a dynamic where website visitors would have had a reason to reach out to me if they were interested. By listing the price up front, I had taken away an important reason for them to connect with me.

Recommendation:

- *Think long and hard before you publicly advertise your pricing. As stated above, if yours is essentially a commodity offering, your primary appeal could be your pricing. If this is not the case, though, readily displaying your prices is likely to undercut the opportunity for personal interaction.*

43. Positioning Your Approach to "Sell What You Have" Instead of Identifying Their Problems and Solving Them

Many sales and business consultants constantly beat this drum, and with good reason. People don't really care about your slick product features. They want you to solve one of their problems. (See Pitfall 35.)

Several years ago, I was at the wrong end of a clunky attempt to get me to buy someone's product instead of getting my problems solved. As I explained under Pitfall 34, I love buying new cars. It's great fun to research various models and then get to road-test the top contenders. I had my eye on one manufacturer's small SUV, so my wife and I visited the local dealership to check it out. I explained to the salesman why a small SUV would be a great fit for our needs at that time.

Although I liked the exterior styling, as soon as we sat in the vehicle, I immediately knew it wasn't right for us, and I told the salesman so. There was no reason to waste either his time or ours.

But in good "buy what I have and not what you need" fashion, he asked. "Can I interest you in this full-size sedan?"

"Seriously," I thought. "Didn't he hear me explain I wanted a small SUV that would accommodate landscaping plants and building supplies? How does his full-size sedan even come close to fitting that bill? Never mind I had also mentioned that driving a somewhat stylish vehicle is important to me, and one of the car magazines described this particular sedan as being so frumpy that it looked like a refugee from a 1960s-era Soviet gulag." But rather than verbalize any of these details, I politely told him I didn't think his for-grandmothers-only vehicle would be a good fit. In one sense, this car salesman had nothing to lose in offering me a lousy alternative, but he did nothing to make me want to ever go back to his dealership.

Recommendation:

- ▪ *Don't default to ticking off all the wonderful features of the product you happen to have instead of assessing the organization's need and determining how well it might solve their problems. If you plan to have continuing contact with these folks, you don't want to develop a reputation for pushing your junk rather than becoming a strategically important resource. Also keep in mind that, as I have said before, the healthcare world is surprisingly small, and people from different institutions and sectors freely talk with each other. Avoid sullying your reputation.*

44. Not Doing Your Homework to Learn about a Potential Client's Situation and Looking Foolish as a Result

One of my friends – I'll call him Chris – is a senior operations executive at a Kansas health system in the process of merging with another system. This merger has been in the works for a couple of years and everyone knows about it. It has also been widely reported that Chris' system will be transitioning from Electronic Health Record (EHR) vendor A to EHR vendor B (the one used by the other system), so his EHR vendor will be out the door in a matter of months. Nevertheless, Chris has received several calls from consultants wanting to help him "enhance" his use of his original EHR. If they had any level of ambition, they would have known that Chris' system would no longer be using that particular EHR. They are obviously trying to sell what they have rather than address the client's real need. How much credibility do you think they have when they haven't even bothered to research what product Chris' system will be using in the future and instead offer something they should have known is totally irrelevant?

Recommendations:

■ *In order to position yourself as a trusted industry asset, do your best to determine in advance your potential client's real need and show how your approach addresses those needs.*

■ *Once you get in front of the client, ask a lot of questions. One senior leader stated, "A great way to get at the specifics of the problems the customer has (and that the product might solve) is to ask a bunch of questions. It shows I genuinely care about what issues you are facing and need to better understand before I go blindly into a speech talking about my product and why you would be a fool not to buy it. In asking the questions, it will help the rep focus the discussion on the product's benefits aimed directly at the issues or problems the customer themselves have verbalized."*

Chapter 12

Return on Investment Pitfalls

Although quality and patient care top the priority list for healthcare providers, neither of these is possible without adequate funding. Back in the 1980s, Sister Irene Kraus, the first president of the Daughters of Charity National Health System, caused quite a stir within the healthcare world by coining the phrase, "No margin, no mission." This catchphrase – surprising coming from a religious leader – explains how the mission side of caregiving is only possible when the financial underpinnings are in place.

Return on Investment (ROI) pitfalls are among the most common and potentially damaging ones I see. Although vendors understand the importance of making a good financial case for their product, they sometimes fail to grasp the complexity of how healthcare services are funded and end up slapping together a haphazard ROI case with more holes in it than a target at the conclusion of a Summer Olympics archery competition.

⇛ Top 10 45. Thinking a Healthcare Organization Will Embrace Your Product or Service Even If You Don't Have a Clear, Demonstrable ROI

Pursuing medicine is one of the highest callings there is. Physicians and other providers devote many years to preparation, often at great personal cost. Medical school and residency program demands and schedules border on the inhumane as students and interns regularly work around the clock. The toll on personal health and marriages can be great. Of course, for many medical specialties, the long-term financial reward is part of the payoff at the end of the long tunnel. However, with healthcare's changing financial dynamics over the last 30 years, becoming a physician is often not considered as attractive as it once was.

Back in the mid-1980s when I was doing my two-year administrative fellowship at Michigan Medicine, I had the chance to spend an entire year working within the School of Medicine. It was a wonderful, formative experience that enlightened me about the physician's mindset. Medicare's new payment system based on Diagnosis-Related Groups (DRGs) was just rolling out, and I recall the many internal discussions we as the health system had about how to adjust to the new payment approach.

Many physicians were almost incensed that finances would even come up when discussing how care should be delivered. "Old school" clinicians take pride in their primary commitment being to the patient's welfare. One physician in particular boasted that he purposely avoided knowing the insurance status of his patients. To him, it didn't matter whether the patient was covered by commercial insurance, Medicare, or Medicaid or didn't have insurance at all. Providing the needed care regardless of the finances was paramount for him.

This admirable attitude still persists to a large extent, but financial realities of the last three decades have forced more discussion about fiscal considerations into care delivery conversations.

One of my recent consulting clients was a physician who had an attractive technology-based approach within her medical specialty, which is not one of the "major" areas like cardiology or orthopedics. Unfortunately, she wasn't getting much traction, and she commented to me, "I thought the clinical value of what my approach brings would convince people to move forward."

That's a nice thought, but in today's tough financial climate, there are too many other factors at work. As we discussed in Chapter 1, most hospitals lose money on substantial parts of their inpatient volume, so they have to fill the hole somehow. This makes it very difficult to justify expenditures with no demonstrated ROI.

I recently heard about a rural hospital administrator in the upper Midwest who experienced fairly significant pushback from his staff over his decision to purchase paintings from local artists to spruce up his somewhat dowdy, 250-bed 1950s-era hospital. He spent about $12,000 buying artwork for some of the public areas and saw it as a win-win: the hospital would be made more attractive, and this purchase would also communicate the hospital's support of the local arts community.

The nurses didn't see it that way. They hadn't received a salary increase in several years and let their displeasure be known. In reality, the $12,000 the hospital spent on artwork would make very little tangible difference in nurses' take-home pay long-term. By the time you spread that relatively small amount over the entire nursing staff salary structure, the ongoing impact would hardly register. But his decision still created conflict.

Every dollar available is being pulled in *many* different directions: staff salary increases, updating OR equipment to support the medical staff, physical plant improvements, IT infrastructure upgrades, etc.

So, unfortunately, clinical value in and of itself is not enough to carry the day. Someone, somewhere along the decision-making process will eventually ask the hard financial questions, and without solid ROI numbers, most projects will die an untimely death. So, a credible ROI projection is crucial.

Recommendation:

■ *Read the rest of this chapter to learn the "ins and outs" of developing believable ROI numbers.*

The following three pitfalls describe a very common fallacy committed by vendors: presenting overly rosy or simplistic ROI numbers.

During the 19 years I was GHA's primary gatekeeper for vendors seeking the association's endorsement for promotional purposes, I heard just about every vendor approach imaginable. I would say the biggest mistake I consistently saw was vendors presenting sloppy, non-credible ROI numbers. I call those, "ROI projections only your mother would believe."

Let me use the following example to explain the three most common ROI fallacies I saw.

⇒
Top 10
46. ROI Fallacy 1 – Not Realizing How Difficult It Is to Actually Capture Potential Savings

Vendors often claim their product will pay for itself, or at least save enough money to make a big dent in the price tag. They typically point to some kind of savings projection as a justification for that statement.

A couple of years ago, I met with a vendor who asserted that his product could speed up a particular department's throughput, thereby increasing efficiency. The product was fairly expensive, but he promised a five-month ROI. In light of the price tag, I found that a bit hard to believe. "You're on," I said. (I'm changing the facts of his product, but let me walk through his logic.)

"Our product can save a physical therapist (PT) five minutes per procedure, and the average PT sees 15 patients a day.

So that saves 75 minutes per eight-hour shift." He did the math assuming fulltime PT's salary and benefits at $90,000 to get to his five-month breakeven.

What's wrong with this picture? His math works but his logic doesn't. Assuming his product did truly save five minutes per procedure, could the healthcare organization really *capture* those savings? In other words, he was asserting a reduced workload – and by implication reduced costs – of 75 minutes per day (5 minutes per procedure times 15 procedures). He then declared you could apply the savings to pay for his product. But since the PT isn't going home after 6 hours and 45 minutes, they are still on the clock and getting paid, and you can't write a check from the reduced minutes.

After I explained to my vendor friend that capturing savings would be tough, he said, "Well, maybe, but the PT can do other things that are really important that they haven't had time to do." True, formerly undone tasks may get done, but they are still getting paid, so there is no salary reduction.

Depending on the nature of the job function, and assuming there are many employees with the same repetitive job function, this logic does have some merit. For example, if you have six Full-Time Equivalents (FTEs) in the same job function and you can eliminate 75 minutes per day for each of them, that translates to 450 minutes or 7.5 hours per day. Now you're talking.

A technology that reduces a few minutes for a billing clerk is likely to be more promising than one that saves time for nurses. Billing staff have one primary task, and larger healthcare organizations typically have enough billing clerks that a streamlined process could potentially eliminate part of a position. On the other hand, nurses conduct many different functions during their shifts, so it is unlikely they do the same activity enough to aggregate enough "saved" minutes to cut staffing.

Another location where a time-saving technology could potentially save some money is a smaller physician practice that employs a relatively small number of support staff or lower acuity clinical staff. Since each employee typically wears many hats and task time demands often vary by day of the week or season, the tight staffing level sometimes results in overtime. If your product truly saves time, you can legitimately make the case that some of the acquisition cost would be off-set by avoided overtime expenses.

But overall, the very common claim that a product will save a few minutes per procedure and "pay for itself" is wildly optimistic. Actually reducing hard operating dollar outlay for labor-saving programs can be difficult.

What's required to avoid ROI Fallacy 1:

- *A technology that introduces efficiency for positions with high volume of a single activity and fairly steady demand throughout the work shift*
- *Enough employees in the affected job category to "gather" the savings to the point where headcount can be reduced or repositioned*
- *A situation where a healthcare organization department or physician's office routinely incurs overtime expenses and the new technology can save enough time to make some of that overtime unnecessary*
  Recommendation:
  - *Be very careful about how you describe potential cost savings. I have heard over and over from my healthcare colleagues that they are extremely suspicious of claims that "this product will pay for itself." They've heard that song more than once and have almost always been disappointed.*

47. ROI Fallacy 2 – Claiming That Using Your Product Will Allow the Provider to Bring in More Revenue

Even though I shot holes in the salesman's logic about saving time for physical therapists as described in ROI Fallacy 1, he wasn't deterred. "Well, even you don't send the therapist home early, reducing the time per procedure ends up increasing the therapist's capacity so he can see more patients and bring in new revenue."

Nice thought – *if* capacity constraints are literally forcing the facility to turn patients away. That may hold true for some clinical areas, but it's certainly not true across all healthcare delivery sites. Depending on the service line, some providers may be idle for parts of their days due to low patient volume. So, increased efficiency doesn't necessarily translate to bringing in new patients. Consequently, the "promised" incremental revenue won't materialize.

There is a further complication to the "increased throughput" argument. There may be bottlenecks involving other staff who are part of a clinical or operational process and who would not be helped by the new technology. A good example relates to operating room scheduling. Even if a new technology saves a few minutes per procedure for the surgeon, those saved minutes evaporate if housekeeping is understaffed and can't turn the room over quickly enough to slip in an additional procedure. So, capturing the "saved" minutes and scheduling extra procedures won't happen.

One of my clients gave me a great example of one salesperson who stumbled over both ROI Fallacy 1 and ROI Fallacy 2. He told me about the time he was with a previous company when he went head-to-head with another vendor in an EHR bid. The other vendor stressed their quicker response time – a full ½ second per click. He used that ½-second savings to make the following economic argument:

½ second saved per click *times*
On average 40 clicks per visit *times*
On average 40 visits per day *yields*
About 13 minutes per day

He claimed this allows for:

1 extra patient visit per day *which generates*
On average $85 per visit *times*

150 days per year *which yields*
$12,750 per year

"So, if you don't go with us, you will lose $12,750 per physician per year."

I would love to see how you capture and operationalize saving ½ second per click. As I said, this poor vendor's logic runs afoul of Fallacy 1 – *Assuming you can capture very small times savings* – and also Fallacy 2 – *Assuming you are literally turning away patients because of internal capacity constraints.*

What's required to avoid ROI Fallacy 2:

■ *A revenue-producing service where the healthcare organization is literally turning away patients due to capacity limitations*
■ *No other volume-based bottlenecks in related service areas upon which the primary service is dependent*

48. ROI Fallacy 3 – Automatically Assuming Additional Patients Are a Financial Plus for the Organization

Even if a facility is literally turning away patients because of capacity constraints that can be addressed by a new product, this doesn't automatically mean that the additional patients provide a net financial positive. If the incremental patients are covered by a fixed or capitated payment (one where the healthcare organization gets a payment for the patient each month and then has to subtract what they spend to take care of them), or if they are uninsured, additional volume could represent a net financial negative rather than a boost. As we discussed in Chapter 1, many hospitals recover only 25% of what they spend on caring for the "average" uninsured patient. If the new patient added because some staff time was freed up and that patient has typical or – even worse – higher than average clinical needs, the hospital could actually lose money. So, is it really financially advantageous to add patients if you take a step backward financially?

On balance, I should point out the difference between covering *total cost* of a patient encounter and covering the *marginal cost* of a patient encounter. When I report that Medicaid on average only covers 87% of the cost of care, that include all overhead costs including insurance, administrative salaries, the cost of debt, utilities, depreciation on the facility, etc. Taking one additional inpatient doesn't increase the hospital CEO's salary or its utility costs.

So, even if the new revenue the healthcare organization gets from treating that extra Medicaid patient falls short of full cost coverage, it can still be financially advantageous to attract them, thus blunting the negative impact of ROI Fallacy 3.

The airline industry provides a parallel analogy. It costs virtually the same to fly a half-full plane as one that is fully booked. Although the passengers love the extra "stretch room," the only advantage of the vacant seats to the airline are the few gallons of jet fuel saved because of the lighter weight and the cost of however many cans of Coke are not consumed. If the airline can add just one more passenger, it generates significant revenue at almost no cost. This shows there can be an advantage to marginal volume. Keep in mind, though, that adding patient volume "on the margin" may eventually require increasing staff, expanding your facility, or adding other costs. Sooner or later, marginal costs begin to get closer to total costs.

The point is that healthcare financial leaders have heard it all, and glibly claiming increased revenue may invite some pushback.

What's required to avoid ROI Fallacy 3:

Either
- *The assumption – based on reasonable evidence – that most new patients are covered by insurance plans that are likely to cover the cost of the care they receive*

Or
- *A conscious decision to move forward, based strictly on* marginal *revenue from patients in categories like Medicaid, Medicare, and the uninsured that do not cover the full cost of care*

Bonus Material – A Better Way to Present ROI Projections

Now that I have trashed the way many ROI numbers are developed, I should address the question of what they should look like.

The most fun part of my job in the planning department of the Midwestern hospital where I worked was projecting future need for various service areas. One project involved a consideration of expanding the number of pediatric inpatient beds. Being a data-driven guy, I enjoyed rooting around the available data to estimate what future volumes might look like. Among the data sets available were current demographics of our service area, future population growth projections, the hospital's pediatric market share, existing inpatient volume by DRG, and physician-based utilization numbers.

Sometimes, if people don't like the implications of an analysis, they try to undercut it by challenging your numbers. Early on in my career as an analyst, I figured out a nearly foolproof way to achieve buy-in from the necessary people. Before I displayed a single number from my analysis, I included one or two slides listing all my data sources and assumptions. For example, these were my data sources for the pediatric project:

- The zip codes in the primary, secondary, and tertiary market areas

- Current pediatric market shares for each of those areas
- Population growth projections from the U.S. Census Bureau
- Our average number of pediatric admissions by DRG within the total market area – derived from the statewide inpatient database
- The fact that the hospital had recruited a new pediatrician who would start in three months
- Average number of inpatient admissions for our hospital's current pediatricians – based on actual experience

These were all the fact-based data inputs. Then I had to make an important assumption about the new pediatrician. Since she was new to the area, she would not have a built-in patient base, and, therefore, it would be unrealistic to expect average regional volume from Day 1. Instead, I assumed 20% of the regional average for Quarter 1, 40% for Quarter 2, 60% for Quarter 3, and 80% for Quarter 4. Starting in Year 2, I assumed 100% of the regional average.

So, before anyone saw a single number from my analysis, they saw my logic and major assumptions. I then asked, "Before I show you the results, did I miss anything in my assumptions, or do any of these data sources or inputs seem wrong?" Sometimes there would be some discussion, but generally there was pretty solid agreement.

After establishing this baseline, I would then show the results. Although I would never state it this way, my implied message was, "Don't argue with my conclusions if you agree with my inputs and assumptions. Essentially, all I'm doing is developing mathematical formulas based on these inputs we all agree on and hitting 'compute' on the keyboard."

I found this method worked like a charm. If someone didn't like the results, we could certainly revisit the assumptions, but how could they argue violently with the conclusions after they bought into my data sources and logic? This approach went a long way to defuse the controversy over my projections.

So, how can you apply this approach to developing ROI projections? Here are the simple steps:

- Identify the variables that go into your financial projection
- Estimate a range of benefit your intervention could offer
- Estimate a range of how much of that benefit can actually be captured operationally and, therefore, financially
- Take the low end (i.e., most conservative) assumption and also the high end (i.e., most optimistic) assumption for each input step

You then multiply the various low-end estimates together and do the same with the high-end ones.

Let me illustrate this methodology with a technology that potentially speeds up the medical coding process in the health information department. Here are my assumptions:

- Savings per chart using the new technology: 3–5 minutes
- Number of charts coded per day: 20–25
- Average coder salary and benefits: $60,000

Taking the low-end assumptions, you would save 60 minutes per coder per day (3-minute savings times 20 charts per day). The high-end yields 125 minutes per day (5-minute savings times 25 charts per day). If there are 10 FTE coders, the expected time saving is 600–1,250 minutes. An eight-hour shift translates to 480 minutes. So, the low-end estimate could save 1.25 FTEs, and the high-end estimate would be 2.6 FTEs. Multiplying that by the $60,000 annual salary results in $75,000 for the low end and $156,000 for the high end.

If the product costs $90,000 one time with a $10,000 annual renewal fee for years two and three, the three-year total cost of ownership is $110,000. So, assuming the low end of the savings, the product would yield positive savings in 1.46 years with the more conservative estimate and 0.7 for the more optimistic one. (Keep in mind that this analysis is based on the three-year total cost of ownership. From a cash flow perspective, it isn't as favorable since the cash outlay is front-loaded.)

And, this can get a bit tricky, if the more conservative ROI still appears pretty reasonable, you might even want to double the break-even period in order to ultra-conservative. Here's how to make your argument:

> We identified the variables that we agreed would factor into any cost savings. Under the most optimistic assumptions, you might be able to expect a payback in a few as about 8.5 months (0.7 years). But assuming all the less favorable numbers, you should be able to recuperate your investment in about 18 months (1.46 years). What if we doubled the most conservative recovery period from 18 months to 36 months? Would this still be an attractive project even if we made the most "pessimistic" set of assumptions?

You see what I am doing. Just as in my pediatric product line example above, I'm inviting the potential client to think through the logic of my analytical inputs so it would be hard for them to argue with the results.

There's an old adage that you should never ask a question when you don't know what the answer will be. If you are either the internal enthusiast supporting a particular project or the vendor, you should be familiar enough with the climate of the clinical or operational area to know whether a 36-month payback estimate would kill the project. If it would, don't go there, and don't do this "doubling the break-even" step. But you might want to consider employing this logic if you think it still makes the project viable. No one can accuse you of "baking" the numbers to make your case.

So, I recommend to my vendor clients that they take this approach of walking through their ROI logic with their own clients and ask them to help develop the high and low ends of each of the assumptions that ultimately lead to the final projection. After agreeing on the inputs, they can run the numbers and see the results. Then, if it seems reasonable, they can consider doubling the payback period.

There are two strong advantages of taking this very conservative approach of doubling the payback period:

1. If your numbers are strong, you have built a rock-solid case for how your product or service can be justified from a financial perspective.
2. Because you have extended the break-even period, you have demonstrated to the prospective client that you are not out to dazzle then with flimflam numbers to make a quick sale. This goes a long way toward establishing your credibility as a person or a company.

Here's an additional approach to consider. Any healthcare organization that signs with you is committing to a certain dollar amount. If you've done a good job of developing credible, conservative ROI numbers that they affirm, they should feel pretty confident in their decision. However, they are still taking on a certain level of financial risk, and nobody likes that.

Why not offer them a money-back guarantee that your product will, indeed, generate the financial advantages the two of you agreed upon? This demonstrates remarkable confidence in both your product and your financial performance projections and removes all financial risk from the customer. Because they will have to assign a certain level of organizational resources for implementation and training, they are still making a tangible commitment, but you've removed money as an excuse for not moving forward. If you take this route, be sure you meticulously define the terms of the guarantee up front so there is no confusion down the road concerning whether your product has indeed accomplished what you said it would.

49. Confusing Average Hospital Cost Per Day and Marginal Cost Per Day

The discussion above demonstrates that you shouldn't trust overly optimistic financial projections. Occasionally, you will also find projections that are downright flawed. I ran into this during the first year of my administrative fellowship at Michigan Medicine. The year was 1984, and the medical center was in the process of moving into a brand-new replacement hospital. One of unanswered questions was what the university would do with the old 1920s-era hospital building.

Many ideas were tossed around, and I ended up heading up a team that analyzed whether we should retain a small part of the old building for a hotel-type facility for visiting families and patients who were well enough to be discharged from inpatient care but might want to stay in the area for additional follow-up. Since the health system draws from all over the state, there are many patients and their families who live too far away to commute.

We found some hospitals around the country that had set up programs like this, so we did a few site visits. One large healthcare organization in the Southwest actually took the concept one step further beyond what we were thinking. They established a facility with around-the-clock *non-medical* supervision in the hotel area to house patients who might be well enough to be discharged a day or two earlier if they could stay *at* the hospital even if they weren't *in* the hospital. Since they were still on the campus, they could conveniently receive outpatient care if necessary. The hospital hired a non-clinical onsite staff member to provide an overnight presence in case a patient experienced a medical setback.

Table 12.1   Original Margin without Hotel

DRG Payment	$12,000
Average length of stay (2 nights @ $80 per day)	6 Days
Average revenue per day ($12,000 DRG payment divided by 6 days)	$2,000
Hospital's cost to provide care (based on hospital records)	$11,600
Average cost per day of 6-day hospital stay ($11,600 divided by 6 days, rounded to nearest dollar)	$1,933
Net margin ($12,000 DRG payment minus $11,600 cost)	$400

In a sense it was like home care, but instead of the care being delivered at the patient's home, it was rendered right on the hospital's campus. This arrangement had the added benefit of allowing family members to stay in the same or an adjacent room if desired.

This particular hospital identified a few medical conditions that lent themselves to earlier discharge as long as there was the "backstop" of non-clinical supervision to monitor patients overnight.

We were intrigued by the concept and spent the better part of a day with the woman who ran the program. Table 12.1 includes the data they used to illustrate the financial benefits.

The hospital's logic was that if a patient could be discharged after four days instead of six and spend the last two days in the hospital-hotel, the hospital would gain financially even if it actually covered the cost of the two-day hotel stay.

Table 12.1 shows the original net margin the hospital could expect *without* the hotel. For many patients, hospitals are paid a flat amount per discharge based on their medical condition under the DRG system.

Table 12.2 illustrates the hospital-hotel logic. Keep in mind, these are 1983 prices and reflect 1983 length of stay.

Table 12.2   Revised Margin with Hotel

Cost to hospital for *just the room* (2 nights @ $120 per night)	$240
Cost to Hospital for non-clinical residential staff (2 nights @ $80 per day)	$160
Total cost to hospital of 2 nights in hotel facility (Room plus staff person)	$400
Total cost for 4-day hospital stay (4 days @$1,933 per day)	$7,732
Total episode cost (4 days in hospital plus 2 days in hotel)	$8,132
DRG Payment	$12,000
New estimated net margin ($12,000 DRG payment minus $8,132 cost of hospital stay plus hotel stay)	$3,868
Net gain to the facility (the difference between the original $400 margin and $3,868 margin with the hotel)	$3,468

Today, costs would obviously be higher, and length of stay would be lower.

There are several liability and licensure issues associated with this concept, but I won't go there. Suffice it to say that we were initially pretty impressed with the potential financial benefit. It wasn't until we returned to Ann Arbor that I recognized the fatal flow in their fiscal logic.

They based their savings on *average cost per day* of a hospital stay. It's true that the $11,600 total cost divided by a six-day stay results in $1,933 *average* cost per day. However, that's not the way costs are actually incurred. Typically, clinical activity (tests, imaging, procedures, etc.) is most intense during the first day or two of a stay, and then it tapers off. So, actual costs might be $4,500 for Day 1, $3,000 for Day 2, and then decrease from there. The actual "recoverable costs" from the last two days of the stay are far less than the $4,000 they touted, thereby invalidating the hospital's estimated net gain of $3,468.

It's interesting that four healthcare professionals sat around nodding our heads in agreement for a whole day while the healthcare organization's representative showed off her facility and explained the financial benefits. It wasn't until a couple of days later that a lowly administrative fellow (me) saw their miscalculation. For the record, this is not an isolated case. Within the last year, I talked with another vendor premising her value proposition on this exact same, flawed "average cost per day" logic.

Recommendation:

- *Never make this mistake! Be sure you thoroughly understand how healthcare finances work as you craft your financial case. As I have said elsewhere, healthcare executives and clinicians have been bombarded with exaggerated ROI promises, and they have understandably grown highly skeptical.*

50. Not Realizing That, Even If You Can Demonstrate a Clear ROI, the Hospital May Still Not Move Forward

You would think that presenting solid, plausible, defensible financial projections would lead to a contract. It often does, but you can't necessarily count on it.

Let me provide an example where one hospital representative failed to move forward with something that made all the financial sense in the world. I was talking with a colleague who worked for a hospital association in one of the mountain states, and he told about the process they were going through with one of their state-funded healthcare coverage programs. They were updating the hospital DRG fee schedule in what proved to be a prolonged and contentious process.

There was one particular clinical area that only two or three hospitals in the state offered, and the effect on them was pretty significant. The largest provider estimated that the proposed change would result in nearly a $2 million annual loss, and, based on somewhat suspect data, the health plan's logic for making the cut for making the cut was pretty flimsy.

My hospital association colleague explained that the discussions with the state's representatives had been dragging on for several months and were frequently antagonistic. By this time, he was ready to dig his heels in, partially to demonstrate that they weren't willing to roll over on every issue. To his surprise, the representative from the hospital that would lose the most money just kind of waved his hand and said, "Well, that's OK. It's only $2 million." My friend was stunned and wanted to say, "Only $2 million!?! Only $2 million?!? If $2 million no big deal, give it to me!"

It's hard to imagine a healthcare organization walking away from that type of money without even trying to change the outcome. They may not have been successful, but shouldn't they at least have tried? This type of behavior is fairly rare, but it does happen.

Lack of moving forward even in the face of clear financial advantage can be caused by other factors:

- You may have brought a prospect to the point of decision when one of the key internal players unexpectedly leaves. This can result in others not wanting to move forward until the vacancy is filled.
- The organization may have suffered an unexpected financial setback requiring resources and attention to be siphoned off in another direction.

- A formerly disengaged stakeholder – like a key physician or a senior executive – may introduce an alternative vendor at the last minute and demand that the decision be revisited.
- Your project may not be perceived as a high enough strategic priority. I had an example of this at a healthcare organization where I worked when we were renegotiating a contract that would have allowed us to increase a commission on certain sales from 3% to 6% with no down side to us. It wasn't a particularly high-volume area, but the change would result in several thousand dollars additional revenue per month. To those of us who worked in that area, it was a classic "no brainer." But for some reason, the senior executive who had to sign off on the change kept dragging his heels, and we ended up losing about five months of the enhanced revenue. He apparently didn't consider moving forward a high enough priority to finally sit down and give final approval or didn't have the emotional bandwidth to address it in a more timely manner.

Recommendation:

- *You may have a terrific product with ironclad financial projections that clearly demonstrate its value. Nevertheless, a potential customer may not feel any sense of urgency to move forward. The best advice I can give is to recognize that these situations pop up from time to time. Do your best to gently remind them of the clear benefits your product offers without becoming pushy to the point of alienating the organization.*

Chapter 13

Other Financial Pitfalls

The fact that I devoted an entire chapter to Return of Investment (ROI) issues demonstrates how significant that issue is. But there are 11 other financially oriented pitfalls in this chapter, and any one of them can also derail a sale.

51. Projecting Overly Rosy and/or Simplistic Sales Numbers

Every entrepreneur is understandably excited about the prospects for their new venture. Even though they recognize inherent risk, they wouldn't move forward unless they believed they had something the market craves.

Although optimism is good, unless it is mixed with a strong dose of reality, the company may be setting itself up for significant hardships.

I was speaking at a healthcare technology conference in California a few years ago when I had the chance to chat with one attendee who was enthusiastic about a new technology he was developing to help patients with chronic pain. During one of the afternoon breaks, he showed me his pitch deck for potential investors. It followed the classic model of describing the clinical problem, showing the potential market size, describing his product, and then projecting sales.

According to his statistics, chronic pain is one of the leading medical complaints worldwide, and he estimated the potential market at 800 million people worldwide. His sales projections traced the classic "hockey stick" with modest sales in Year 1, good growth in Year 2, and explosive growth starting in Year 3, and continuing forward. (This type of sales projection gets its name from the fact that the sales curve resembles a hockey stick.)

From what I could tell, he had a potentially valuable clinical product, but his market size and market growth estimates were absurd. When he identified 800 million people who could potentially use his product, was he seriously considering selling to patients in Fiji, Uganda, and Iceland? And what basis, beyond wishful thinking, did he have for projecting exponential growth starting in Year 3?

His wild-eyed enthusiasm creates two significant issues:

1. A credibility problem with potential investors and customers – I recognize that including outrageously optimistic market size numbers is fairly common in investment pitches, but claiming potential market size of 800 million without any discussion of a sales structure or consideration of whether or not potential patients in Vietnam could pay for the technology seems highly nonsensical.
2. Potential cash flow issues for the entrepreneur – If he ends up believing his own sales projections, he could foolishly build his infrastructure to support his numbers. As I will address in Pitfall 76, healthcare sales cycles are notoriously long. I tell my clients new to healthcare to develop a conservative projection about how long it will take to reach a critical mass of sales, double that number, and then recognize that it may still be optimistic. More than one start-up has been forced to fold because sales failed to materialize according to their business plan projections.

Recommendations:

- *When it comes to your "public" sales projections, of course you need to be upbeat. Few investors are likely to fund a company that projects breakeven six years out. But keep in mind that both investors and potential healthcare clients have been barraged by unrealistically rosy sales numbers, and your credibility with both groups will suffer if you display naïveté by your financial projections being improbably favorable.*
- *When it comes to developing your internal sales numbers, do yourself a favor and be extremely conservative in your growth projections. It's OK to be a bit more sanguine publicly and plan for a less optimistic growth curve privately to make sure you don't run out of capital. If you can survive a six-year breakeven, you should be in great shape. My budget approach has always been to assume revenue growth on the low side and expenses on the high side. If the budget works with those assumptions, there's a good chance you will come in at budget or even more favorably.*
- *Early in your conversation with potential healthcare clients, be sure to discuss their capital budgeting calendars and do everything you can to meet each window, recognizing that each step may take longer than you would like. Be sure to consider these timelines as you develop your revenue projections.*

52. Triggering Financial Thresholds for Budget Limits, Board Approval, and/or Other Fiduciary Requirements

Healthcare organizations have strict requirements regarding purchasing approvals. Hospital department heads are typically authorized to spend up to relatively modest levels, often $10,000–25,000. VPs and CEOs have higher limits, but even they must seek board approval over a certain level, often $100,000. A few organizations require CEO approval for all capital items. These limits are not necessarily a problem but can add extra steps and time to the purchasing process. Furthermore, there may be provisions in a healthcare organization's debt structure that require higher level approvals for expenditures above a certain amount.

Recommendations:

- *Be aware of this issue and be sure to allow for the possible extension of the acquisition time frame.*
- *You may be able to avoid some of these trigger points by restructuring your financial offering. The thresholds typically apply to capital acquisitions or capitalized leases. You might be able to offload some costs to the hospital's operating budget or into different modules that could be phased in over subsequent fiscal years or assigned to different departments. Just be sure to maintain transparency and integrity in your alternative financing proposal.*

53. Triggering Additional Insurance Requirements, Plus Possibly Having to Name the Health System a Beneficiary

Healthcare organizations have become extremely concerned about data breaches and cyber-security issues. Any product that touches a hospital's IT infrastructure or databases raises significant security red flags. Some healthcare organizations now require vendors to secure additional cybersecurity insurance coverage and possibly name them as a beneficiary on the policy.

Additionally, they may require enhanced limits on errors & omissions, professional liability, workers' compensation, or even automobile coverage.

Recommendations:

■ *Be aware of this possible requirement and budget for it, both in terms of your financial planning and in your implementation timelines.*

■ *You might consider proactively mentioning your willingness to secure additional insurance. It will demonstrate your awareness of and responsiveness to cybersecurity issues.*

⇛ **54. Not Fully Understanding Overall**
Top 10 **Financial Incentives**

Many new hospital offerings promise to save money by better coordinating care, lowering length of stay, and/or reducing readmissions. Entrepreneurs are aware of Medicare's efforts to reduce unnecessary readmissions through a program called the Hospital Readmissions Reduction Program (HRRP). HRRP is a penalties-only program – there is no "bonus" for doing well – where hospitals are financially penalized on payments for all Medicare patients in a subsequent fiscal year if they had excessive readmissions within 30 days of patient discharge. Medicare only tracks readmissions in a few diagnostic categories, but the future penalties apply to *all* Medicare patients, not just the ones in the categories that are measured. Since so many inpatients are covered under Medicare, this penalty can be a real financial blow. As often happens, Medicare sets the pace for other payers, and several of them have recently started similar programs.

Some vendors don't understand that not every single readmission results in a direct financial loss. Penalties kick in when the facility exceeds the "allowable" level.

There are several factors that affect the financial impact of any given, single readmission:

■ Which payer covers the patient – Medicare was the first – and for a while the only – major payer imposing readmission penalties. Many commercial payers have recently started to follow suit. So, although this is a growing trend, readmissions penalties are not yet universal.

■ What the diagnosis is – There are currently only six clinical categories – all high volume – that count toward the Medicare penalty. Many Medicare readmissions fall outside the six. Additionally, each commercial payer that imposes this type of penalties has its own set of cases they track.

■ Whether the hospital is bearing financial risk for entire episode of care – If the healthcare provider has assumed full financial risk for an entire episode of care, every readmission represents a financial expense to the hospital without additional payment. But if it is a fee-for-service patient – and many Medicare patients are – the hospital receives a separate payment for that readmission. So, avoiding the readmission means losing revenue in the short term.

■ Whether new readmission will trigger a higher penalty or any penalty at all – As I stated, hospitals are allowed a certain number of Medicare readmissions in the covered categories before penalties kick in, and the magnitude of the penalties increases if readmissions reach higher thresholds. If a hospital's current "baseline" readmission rate is already very low, a few additional readmissions may not thrust it into the penalty box. So, not every single readmission, even within the Medicare six covered clinical categories, necessarily results in a financial loss.

■ The time frame under consideration – There is a lag of up to four years between the time a patient is discharged and when Medicare penalties take effect. For example, penalties imposed in federal fiscal year 2019 (October 1, 2018 through September 30, 2019) consider discharges from July 1, 2014 through June 30, 2017. Some hospitals are so financially stressed that they may prefer to receive the additional payment now and worry about any possible penalty down the road. A very small number of executives might conclude that, for a variety of reasons, they might not be working at the same hospital three or four years down the road. If they may not still be there when the penalties start, and if the hospital is hard-pressed for revenue right now, they might not be quite as concerned about excessive readmissions and any subsequent penalties. This dynamic is reminiscent of a recent *Dilbert* cartoon where the slacker Wally is making a presentation about a new product he says would be unprofitable for the first nine years but then surge into profitability in year ten. When his boss points out that Wally is scheduled to retire in nine years, Wally waffles and has nothing to say.[1] I'm not implying any dishonesty on anyone's part, but time frames sometimes do enter into mental calculations.

Recommendation:

■ *Stress the positive impact your product or service has on addressing the readmissions issue. Reducing them is a clinical goal all hospitals embrace. However, recognize that the qualifiers listed above might affect any given hospital's sense of urgency about reducing readmissions, thereby rendering your offering somewhat less compelling than you think it might be.*

⇛ **55. Not Appreciating the Misaligned**
Top 10 **Financial Incentives between the Environment Asking for Greater Care Coordination Utilizing the Lowest Acuity Interventions Possible and Most Payers Reimbursing on a Fee-for-Service Basis**

Although medical care is clearly based in science, not every care decision is black and white. For example, as a patient in a post-acute rehab facility approaches discharge, the supervising physician must decide whether or not they are ready to go home. Many patients discharged from a post-acute rehab hospital require home care. Depending on the level of care needed, the cost of the home visits may be less than an additional day in the rehab facility. However, revenue to the rehab physician and facility stops once the patient leaves. So, if the decision to discharge vs. keep the patient for another day is 50/50 and both options are equally clinically responsible, the financial aspect may tip the decision in favor of keeping the patient the extra day.

A product that makes it easier to treat a patient at home or in some alternate setting can move the needle toward earlier discharges. This may be in the patient's best interest, but you must realize that you may be asking the healthcare organization to forego some revenue.

This dynamic would be minimized if all providers were paid based on total cost of an episode of care and the provider organization either owned or contracted for all "downstream" services. In that case, if the health system bears 100% of the financial risk, offering care in the last expensive setting clearly makes financial sense. Remember, though, that I reported in Chapter 1 that 78% of care is still paid under a fee-for-service rather than any type of bundled or incentivized care.[2] The good news is that there are a number of initiatives – Value-Based Purchasing, bundled payments, Pay for Performance and others – designed to better align care across the continuum.

Recommendations:

- *Until and unless the industry fully arrives at the point of strong incentive alignment, providers will be living in a somewhat-schizophrenic financing climate. As early on as possible, try to assess what percentage of their revenue comes from traditional fee-for-service care whether they get paid for every procedure or service they provide instead of being part of a unified payment or incentivized arrangement.*

■ *Remember that providers' default is to always do what's best for the patient. However, you must recognize that you may be asking them to cut into their revenue stream on top of having to pay for whatever product or service you are offering. This can be especially difficult if they are financially stressed.*

56. Not Knowing the Specific Payment Rules

As I explained in Chapter 1, the term "reimbursement" is really a misnomer. Reimbursement usually means someone spent money for an approved expenditure, subsequently submitted a receipt, and ultimately got paid back all they spent.

This is not how it works for inpatient care, where hospitals are paid for most inpatient admissions on a fixed fee basis. As I've mentioned elsewhere, back in 1984, the Medicare program implemented a payment system called Diagnosis-Related Groups (DRGs) where inpatients were categorized into one of about 500 (since expanded to about 1,000) categories based on their underlying clinical condition, severity of their case, some additional medical conditions, and other factors. Most other payers have since adopted the DRG approach, so the amount hospitals are paid for inpatient care does not go up if they provide additional services while they are hospitalized unless the patient ultimately gets classified to a more intensive DRG.

As I explained in Pitfall 3, new technologies sometimes face an uphill battle if they can't replace an older one that is already baked into the DRG payment level. Another way of stating this is that the existing DRG takes into account average costs of providing care using the technologies that are currently employed most frequently. A vendor offering a new product introduces a new cost element that has not been incorporated into the DRG payment, and the payment doesn't go up even though a new element is added. If the new product *replaces* an older one and the cost of the new approach is less than or equal to the old method, that supports moving forward. Not every newer approach, though, replaces an existing one, so the net impact is increased cost without increased payments. It's not hard to conclude why hospitals don't always jump at these new approaches.

I once met with an entrepreneur who developed a new device for cardiac care. He had just completed a technology incubator program based on the West Coast and approached me about getting some market insights. I asked him which DRGs he thought most of his patients would fall into and, to my surprise, he didn't have any idea. I was amazed he could go through a technology incubator without ever having had to come to grips with something as basic as knowing which DRGs he would likely encounter. He clearly needed help with his financial projections.

A few resource-intensive DRG categories do allow carve-out or additional payments for unusually expensive technologies such as certain implantable devices, but these are definitely the exception, and getting insurance companies to offer additional payments can be a lengthy process.

Recommendation:

■ *If you are new to the healthcare field, you would be wise to find a trusted advisor who can help you think through the financial implications of your product and proposed financial logic.*

57. Offering a Project with Negative Implications on the Workforce or Other Operational Areas

Vendors often focus largely on the acquisition costs of their product and don't always discuss possible impact on either workforce or other operating costs.

Technology can affect staffing in three ways:

1. Reducing head count through increased efficiencies – This can be seen as either a plus or a minus, depending on who is viewing the possible change. From an overall budget standpoint, reducing staff can help the organization's budget, but department heads who stand to lose head count might see this a threat to their status within the organization.
2. Freeing up some employees to be redeployed to other functions within the organization – This may be well received if the organization perceives a need to reconfigure its workforce without reducing total count. A technology that automates fairly routine processes may make it possible to reassign some people to other, less-automated areas. However, there must be a match of skill levels between the old job and the possible new assignment. A clerical person cannot shift to a job requiring clinical skills. Furthermore, any move could involve some kind of training period, which could create some down time during the learning curve and probably some incremental training costs.
3. Requiring additional staffing – In this day of relentless cost pressure, adding staff can be a deal-breaker. Staff in many departments are often stretched to the max. One area potentially susceptible to needing additional staffing with a new technology is the IT department. A product that allows the department to bring a formerly outsourced function in-house might be appealing from a product control and flexibility standpoint, but if it required extra bodies, approval might be hard to come by.

Recommendations:

■ *If your project would likely reduce staff, try to determine if that would be perceived as a positive or a negative and shape your messaging accordingly.*

- *If it would allow redeployment, bring examples from other clients who have successfully followed this strategy and how it benefited them in the long run.*
- *If it requires additional staff, do your best to show how the benefits of adopting your product offset the negatives.*
- *Be upfront about additional operational costs – and also capital expenditures – the organization must consider as they evaluate your project. They will eventually figure out the extra costs involved, and you want to avoid creating suspicions that you are not being entirely transparent with them.*

58. Potentially Squeezing Some Providers Out of the Revenue Stream

An old saying goes, "One person's expense is another person's revenue." As I have said, people in the healthcare field are dedicated to address human ailments. At the same time, individuals always act with a certain amount of self-interest, including protecting their financial well-being. New technologies can threaten someone's finances in several possible ways.

- Displacing existing approaches – The Apple Watch 4's ability to provide Food and Drug Administration (FDA)-approved screening electrocardiograms (EKGs) is an example of largely eliminating a clinical function from the traditional provider setting. Instead of paying hundreds of dollars for an EKG in a cardiologist's office, clinic, or hospital setting, patients can spend the $400 needed to buy the watch (or use the watch they may have already purchased) to get screening results that can be transmitted to their physician. If the screening results indicate a possible concern, the physician can order a more traditional EKG. And remember that another advantage of using the Apple Watch as a screening device is that it is the patient's to keep. In this Apple Watch scenario, the cardiologist is still engaged with reading the results, but using the watch eliminates the facility-based EKG, which saves money for the patient but also decreases the healthcare organization's revenue.

In April 2019, the FDA cleared a plug-in device for iPhones with an EKG function that is even more robust that of the Apple Watch.[3] This development has the potential to further erode institutional providers' revenue stream.

■ Patient portals, telephone consultations, and other forms of virtual visits for less serious conditions can be very convenient for patients. If insurance companies cover virtual encounters at all, they often pay less than they do for the in-person visits they are replacing. To the extent payers don't reimburse these patient encounters, every online interaction that supplants an office visit could represent lost revenue for the clinician.

However, there are still two ways adding virtual visits may be financially attractive:
- If the eliminated "unnecessary" office visits open up the schedule for additional patients with more serious conditions and for which the physician would get a higher payment
- If the provider has available capacity. A *Health Affairs* research article on direct-to-consumer telehealth (where patients have phone or videoconferencing access to physicians) concludes that only about 12% of 300,000 direct-to-consumer telehealth visits between 2011 and 2013 replaced in-person encounters while the other 88% represented new visits, tapping into previously unmet needs. The article's abstract

concludes, "Direct-to-consumer telehealth may increase access by making care more convenient for certain patients, but it may also increase utilization and health care spending."[4]

■ Playing into professional rivalries among different provider groups – Technology can make "turf wars" among physician specialties worse. For example, a technology that might allow general surgeons to perform procedures that are traditionally the purview of surgical specialists is likely to be celebrated by the general surgeons but lambasted by the specialists. If a vendor presents such a proposal in a healthcare organization with both general surgeons and surgical specialists, they should expect vastly differing reactions. Similarly, internists, family practitioners, and obstetricians/gynecologists often offer overlapping services, and a new technology targeted at, for example, OB/GYNs could create suspicion from the other specialty areas.

■ Shifting care delivery location – Telemedicine allowing patients in remote areas to consult specialists in other geographies could lead to the patient transferring much of their care to the new location. For example, a telemedicine visit may ultimately result in the patient traveling to visit the remote delivery site if advanced services are not available locally. The patient may decide that the care at the new location is so good that they transfer some of their loyalties there, even for needs currently being treated locally. This may not happen routinely, but the possibility may still lurk in the back of the referring organization's thinking and perhaps lessen their enthusiasm for the new technology.

So, there are several ways introducing a new technology could negatively affect some providers' revenue sources, and you should take steps to minimize the impact.

Recommendations:

- *Until more insurance companies pay adequately for electronic visits, you must recognize that providers must always consider the potential negative impact of replacing certain patient visits with lower paying virtual visits. Be sure you can present a credible "payment strategy."*
- *If your product facilitates virtual visits, try to ascertain if the practice you are targeting has a schedule with a lot of "unnecessary" visits. If that is the case, your product could open up additional appointment slots for more seriously ill patients and which command higher fees. It could also allow the practice to bring in additional revenue from the virtual visits. Alternatively, if the office has excess capacity it may be able to attract patients currently not receiving any care or getting it elsewhere.*
- *Although no one will buy your product if you can't make a reasonable case for additional net revenue, you can also stress the patient satisfaction aspects resulting from the added convenience. Just realize that the patient satisfaction argument won't carry the day if you can't present a solid financial picture.*
- *If you are likely to encounter the problem of allowing lower levels of clinicians to treat more acute cases than they traditionally have, expect those who potentially lose out to raise quality of care issues. Although quality should always be first and foremost, some providers may use this argument as a defensive lever. The most effective thing you can do is load up with as much credible clinical research that supports your contention that some screening-type visits can be handled by appropriately credentialed staff extenders.*
- *Regarding the telemedicine example, few sending organizations will verbalize the fear of patient "leakage," but recognize that this apprehension may exist. You can stress with the potential "sending" party the benefits of*

*stronger working relationships with remote "receiving"
providers. Perhaps the larger healthcare organization
would be willing to send clinicians representing a variety of specialties to the smaller facility in the remote area
one day a week, thus strengthening the services available
locally.*

59. Experiencing One or More of Four Situations That Handcuff a Potential Customer

There are four things that could potentially prevent an organization from working with you even if you have significant
internal support:

1. Running into the requirement that all purchasing decisions be made at the corporate level – Since many healthcare organizations require centralized approval for many
   or most purchases, the local facility has little ability to
   approve moving forward. Sometimes, the best you can
   hope for is that someone at the local level likes what you
   have and is willing to push it upstream. But this sets in
   motion an entirely different and complex set of approval
   requirements.
2. Coming out on the wrong end of "contract lock" – This
   can be a problem for a vendor who is either:
   – Offering a commodity-type product and is trying to
     displace a competitor
   – Proposing an innovative product that introduces a new
     way to address a problem
       In either case, the potential client may have
     limited flexibility because of preexisting contrac-
     tual restrictions. Even if you have a revolutionary
     approach with a tech product that leapfrogs the status
     quo, a binding agreement may keep you on the
     bench until the clock runs out.

3. Asking a prospective client to abandon their previous technology investment – Some technologies like Electronic Health Records (EHRs) require tens of millions of development or implementation dollars. If the potential client has recently made a significant investment in their current solution, the likelihood of them abandoning it before the projected depreciation date is very small.
4. Losing out because of the hospital's commitment to their Group Purchasing Organization (GPO) – Some GPOs link significant rebates or other financial benefits to customer loyalty. An internal purchasing manager may have great difficulty going outside their GPO.

Recommendations:

- *If the issue is decisions being made at the corporate level, you will have to decide if you want to go down that road with the central office. In general, some corporate offices can be somewhat less likely to go with a start-up than with a more established company, so take that into account.*
- *There is little you can do about the contract lock problem or the "sunk" investment in another technology if the existing vendor is delivering on the agreement and can't be terminated "with cause." If you suspect either contact lock or sunk costs may be an issue, try to identify this early on in your conversations with your potential client and agree to the best time to pick up the conversation in the future.*
- *In some cases, your potential client may be experiencing unacceptable performance from their current supplier which might form the basis of a breach of contract situation and possibly allowing for an early termination. You should not get in the middle of that fight, but it may be a question you could at least raise.*
- *If you consistently run into the GPO restriction, consider approaching some of the major GPOs to see if it makes sense for you to affiliate with them to circumvent this problem.*

60. Failing to Offer an Adequate Tiered Structure in Your Pricing Schedule

People who are newer to the healthcare world don't always appreciate the huge variability within the market. As we discussed in Chapter 1, hospitals vary from huge 800+-bed facilities that anchor a large health system to rural, 25-bed Critical Access Hospitals. Some rural facilities may only have an average daily census of three or four patients.

Similarly, physician practices vary tremendously, from a huge, multi-specialty practice that is part of a major healthcare delivery system to a single-physician, solo practice. Of course, most vendors know this, but, when it comes to doing business with various healthcare organizations, they may not fully appreciate the implications of these differences.

Everyone within healthcare is used to the fact that bigger providers often pay far more than smaller ones do, but this can look very different depending on which of these three types of product or service is under consideration.

1. Ones involving physical assets such as plastic, metal, textiles, etc. Examples include hospital beds, or equipment, medical supplies, and construction materials. Each item sold has a direct cost to the supplier, and margins are sometimes very slim. Vendors are used to offering volume-based discounts for these products. It only makes sense that a hospital buying 200 hospital beds for their expansion would pay less per bed than one purchasing three replacement beds. Consequently, vendors often develop a pricing schedule that reflects volume but only offers maximum discounts that might be in the 30–40% range.

2. Ones that require a vendor's dedicated staffing efforts such as customized throughput studies, individual market analyses, or other tailored consulting projects. Analyses

at a larger organization might involve talking with more individuals than at a simpler organization, but both are still labor-intensive, meaning a project for a smaller facility might require nearly as many staff hours as one for a larger organization. Assuming the same hourly rate, total price for both types of institutions may not be all that different.

Vendors also realize that the cost of closing a deal at a rural facility could be nearly as high as it is for a major medical center. Both typically involve multiple visits, and many rural hospitals are located hours away from major airports, requiring additional travel time.

3. Software-driven analyses that include establishing processes for data collection, cleansing and loading. After the protocols are in place, future data submissions for data projects can pretty much run themselves. A good example of this type of project is a state-wide patient discharge data program where every hospital contributes data and can then access software that allows them to analyze their market areas.

Much of the work after the initial setup can be automated. Participants submit their data on a quarterly basis, and algorithms detect high-level data anomalies. The vendor's staff then steps in to individually work with the submitting hospital to correct the errors, but most of the other program's processes are automated.

After the statewide database is stable, all hospitals can access the software to conduct whatever analyses they wish to do. Group training classes are available to all participants, so there is relatively little incremental cost to the vendor for adding a new hospital.

The bulk of the vendor's costs for these programs lies in the initial intellectual property that went into establishing the data cleansing protocols and algorithms, into securing the hardware required to house the data and the analytic software, into designing the software itself, into actually collecting the data, and into conducting the ongoing collective meetings available to all participants, regardless of size.

The very largest hospitals that are a part of projects like this can sometimes pay as much as 30 times what the smallest ones pay. Because there are no tangible products or materials involved, the vendor can pool the total project costs and divide them however they see fit. This can appear very arbitrary, but it does allow the vendor to create a pricing structure that is not likely to categorically exclude any particular type of participant.

The dynamics are similar for mobile apps. By the time the developer is ready to start selling the app, the majority of the costs have already been incurred through the development process. Since adding a new healthcare organization user adds virtually no cost, the vendor is free to charge whatever amount they feel is needed to cover development costs, sales costs, ongoing support, and profit.

So, as you develop your pricing approach, your first step is to determine if you will offer volume-based discounts for physical products (category 1) or customized personnel-driven work (category 2), or if you will develop a sliding scale for a less tangible service (category 3). Discounts (for categories 1 and 2) are pretty standard and straightforward: the higher the volume, the greater the discount. Category 3 requires some creativity.

I have seen that for category 3 projects, most vendors recognize to some extent the differences among organizations. Consequently, they often have a few – but not enough – price categories. Just having three or four buckets is not adequate. Some products have as many as eight or ten.

Once you determine that you need a sliding scale, the next question becomes the basis by which you categorize hospitals.

Here are some possibilities, along with the issues you might encounter:

▪ Number of beds – The number of *licensed* beds is publicly available, since this is regulated by each state. However, most hospitals actually staff and operate fewer beds than they are licensed for. They are typically reluctant to delicense beds since getting them back may be hard. In states with Certificate of Need (CON) regulations, a hospital can sometimes agree to reduce its bed count as part of a CON approval for a different project like adding operating rooms, so licensed beds have real value in those cases. An alternative is using the number of *staffed* beds to determine cost. But since the number of staffed beds can change rather frequently, getting accurate counts can be difficult. So, setting price based on the number of licensed beds rather than staffed beds is more straightforward.

▪ Number of admissions per year – This information is generally available, but it is becoming less relevant as hospitals shift more of their focus to outpatient care. There are some formulas that "translate" a certain level of outpatient volume to "inpatient equivalents." Getting access to uniform inpatient equivalent data may be a challenge.

▪ Financial information, either revenue or expenses – This can also be difficult to get on a timely basis. Some states require this information to be published, but vendors who operate in multiple states face the additional challenges of slightly varying definitions of costs or reporting timelines that may not match up from state to state.

Based on ease of getting the information needed, using licensed beds or annual admissions may be the best options.

There are two other issues relating to price schedules you must consider. The first is whether you charge a system based on each hospital individually or if you roll them up together and consider them a single entity. This is a growing issue as more and more hospitals join systems. Many price schedules I have seen that charge hospitals individually – adding up the cost each hospital pays – result in a very high total cost and a very high cost per hospital. This is true even if the pricing approach includes discounts for multiple hospitals within the system.

Figure 13.1 compares discounts based on bed size – charging each hospital individually – and using a fee schedule based on bed size and rolling up the system hospitals into a single entity.

The top of the chart displays two different pricing approaches:

1. One with discounts decreasing with bed size – It may seem counter-intuitive to give a bigger discount to the smallest participants, but this is done to acknowledge smaller hospitals' tighter financial situations.
2. A second with a flat fee that increases with bed size

The bottom half shows pricing under each method. Under the discount approach, each of the five hospitals in the Big System is charged as a separate entity. The starting price is $7,000 per hospital, but various discounts based on bed size are applied. This approach results in a total system cost of $22,050, or an average of $4,410 per hospital. As seen at the bottom of the chart, a single Big Hospital with 661 beds would pay $5,950 ($7,000 minus a 15% discount).

The alternative fee schedule approach combines all five of the Big System hospitals and treats the system as a single entity. There is a certain logic in doing this since, typically, the sales and negotiating process involves one set of people representing the whole system instead of five sets of players,

Bed Size	Discount		List Price = $7,000	vs. Fee	
25 beds or less	50%			$1,000	
26–100	45%			$1,700	
100–200	40%			$2,400	
201–300	35%			$3,100	
301–400	30%			$3,800	
401–500	25%			$4,500	
501–600	20%			$5,200	
601–700	15%			$5,900	
701–800	10%			$6,600	
801–900	5%			$7,300	
901 or more	0%			$8,000	
	Percentage Discount			**Fee Schedule**	
Big System					
	Beds	Price	Discount	Cost	.
Hospital A	497	$7,000	25%	$5,250	
Hospital B	25	$7,000	50%	$3,500	
Hospital C	78	$7,000	45%	$3,850	
Hospital D	345	$7,000	30%	$4,900	
Hospital E	201	$7,000	35%	$4,550	
Total	**1,146**			**$22,050**	$8,000
Cost per Hospital				$4,410	$1,600
Big Hospital	661	$7,000	15%	$5,950	$5,900

Figure 13.1 Contrasting Pricing Approaches.

one from each of the hospitals. Similarly, if there is data sub-
mission involved, it is usually coordinated through a single
point. So, the vendor's workload is reduced a bit because of
the streamlined operating process of funneling all activities
through one person instead of five.

Since the total bed count for Big System is 1,146 it ends up
in the highest category, resulting in a $8,000 charge for all five
hospitals. This translates to an average cost per hospital of
$1,600, which is far better than the $4,410 per hospital under
the discount model.

If you stand back and view these alternative methods from
the perspective of both the Big System and the Big Hospital,
the aggregated fee schedule approach seems more equitable.
Under the discount arrangement that treats each hospital individually, the Big System must pay $22,050 while the single Big
Hospital pays only $5,950. I could easily imagine Big System
declining to participate because of the perceived inequity
of having to pay nearly four times as much as Big Hospital,
which they might consider to be a competitor to some extent.

The fee schedule model with the Big System hospitals
rolled up results in a total charge of $8,000 for the Big System
and a charge of $5,900 for Big Hospital. This seems to be a
more equitable differential.

I should also point out that the total payment to the vendor
under the fee schedule model ($8,000 for Big System + $5,900
for Big Hospital = $13,900) is far less than the one under the
discount arrangement ($22,050 + $5,950 = $28,000). However,
you must weigh the likelihood of the Big System taking a pass
entirely because of the high price. If they were to do this, you
would not only lose all the revenue from the Big System, but
you would also lose the prestige of having them in your project.

Clearly, setting a pricing schedule is more of an art than it
is a science. Before you go public with the final pricing, you
should create several versions and brainstorm internally to
evaluate whether it appears reasonable and equitable for all
potential participants. When all is said and done, you have to

make sure that your estimated revenue will fully cover your costs plus whatever profit you need, so it's important to thoroughly weigh your options and the likelihood of various organizations joining in at different financial levels.

As I said, there are two additional issues that must be considered in setting your pricing. The first is whether or not to consider system hospitals as a single entity for billing purposes. To me, the clear answer is yes.

The second issue matters if you are using a pricing schedule and are simultaneously selling your product to various types of organizations such as hospitals, physician practices, nursing home, hospice programs, etc. If you are using bed counts or admissions for hospitals, you must determine an appropriate equivalent measure for the other provider types. It is a challenge to develop measures that will be perceived as fair to all parties. Even using revenue as the basis for a fee schedule can be tricky since health system revenues can be in the billions while many smaller organizations have far less income. Determining break points for your pricing tiers is challenging, but it can be done.

Recommendations:

- *Using discounts based on volume generally make sense for projects involving physical assets or require dedicated staff times (categories 1 and 2 above).*
- *If you use a sliding scale, make sure you develop a pricing structure that is perceived as fair to all your potential clients. Be ready to explain your logic if you start getting pushback.*
- *Carefully consider which approach (beds, revenue, expenses, etc.) is the most appropriate for setting your price schedule. Licensed beds or annual admissions are probably the simplest to administer, and hospitals are used to these methodologies.*
- *Generally, you are better off treating a system as a single entity rather than individual hospitals.*

■ *Before you "go public" with your pricing, make sure there are no logical inconsistencies in your pricing, such as a small clinic having to pay more than a medium-sized hospital.*

61. Failing to Offer Flexibility in Your Payment Structure

As I have repeatedly said, healthcare organizations face widely diverse circumstances, and some flourish while others struggle. For example, a 300-bed hospital with a new facility in an affluent suburban area is far more likely to have a favorable financial position than is a similarly sized inner-city institution operating in a worn-out 1950s-era building.

The suburban hospital may be able to write a check for your project while you may have to get creative for the other one. As a result, you should take these differences into account as you structure your financial terms.

Recommendations:

■ *Consider whether you are potentially losing customers by not offering some flexibility in your payment approach.*

■ *Develop various financing options, such as purchasing your product out-right, signing an extended lease, agreeing to a lease-purchase option, or combining cash outlay with a percentage of new revenue generated by or savings resulting from your product. This last approach can become a bit cumbersome since you have to develop a mechanism to verify actual volumes or agree on how savings will be defined. Also, you must consult competent legal counsel to be sure you avoid any payment approach that violates anti-kickback regulations tied to patient volume. Finally, since offering extended payments increases your financial exposure, consider building in extra compensation to balance your increased risk.*

End Notes

1. Scott Adams, *Dilbert*, April 14, 2019.
2. Kelly Gooch, "Health system executives expect 25% of care delivery payments to be value-based in 2019," Becker's Hospital CFO Report, February 21, 2019, accessed March 8, 2019.
3. Amanda Capritto, "The FDA just cleared an iPhone ECG sensor that beats the Apple Watch," https://www.cnet.com/news/the-fda-just-cleared-an-iphone-ecg-sensor-that-beats-the-apple-watch/, accessed April 26, 2019.
4. J. Scott Ashwood, et al., "Direct-to-consumer teleheatlh may increase access to care but does not decrease spending," *Health Affairs*, vol. 36 , No. 3, March 2017, article abstract accessed online December 19, 2018.

Chapter 14

Legal and Regulatory Pitfalls

Thousands of laws govern healthcare delivery. This book is not designed to provide legal advice. There are many qualified resources that can do that, but I don't happen to be one of them. In this chapter, I only point out two legal problems I have seen trip up more than one vendor and highlight two regulatory requirements you must remember.

Regulations play a crucial role in ensuring compliance with recognized safety standards and best practices. Few industries are as regulated as healthcare is, and it's vital that vendors understand and fully comply with all relevant federal and state regulations. Most of these requirements apply to healthcare providers, but there are a few that you as a vendor should understand and comply with.

62. Shooting Yourself in the Foot by Insisting on Overly Restrictive Non-Disclosure Agreements

I already addressed the Non-Disclosure Agreements (NDAs) in Pitfall 18 (the possible negative effect on recruiting qualified advisors) and Pitfall 36 (being so protective of your intellectual property to the point that you scare off potential customers by requiring them to sign an NDA to even figure out what you do). I'm revisiting the NDA issue under the legal pitfalls chapter simply as a reminder that you might have to have a serious discussion with your legal counsel – or with yourself if you are the one insisting on a top-secret "cone of silence" – to make sure you're not backing yourself into a corner with either your advisors or potential customers through over-zealous legal language in your NDA, thereby losing sight of the balance between protecting your intellectual property and moving forward.

Recommendations:

- ■ *Be careful how openly you talk about your concept in order to keep it under wraps. But don't make the opposite mistake of developing it in a vacuum so you end up designing something no one really wants or set up barriers for potential customers to learn enough about your product to make an educated evaluation of your product.*
- ■ *Review my suggestions under Pitfall 19 and Pitfall 36.*

63. Assuming That Having Access to Additional Data Is Always a Plus

This pitfall is related to the "Alarm Fatigue Syndrome" (Pitfall 26). As I said there, if everything is flagged as urgent, nothing is really urgent. Three trends in recent years have led to the explosion of patient-specific health information:

1. Widespread adoption of Electronic Health Records
2. The fitness device wearables craze, which generates endless streams of biometric patient data
3. Growth in Big Data, which makes robust consumer profiles and predictions possible

Many people don't realize that access to data can actually create a liability for healthcare providers. In our highly litigious world, it's easy to envision a physician on a courtroom defense stand five years after an untoward medical event being interrogated about why they didn't detect an impending medical crisis. "Didn't you have ready access, Dr. Richardson, to Mrs. Armfield's biometric data? Why didn't you spot the impending problem and intervene right away?"

No one has time to constantly monitor reams of raw data. So, although additional data can contribute to nuanced insights in a patient's situation, some clinicians may prefer not to have it at all, especially if it is presented without a reliable interpretive framework.

Recommendations:

- *Repeating what I suggested in Pitfall 26, be very judicious with how many flags and alerts your technology sends. As one CEO said, "Only create an alert under narrow circumstances or the whole forest becomes an alert, and nothing can be nuanced out that is really important."*
- *If your product generates or reports data, allow hospitals and physicians to customize their data feeds so they receive only what they deem valuable.*
- *Be sure to provide a robust analytical framework that helps clinicians interpret the data you are sending them. There should be immediately identifiable thresholds that alert providers to when intervention is needed. More and more app developers are adopting the "red/yellow/green" color coding approach to flagging patients in need of possible intervention so clinicians can immediately spot and address the need.*
- *As you are presenting your product, make sure you communicate that you know that some data is not particularly helpful and may actually be counterproductive. Otherwise, you run the risk of being marginalized as an "industry outsider" who doesn't understand providers' legal climate.*

64. Having to Comply with Strict Regulations Regarding Selling to Physicians and Other Clinicians

In order to minimize the likelihood of prescribers allowing financial self-interest entering their care decisions, regulators have established narrow lanes within which vendors must operate. There are strict rules about how salespeople interact with clinicians and what they can tell them about how various drugs can be used. All medications have defined clinical conditions for which they can be prescribed. Some of them have other potential applications, but unless they have been cleared by the Food and Drug Administration (FDA) for those other conditions, pharmaceutical salespeople cannot even suggest they can be used for those purposes. This is considered "off-label marketing."

Provisions in the Affordable Care Act of 2010 further define acceptable and unacceptable activities. Vendors cannot leave items with any tangible value, including something as simple as a pen, but they are allowed to conduct business over a meal.

Another important piece of legislation is the Physician Payment Sunshine Act, designed to:

■ Identify possible conflicts of interest initiated by either the pharmaceutical industry or the physician
■ Make the financial relationships between healthcare providers and the pharmaceutical industry more transparent to the public

All financial transactions between pharmaceutical representatives and teaching hospitals or physicians must be tracked and reported to the federal government.

Recommendation:

■ *Possible conflict of interest is a high-visibility/high-risk area, especially when you are dealing directly with physicians. Make sure you fully understand and comply with all relevant requirements.*

65. Not Fully Understanding Human Research Protection Protocol Requirements/FDA Regulations/Certificate of Need Triggers/ Licensure Regulations

I have seen vendors make the "rookie mistake" of not fully appreciating the complexity of these regulatory requirements. The Office of Human Research Protection is part of the Department of Health and Human Services and has developed strict guidelines for all research to protect the "rights, welfare, and wellbeing of human subjects involved in research conducted or supported by the U.S. Department of Health and Human Services (HHS)."[1] Additionally, any research that directly affects patients conducted in an academic medical center must comply with institutional guidelines. Beyond research-oriented constraints, the FDA also has complicated requirements for all medical devices. These must be met before these devices can be offered to patients. Almost all affected vendors learn about these early on, but they sometimes underestimate the expense and extended timelines involved.

Because they vary from state to state, Certificate of Need (CON) and licensure requirements can be a bit more complicated. Some states retain rather restrictive CON regulations while others have eliminated them entirely. Similarly, facility and personnel licensure rules are state-specific. Vendors who sell in multiple states run the risk of appearing naïve if they start offering a product or service in a new state without understanding the exact requirements in that state.

I once met with a company that was proposing a service that would expand the clinical capacity in their particular state, which happened to be a CON state, without fully appreciating the pushback they would get from other area providers. Because the owner's product would address an unmet need in an underserved community with economic challenges, she felt she could garner enough support from local politicians to ram a CON exception through the process. I told her several times that, although support from elected officials wouldn't hurt, she would have to demonstrate true need as defined by that state's regulations and that other providers would certainly fight the project tooth and nail.

Recommendations:

- *In order to maintain your reputation, before "going public" with any product or service that bumps up against any of these legal dynamics or regulatory requirements, make sure you completely understand exactly what's required.*
- *Factor generous time allowances into your planning process if any of these regulations are likely to come into play.*

End Note

1. https://www.hhs.gov/ohrp/, accessed January 7, 2019.

Chapter 15

External Political Pitfalls

With only two pitfalls, this chapter is tied with the market misreading chapter for the fewest problems to avoid. Although these two will probably not entrap too many vendors, you should still consider to what extent they may affect you.

66. Possibly Running Afoul of Hyper-Vigilant Privacy Advocates

Of all the pitfalls in this book, this is the only one I haven't actually seen yet, and that surprises me. By nature, I'm not a suspicious person, a libertarian or a survivalist. But I grew up in New York where there is a certain level of reservedness about interacting with others. Although I was actually brought up in a small town of about 5,000, we were close enough to New York City and had enough relatives living there that we typically visited the "big city" a couple of times a year. The rule for walking the streets of Manhattan is, "Never make eye contact." In reality, New Yorkers can be the warmest people in the country once they determine you're "safe," and I still love getting back there. However, growing up in this climate taught me to be a bit cautious around strangers in unknown situations. So, I "get" that we need to be careful.

The Internet provides plenty of opportunity to "meet" strangers in unknown situations. I read an article about 20 years ago, just as the Internet was beginning to fully blossom, marveling at the willingness of many people to share their personal information online. The writer was amazed that many people – particularly millennials – seem surprisingly willing to key personal data into retail websites in exchange for a modest benefit such as a free Starbucks coffee coupon. Again, I'm not an alarmist, but I recognize that the current generation of 20- and 30-somethings has grown up never knowing a time when sharing personal information was not common.

The advent of Big Data has created unprecedented opportunities to generate surprisingly specific guesses about individuals and their behaviors. Add to this the social media trend of posting all kinds of very personal information and pictures for all the world to see, and we realize that we have entered a new world. People with less-than-honorable motives troll for data to exploit unsuspecting victims. Feeding information gleaned from social media sites or hacked Electronic Health Records (EHRs) into Big Data programs can magnify the danger of this trend.

Having said all this, I wonder if we are not heading for some kind of "tipping point" in the public's perception of data privacy. The incidence and size of recent data breaches and the misuse of data has escalated in recent years. Besides malicious hacker activity, some of the largest holders of personal data have recently come under attack for allegedly misusing data and violating their subscribers' confidences.

Healthcare, of course, has been operating under stringent Health Insurance Portability and Accountability Act of 1996 (HIPAA) regulations for many years now, and the public fully understands that their Personal Health Information is to be strictly protected. Although I haven't seen any specific evidence of this yet, I wouldn't be surprised if we start seeing a significant uprising among privacy advocates demanding stricter controls over data usage. Questionable activity could sour the public on the practice of sharing data as freely as we currently do.

What does all this have to do with healthcare? A lot. My health and my financial dealings are extremely personal and must be kept private and secure. Many argue that, because they can contain potentially embarrassing information about substance abuse, mental health, and other behaviors, someone's health record is far more sensitive than even their financial data. I have a relative who won't subscribe to any of the genetic testing services because he fears that somewhere down the road that information could find its way into his EHR or an insurance company's database and adversely affect his coverage.

Data is becoming the name of the game in the emerging healthcare universe. It is the oil that lubricates the complexities of care delivery decisions and makes the tracking of a patient's progress possible. As we have seen, the myriad of new smartphone and tablet apps is revolutionizing how care is delivered. And the worlds of medical devices and data analytics are quickly converging. Many devices now spin off data that can fold into care decisions and plans. But if the culture "turns" on this type of data collection, physicians and other providers may become somewhat less likely to want to use apps or other technology that gathers potentially sensitive data.

Recommendation:

■ *Since this threat is still somewhat theoretical, there is not much of a current action point. However, if you believe this will become a greater issue, you should continue to build in the highest levels of security protection into your offerings and consistently communicate this to your current and potential customers. Even if you don't think this issue will continue to dominate future discussions, ramping up your privacy and security practices is still a great idea.*

67. Selling a Product That Requires Hospitals to Share Data with Others

There are three types of programs that require providers to share their data with outside organizations:

1. Benchmarking projects – This type of initiative provides invaluable comparison data. The most meaningful benchmarks come from similar hospitals in the same market. Of course, the quid pro quo is that hospitals must give data to get data. Some balk at the thought of letting their competitors see their numbers.

   Vendors sometimes try to skirt this problem by masking data in comparative projects, referring to Hospital A, Hospital B, etc. instead of using names. Making educated guesses about which hospital is which can be pretty easy if any types of volume statistics are reported. Other vendors form aggregated group averages against which individual hospitals are compared. That way each hospital compares its number to aggregated averages. Reluctant participants are more likely to accept this methodology.

2. Projects where an insurance company gets to see a healthcare organization's data – As touchy as sharing data with competitors is, an even more volatile proposition is allowing payers to access hospital or physician data. With the advent of population health initiatives, all parties in the healthcare ecosystem are trying to find ways to maximize patients' health statuses. Data – especially Big Data where information is drawn from multiple databases – can yield incredibly helpful insights into a patient's health status and how to manage it.

   However, healthcare organizations are extremely suspicious of payers' motives. In their minds, the only reason they want a healthcare organization's data is to find additional ways to cut their payments. Consequently, many healthcare organizations dig their heels in and refuse to participate in any initiative that allows an insurance company to access their data even if it's for improving care.

3. Capacity reporting projects – These projects can also meet with provider resistance. Discharge planners love knowing in real time how many open nursing home, inpatient rehab, psychiatric, or inpatient hospice beds are available so they can conveniently find the best clinical fit for patients being discharged, but others in the organization may not be as enthusiastic.

    I once spoke with a vendor who was launching a near-real-time project that reported open nursing home beds in a particular market. This company was surprised that some nursing homes resisted because they didn't want competitors to know how successful (or not) they were at attracting and/or retaining patients. The institutions most likely to react this way often perceive themselves as the market leader in their category and fear that by providing specific data, they are inviting competitors to chip away at their success.

Beyond these resistance points, vendors must also recognize that federal anti-trust regulations prohibit the sharing of certain financial data unless strict guidelines are in place and rigorously enforced. Do not, under any circumstances, cross any of these lines.

Recommendations:

■ *Be prepared for provider reluctance if you are proposing a project that involves data sharing among potential competitors and especially between providers and payers.*

■ *Recognize that resistance to a program requiring readily identifiable data might be a default response, especially if it reports on capacity or patient volume. Stress the benefits of these projects to both patients and program participants.*

■ *Be sure to obtain a thorough legal review for any projects that deal with data covered by anti-trust regulations.*

Chapter 16

Internal Political Pitfalls

The reading plan presented in the introductory material identified this chapter on internal political pitfalls as one of the key
chapters. Throughout my career, I have been blessed to work
with many fine people. But human nature is such that it's easy
for misunderstandings and mistrust to creep into even the best
of working relationships. Although people in every industry
have encountered many of these problems, these difficulties
within healthcare have their own "flavor." I hope my insights
help you circumvent these eight problems.

⇛ 68. Playing into Professional Rivalries
Top 10

Unfortunately, jealousy and potentially harmful competition
exist everywhere, including the healthcare world. Some of this
comes from overlapping areas of clinical focus or job function,
and some of it stems from individual personality clashes.

Pitfall 58 addresses the potential for technology to allow a
particular medical department to encroach on what has traditionally been another department's "territory" and adversely
affect its revenue stream. The problem can actually be broader
than just revenue. Relative standing within an organization can

251

also come into play. Not surprisingly, the most fertile grounds for professional rivalries among departments exist where there is overlap in services. As indicated in Pitfall 58 internal medicine, family medicine, and OB/GYN all offer primary care, but with different emphases. Areas of overlap also exist among nursing, discharge planning, care coordination, and social work. I do not want to imply that all departments are constantly at war with each other, but depending on how the hospital is organized, there can be areas of disagreement.

Add to this individual personalities and personal histories, and the climate can get pretty messy. Again, I don't wish to malign anyone, but we all have worked in organizations where a few people just don't get along.

Another twist may be a potential Return on Investment (ROI) conflicts between a medical specialty area and the hospital. The physicians may fall in love with a particular technology that will enhance their practices and expect the hospital to buy it. That could result in yet another demand on the hospital's capital budget without any offsetting marginal revenue.

A vendor entering a conference room filled with people representing various disciplines within the healthcare organization has no idea of the underlying psychodrama that may be bubbling below the surface. A product that could inflate the status of one particular department at the expense of another – or one particular executive over others – could trigger resistance from those adversely affected. Of course, no one in the room is going to acknowledge that publicly. (This dynamic is not limited to healthcare organizations, and experienced salespeople have undoubtedly encountered this in other settings.)

Recommendations:

■ *You should thoroughly understand the possibility that your product could shift the relative balance of power within a healthcare organization. Stress the benefit to the organization as a whole and not necessarily to any particular department. If possible, identify your product's potential organization-wide advantages to the areas that might possibly perceive their role as diminishing.*

■ *If at all possible, try to determine the lay of the land early on in the sales process. Never get in the middle of institutional turf battles but attempt to locate an internal advocate who might be able to alert you to possible sensitivities, especially as they relate to individual personalities. It's ideal if you are able to identify all the key figures and, if you can, meet with any potentially problematic people in advance to hear and address their concerns. I have been in some very uncomfortable meetings where an unsuspecting vendor got ambushed by an executive carrying out a vendetta against the "sponsoring" executive. You may not be able to entirely defang the situation, but at least you will have a better sense of what you might be up against and might be able to think through in advance what to say in case the worst happens.*

⇒ Top 10 **69. Threatening Someone's Job or Stature within the Organization**

This may be one of vendors' most common mistakes. Here two typical scenarios:

■ *Scenario 1* – A vendor discovers a way to capture revenue that hospitals may be missing. Perhaps the vendor has identified a technical loophole in Medicare or other payer provisions that the hospital is not taking advantage of. This oversight means they are not collecting revenue they are legitimately entitled to. I had one vendor claim his product would help one hospital (which he named by name) start collecting up to $4.2 million dollars a year it was leaving on the table.

■ *Scenario 2* – A vendor presents a way to streamline operations, thereby generating cost savings. For example, they might have a technology-related labor-saving approach that will reduce headcount in a particular department.

The vendor proudly makes their case for how their product will enhance the hospital's financial position. If they are fortunate enough to secure a meeting with the CEO and has a compelling story, the first thing the CEO will do is bring in the CFO, VP, or director with responsibility for the relevant area.
Here is how the two situations sometimes play out:

■ *Scenario 1* – Put yourself in the CFO's position. If the CEO calls you in to comment on the vendor's approach, agreeing with his assessment is tantamount to admitting that you're an idiot who has cost the organization hundreds of thousands or even millions of dollars.
■ *Scenario 2* – In many organizations, the number of employees within a VP's or director's domain is subconsciously interpreted as a statement of power. Any product that could potentially reduce significantly that influence can threaten the person's status.

In both cases, the affected CFO, VP, or director may sense the danger and do everything possible to discredit the potentially damaging product. The more technical the product or service is, the less likely that the CEO will understand the mechanics of the operational area, giving the threatened executive more room to obfuscate the issues and undermine the product.

Recommendations: Tread very lightly in this area. The last thing you want to do is create an internal enemy. Here are some strategies that may help:

■ *If your product taps into a new technology or new insights, you can downplay the likelihood that you are*

*implicitly criticizing the organization or the individuals
who oversee that area. For example, before Software as a
Service (SaaS) – which provides a more economical and
efficient way to meet the organization's IT needs – hit the
market, every enterprise hosted its own software. There was
no alternative. The first vendors offering SaaS could legitimately introduce the revolutionary approach in a blame-
free way. No one was doing it, so that fact that a particular
healthcare organization hadn't yet adopted SaaS was no
reason for shame or blame. So, as you approach healthcare
organizations, focus on any new-to-the-market aspects of
your product to provide "cover" for internal staff.*

■ *If your offering is triggered by a new development in the
overall environment, you can diffuse the implied criticism,
even if your target healthcare organization is guilty of the
same shortcoming as the rest of the industry. This scenario
sometimes develops when a regulatory body suddenly offers
an unfavorable interpretation in an ambiguous regulation,
causing the entire industry to scramble. Few CEOs would
blame a VP if the organization must reverse course because
of a newly established interpretation of a vague regulation.
Point out that the industry is just now realizing how to deal
with the problem and that the target healthcare organization
can help lead the way for others. Again, this diminishes any
implied blame.*

■ *Similarly, occasionally a vendor will discover a legitimate
loophole in a regulation that no one has seen before. They
typically make the rounds to every potentially affected
organization to inform them of this new legitimate interpretation. If you find yourself in this enviable position of
being the vendor who has discovered something big, you
can confidently approach the healthcare organization
to announce your good news without fear of threatening
anyone internally.*

■ *If neither of these situations apply, do everything you
can to minimize the likelihood that someone within the*

organization will feel they are being criticized. Choose your words very carefully.

- *Especially in cases where your product could reduce staffing or operating costs, you may want to start with the executive over that area (instead of the CEO) and help them understand they have an opportunity to be a hero within the organization if they introduce a cost-saving innovation.* In other words, enlist them as an ally right from the start.

70. Finding the Wrong Internal Champion

The immediately preceding pitfall recommends enlisting the services of an internal champion to smooth your way. Having someone in the know is invaluable. However, you must attempt to assess that person's internal stature. The healthcare world has a definite pecking order in terms of both clinical clout and position within the organization.

Clinically, physicians are at the apex. But an organization's medical staff is not a monolithic entity. Even though a hospital chief of staff, physician group practice president, or equivalent leader may be the highest-level physician on the organizational chart, they may or not have the same clout as a key admitting physician or the head of an important department such as cardiology. Chiefs of staff sometimes face some of the same resistance executives face since some of their colleagues might consider them one of the "suits" instead one of the "white coats."

The next level of clinical prestige is generally the VPs of nursing, followed by head nurses, therapists, and other clinical technicians.

On the non-clinical side, the CEO, of course, is the pinnacle of decision-making. (But remember, they must answer to the hospital's board.) Next come other C-suite executives. By the time you get to directors and managers, the organizational status is significantly diminished.

I have seen situations where a person of relatively lower position within an organization latches on to a product that would greatly enhance his area's operations. Sometimes people at this level are overlooked or don't get a lot of attention. They usually appreciate the chance to introduce something that will truly help the organization. It's wonderful to see their enthusiasm, but if they are not perceived as a dynamic leader, that may not be enough to carry the day, and their lack of clout could rub off on you. I'm not trying to be unkind, but some organizational positions just don't garner the same level of respect that others do.

Beyond organizational hierarchy, the dynamic of individual personality is the "X-Factor" that can come into play. Even if you have gained the support of a senior executive, unbeknownst to you, that person may be on shaky ground and may not be long for this world. Similarly, your potential champion may have the reputation of incompetence or being a chronic complainer. Having such a person as your champion does not help your case.

Recommendation:

■ *Clearly, your objective is to enlist the support of the highest-ranking clinician or management person you can get. But attempt to get an informal read on how respected they are within the healthcare organization, how much influence they have, and who the real decision-makers are.*

71. Failing to Get Strong Physician Buy-In Right from the Start on a Clinically Related Project

Vendors must fully understand that, when it comes to quality of care or efficiency enhancement efforts, you will get absolutely nowhere without strong or even enthusiastic support from key clinicians. And this backing must be solicited at the very beginning of the discussions. The later physicians are brought into the process, the less likely their support will be. Sometimes vendors find an enthusiastic administrative staff member who dives into a project and lets it progress several levels before soliciting physician input. If a proposal is fully or even partially "baked," the key physicians involved could possibly view it as something shoved at them by administration.

There are two objections physicians often raise to quality- or efficiency-related efforts. Clinical data programs inevitably involve comparisons of physicians, either at the departmental or individual levels. Physicians are understandably wary of any such evaluation since it has the potential to make them look bad. Furthermore, this type of effort has been around long enough that most physicians have participated in poorly designed or implemented comparison projects. Sometimes well-meaning analysts overstate the reliability of their methodology. No matter how well-thought-out a comparative effort is, it will always have at least some inherent limitations. Poorly designed or heavy-handed projects understandably raise clinicians' ire.

A second possible resistance point relates to the very existence of clinical Artificial Intelligence (AI) algorithms. Some doctors may feel they are trying to be displaced by a computer. "You're telling me that some machine can do a better job than I can?" In reality, AI can provide an extremely helpful diagnostic *starting point* that narrows down the range of possible medical issues and allows the physician to apply their experience and knowledge base as they develop the treatment plan.

Recommendations:

- ■ *Recognize that it's never too early to engage prominent physicians in clinical initiatives.*

■ *Be very humble about what your technology can and cannot do. Nothing will torpedo a project faster than implying that your technology offers the final word. No technology is definitive, and it should be presented as a launching pad for further investigation and discussion. This applies both to projects that compare clinical departments or individual physicians and to AI diagnostic or treatment software.*

72. Creating an Internal "Enemy" Whose Mission in Life Becomes to Prevent Your Success

This pitfall is an extension of the previous one and may seem a bit far-fetched. However, I personally encountered this at one of the hospital associations I worked at. Through my relationship with a terrific software vendor, I recognized the opportunity to develop the first quality comparison project in the state. Since you can't do a comparison project without a robust group of relevant organizations with which to compare yourself, this was one of those projects described in Pitfall 67 that requires broad participation and relevant peer groupings.

This was the first large-scale quality comparison project in the region. The field of cross-institutional quality studies was still in its infancy, and the algorithms that drove this project's comparisons were somewhat crude, largely because they drew on administrative billing data rather than using clinically robust data. (Pitfall 23 elaborates on the data limitations of this type of project.) In an effort to not oversell the initiative, I tried to be candid about the inherent shortcomings.

It turned out that the head quality director at a large and influential Cleveland hospital was a Ph.D. statistician who personally knew and had previously worked with some of the leading thought leaders in the clinical data field. Due to the unavoidable limitations with our project's data and methodology, he didn't like it – at all. In fact, he felt it was downright counter-productive. And he made it his "mission in life" to publicly denounce the project.

I will never forget meeting in his office where he gave me about five reasons why he thought the project was terrible. After he accused me of being a snake oil salesman, he threw me out of his office. That's the first and last time that ever happened during my career. Not one of the highlights!

In his defense, our process was less than perfect. And this is why I included my comments in Chapter 9 about the "art" of data interpretation where I said it's imperative to acknowledge the limitations of your data and methodology and not come across as if your results are magically accurate.

My response to my critic's charges was that this project was designed to identify *possible* problem areas that warrant further discussion. The point is that, if there are potentially thousands of areas to investigate based on the patient's severity of illness, which specific procedures were done, which physicians were involved, and many other factors, it makes sense to focus efforts on the combinations that appear most out of line. As I was introducing this project to various hospitals, I repeatedly told them that no one should be promoted or fired based on these reports' results. They are not that laser-focused.

I'm happy to report that, despite my friend's best effort, the project did launch – without his hospital of course – and was subsequently recognized as an important step forward for hospitals in the region.

Although encountering such a harsh antagonist is rare, there is still a fair degree of hostility to some types of data projects and technologies. During the June 2016 American Medical Association annual meeting, Dr. James Madara, the organization's CEO, charged the digital health industry with promoting devices and applications that "impede care, confuse patients, and waste our time…. This is the digital snake oil of the early 21st century."[1] Where have I heard the charge of "snake oil" before? Dr. Madara also referenced ineffective Electronic Health Records (EHRs), direct-to-consumer digital health products, and apps of "mixed quality."[2]

So, this issue is alive and well. And it harkens back to my comments under Pitfalls 9 and 10 about the need to have scientifically backed clinical data and/or credible clinicians as part of your product development team. Having that type of trusted backing may help counter some of the backlash expressed in Dr. Madara's comments.

Recommendations:

- *If you have a product that could potentially invoke the wrath of a clinician, work with your internal clinical advisers to identify the specific points of potential objection and think through credible responses. Never dismiss them as irrelevant. Even if your antagonist is dead wrong – which they probably are not – just having a prominent critic verbalize objections could be enough to destroy your initiative. Whenever controversy surrounds a project, many people – especially those who may have limited technical understanding of the issues – choose to walk away rather than wade into the murky waters.*

- *Be very humble about your data project. Avoid any language that sounds like you can definitively identify or solve problems. You don't have to be apologetic about your offering, but it is usually best to preface any type of detailed presentation with an acknowledgment of its limitations. That way, if a critic emerges, you can agree that he has correctly assessed the situation and point back to your earlier comments that were consistent with his point. This will go a long way toward maintaining your credibility.*

73. Losing a Sale Because an Incumbent Vendor Claims They Can Do the Same Thing, or Your Innovative Approach Teaches Them How to Do It Themselves

This one provides a "double-whammy." You could lose a potential sale to an existing vendor who somewhat falsely claims they can do what you do, or you could inspire them to copy your great new idea. Either way, you lose.

There's an old sentiment that states you will never find a consultant who admits they can't solve your problem. (For the record, I *do* turn down engagements when I don't feel I can do an excellent job.) This saying can also be true of technology vendors.

If you have an innovative take on a recognized problem, it's possible that there are other vendors who may be trying to address the same issue, but perhaps you are using a different approach. Technology is often confusing to executives who don't necessarily use it every day. So, if the executive tells an incumbent vendor that your company approached them with an allegedly superior product, the vendor will, naturally, try to retain them as a client. It may be difficult for the executive to ascertain whether their existing vendor can, indeed, effectively tackle the problem you are proposing to solve.

Another factor is that, if the existing vendor is doing a good job for your target healthcare organization, the loyalty factor will make it harder for you to displace them.

A variation on this problem is where the end-user explains your new approach to their current vendor who then decides you have a great idea and tells the client they'll be happy to develop the same thing for them. Besides losing revenue, you've essentially inspired a competitor to mimic your work.

To make matters worse, you may discover that an incumbent vendor may have actually inserted a right of first refusal clause into their client contract. I once had this very thing happen to me. I managed the data function for my organization. My department was responsible to collect and process the data, and then we handed it off to a peer senior executive who used the data my area produced to feed into one of his projects. When it came to renew our data vendor's contract, the company wanted to insert a right of first refusal clause for essentially *any* future data-related project.

I had no problem with that concept for conventional or existing types of data projects where there are already several companies to choose from. But there are many innovative data and analytics companies that steadily introduce brand new approaches and methodologies. If one of those companies approached me with an awesome new idea that no one else had thought of yet, I didn't want to feel constrained to go to our current supplier to essentially "ask their permission" to work with someone else who had the foresight to create a dynamic new product. Let me remind you that many vendors' default is to claim they can do anything, so the chance of them declining was pretty small.

Complying with this step would also prolong the timeline for acquiring a new technology. The current company would have to take time to evaluate whether or not they could really replicate the technology, and then if they decided they could, it would take them many months of development time. Furthermore, giving them the inside track could potentially hinder our ability to negotiate favorable terms if they came back with an offer to develop the product for us. They could claim to replicate the other vendor's product, but the price could be twice as high. So, this concept of right of first refusal was a terrible idea all around.

Unfortunately, my colleague thought he knew more about data and technology then he really did, and he absolutely insisted in bowing to our incumbent's requirement for taking a first shot at anything new. About a year later, after I had seen an innovative take on a pesky problem, I was forced to abide by this clause and asked our existing data vendor if they could replicate the idea I had seen elsewhere. They naturally wanted to take a crack at it and spent four months looking into the concept before they finally recognized they couldn't deliver what we wanted. We lost valuable time, and it was all I could do to keep from telling my internal peer, "I told you so."

Recommendations:

■ *If you find yourself trying to displace an existing vendor, recognize that the momentum is not in your favor. This dynamic holds true any time you try to change vendors, whether you are selling a technology product, banking services, or any other item. Since many business decisions are based largely on relationships, the existing supplier may have strong personnel connections with on the organization's executives or board members, making your task all-the-more difficult.*

It's disruptive for the client to yank out one technology or product and replace it with yours. At a minimum, staff will have to be retrained, and it's entirely possible that work processes may have to be adjusted. You have to make it worth a client's while to do so. If your product pretty much replicates what the other vendor's does, you may be able to stand apart through either enhanced features or functionality, superior customer service, and/or favorable pricing.

■ *If you happen to run into a right of first refusal situation, get a thorough understanding of exactly what the current company does. Your objective is to demonstrate to your potential client that your approach is different enough from what the other vendor does that it falls outside the right of first refusal requirement. Of course, whether or not it does may be a matter of degrees, and the final outcome depends on the exact contract language.*

74. Losing Out Because the Organization Prefers a Single Source Vendor

The battle between Single Source vs. Best-of-Breed installations has raged on for decades. According to a blog posted on www. binarystream.com,[3] Single Source can work well in smaller organizations with relatively simple needs or very large organizations that are strong in a particular vertical. Twenty years ago, Single Source vendors could credibly claim the advantage of easier integration over a patch-worked Best-of-Breed hodge podge. However, Binary Stream argues that the current marketplace offers integration tools that have made this less of an issue. The biggest weakness of Single Source systems is that they almost never offer the absolute best application for everything they offer.

Best-of-Breed works best where maximum performance is essential in complex, financial, or competitive markets. "Progressive IT departments where system change is not feared or considered as risk averse is another essential success factor in implementing Best-of-Breed solutions,"[4] according to BinaryStream. These vendors claim with some credibility that, since they are literally on the leading or even bleeding edge, the Single Source vendors with whom they compete must play catch up.

Although most experts lean one way or the other, there is no clear consensus within the user community. The "right" answer depends on the organization's needs and the preferences of its IT professionals.

Typically, entrepreneurs offering disruptive products fall into the Best-of-Breed camp. This can be challenging if you are targeting a Single Source-leaning organization.

Recommendation:

- ■ *If you are up against an organization that clearly prefers Single Source, there is little you can do beyond stressing the advantages of your product and the possible opportunity costs of going with a suboptimal product. Quantifying opportunity costs can sometimes carry the day.[5]*

75. Facing a Very Cautious Decision-Maker or Purchasing Agent Who May Be "Technophobic" or Prefers a "Safe" Option over an Untested, Innovative One

As I mentioned in Chapter 4, everyone agrees that healthcare is about a decade behind other industries when it comes to embracing technology. The industry's complex environment means multiple interests must support any significant decisions, and project failure is often swiftly punished. This dynamic makes some executives highly cautious, and the problem is amplified when they feel intimidated by technology.

About two years, I was at a professional conference in Chicago where I ran into an old colleague I used to work with in Michigan years ago. When I explained that many of my clients are developers and entrepreneurs who are trying to introduce technology innovations into healthcare, he commented, "Good luck with that. They wouldn't get very far with me. I've worked in hospital operations for over 30 years and have been able to avoid technology the whole time. If I can keep it that way until I retire, I'll be a happy man." Not everyone feels this way, but at least some do.

One of my earliest blogs was entitled, "Would You Rather Manage a Nuclear Power Plant or Buy Healthcare Technology?" You might be wondering what kind of choice that is. What could those two things possibly have in common?

Think about the nuclear power plant situation. Even though someone might be a highly intelligent leader, unless they have worked in the nuclear energy field, what could they possibly know about the technical aspects of the nuclear power industry? They are completely dependent on their technical advisors' recommendations.

What if the experts are wrong when they say the early warning alarm system in Reactor 2 is just fine? Whose head would roll if a failed alarm resulted in a nuclear incident? Or what is the technical experts' real motive for seeking a 30% budget increase? Is it a genuine fear of avoiding technological obsolescence, or is it to expand their own power base? It can be hard for the uninformed executive to tell what the real spending priorities should be. Of course, they can seek input from multiple outside sources, but all that information is still second-hand, and this makes the situation a bit unsettling.

These feelings of uncertainty often parallel the stomach-churning experienced by healthcare leaders thrust into medical technology or healthcare IT, some of which may be untested. There are four reasons for this:

1. As with nuclear plants, many executives know little about the nuts and bolts of healthtech. Even if they are fairly comfortable with it, tech is such an ever-changing world that what they knew a year ago is probably obsolete today. So, as they are being asked to manage something they don't really "get," they can't turn to their personal experience base but have to rely on technical experts.
2. They have seen technology – even technology released from major companies – flop spectacularly. I referenced Apple's dismal launch of its revised Maps app in 2012 under Pitfall 1. Someone who is slightly nervous about technology will correctly reason that if a company as huge and progressive as Apple can botch a roll-out, how do they know they won't suffer the same fate?
3. There's a good chance they have personally been burned by a major technology fail, through either incompetent installations, unfulfilled promises, or major cost overruns.
4. Maybe, just maybe, they know a CEO or other senior executive who literally lost their job because of a bungled EHR implementation or other major technology project disaster.

Add to this the knowledge described in Pitfall 72 above that some in the medical field consider much of the newer technology being launched "snake oil," and you have very reluctant and cautious decision-makers. Who wants to have their name on the snake oil purchase order? Many executives are much more comfortable with taking the safe route, and their operating philosophy appears to be: No one ever got fired for buying an IBM computer.

The following table presents a helpful mental framework for assessing the likelihood of a particular healthcare organization coming on board. In a classic 2 × 2 analysis (as shown below), one dimension is the organization's financial position and the other is the leadership's degree of enthusiasm for technology.

	Enthusiastic	Financially challenged with enthusiastic leadership	Resource-rich with enthusiastic leadership
Leadership	Reluctant	Financially challenged with reluctant leadership	Resource-rich with reluctant leadership
		Challenged	Resource-rich
		Financial Condition	

You clearly want to identify organizations in the upper right quadrant, and you can pretty much write off healthcare organizations in the lower left box.

Recommendations:

- *If you regularly show senior executives or clinicians the virtues of your technology, don't be surprised if some of them treat you like the ex-spouse they accidentally bump into on a family vacation. You can't change people's apprehensions, so think through ways to put them at ease and build your credibility.*

- *Do what you can to minimize their feelings of intimidation. Leave the technical jargon home. Explain your product in language mortal humans can understand.*
- *Don't join the ranks of vendors who overpromise and under-deliver. Be upbeat but realistic about what your product can and can't do. And be honest about installation and timeline challenges. Vendors love to talk about "long-term partnerships." It's hard to consider someone a partner once they have shown themselves to be unreliable just to make a sale.*

End Notes

1. "Is Health IT really 'digital snake oil?' 8 leaders react to Dr. James Madera's speech," *Beckers' Health IT 7 CIO Report*, June 23, 2016.
2. ibid.
3. Aidan McCrea, "The Advantages and Disadvantages of Single Source vs. Best-of-Breed," www.binarystream.com, December 25, 2018, accessed January 11, 2019.
4. ibid.
5. Ibid.

Chapter 17

Organizational/ Operational Pitfalls

The healthcare delivery world has reached an uneasy operational equilibrium where the thousands of moving parts have settled into temporary stability. You may be familiar with the game Jenga where players progressively remove wooden blocks from a tower of 54 blocks and move them to the top of the structure, making it increasingly unstable. The last person to successfully remove and relocate a block before the tower collapses wins the game.

Introducing change into a healthcare delivery system can require the same level of dexterity as playing Jenga, and here are some mistakes you must avoid as you try to do so.

⇛ Top 10 76. Not Recognizing the High Threshold Required for Decisions and Action due to Organizational Complexities

Management expert Peter Drucker has called hospitals "the most complex human organization ever devised."[1] People who have never worked in this climate cannot fully appreciate the truth of his statement. As I described in Chapter 1, the range of variation among different hospitals and health systems is huge. Generally, the larger the healthcare organization, the more complex it is. But even the smallest Critical Access Hospitals have various decision-making layers, including numerous executive, clinical and operational departments, committees, and boards.

If you are trying to sell a product targeting frontline end-users, you must first sell them on its usefulness. If the product touches on clinical care, you must obtain the blessing of physicians, nurses, therapists, or others in the patient care area. (See Pitfall 71 about needing to get physician support as early in the process as possible.)

Assuming executive leadership has not been engaged up to this point. The next step is for you and the internal people who support the product to convince them of its worth. If the product involves a large financial commitment, it must be folded into the subsequent year's budget and may even have to get board approval if it exceeds a certain dollar threshold. (See Pitfall 52.) And if you miss the budget cut-off date, you will have to wait an entire budget cycle before the project can gain approval. I've talked with several experienced sales executives who say that government is the only other sector with as long a sales timeline as healthcare.

And things happen along the way. More than one client has "spun" the following tale of woe: "It looked like we were all set to go, but then at the last minute the _____ (fill in the blank) department stepped in and mucked everything up." This blank has been populated by the legal, compliance, human resources, and many other departments. One of my clients told me that even though he and his client hospital had agreed to terms in a straightforward, four-page agreement, the legal department jumped in – almost at the moment he had his hand poised above the agreement to sign it – and started a lengthy process that lasted months and resulted in a bloated, ten-page contract. Another client told me that the compliance department from the targeted healthcare system swooped in at the last minute and scuttled the entire project.

This complexity within healthcare organizations can add layers and possibly months to the approval process.

Recommendation:

- *Be sure you factor this reality into your internal sales projections and as you plan your cash flow needs. You need to have a long financial runway. See Pitfall 51 for further advice on sales projections.*

⇛ 77. Underestimating the Complexity of Streamlining a Process or Changing Procedures, Especially If It Creates Additional Workload Requirements for Some Departments or Individuals

Top 10

Don't underestimate the power of resistance to change. Of course, this problem exists in every organization and industry, but it takes on its own unique shape in the healthcare world, primarily because of its incredible complexity as described in the preceding pitfall.

One factor in healthcare is the tenuous "balance of power" within the organization, as highlighted in Pitfall 68. As I stated there, any operational change can potentially increase one department's influence within the organization and generate resistance from others. Change invites controversy.

This problem can be exacerbated if the change requires others to do additional work. Even if the new process is a net positive to the overall organization, those people whose workload is adversely affected often make their displeasure known. The increasing financial pressure on healthcare organizations over the last few decades has forced them to dramatically streamline operations while trying to maintain and even improve quality of care. Adding workload expectations in a climate that is often stretched to the max is seldom appreciated.

Some technology – particularly software programs – can make life easier for a particular department but have a spill-over effect on other areas that might have to modify their operations or pick up extra responsibilities. Although the department that primarily benefits from the software may be very happy with the new operating state of affairs, others might not be so thrilled.

We saw this at one association I worked at when we adopted our member contact management software program a number of years ago. It brought a needed level of structure to our member relations function but required absolutely every-one in the organization to change some of their day-to-day activities. Since this was mandated from the top down, there wasn't much resistance (although there was a bit of grum-bling). But had this been initiated by just one department resulting in everyone else having to comply with new operat-ing procedures, I suspect there would have been considerable pushback.

This scenario is played out in every healthcare organiza-tion whenever a new way of doing things is introduced, and changes can be all-the-harder if they involve a steep learning curve. The old cliché about the difficulty of turning a battle-ship around aptly describes the effort needed to get a health-care organization to change.

Recommendations:

■ *If you are newer to the healthcare market and are just now starting to sell your product, you may not fully appre-ciate the operational impact your approach may have on a healthcare organization. Soliciting input from the "friend-lies" in your pilots or first clients can be especially helpful.*

■ *Do all you can to paint a realistic picture of what adopt-ing your product or service will mean to the healthcare organization. You are the expert on your own technology, and you have the deepest understanding the positive impact it can have. However, every healthcare organization is unique and has its own quirks. Just because one institution embraces your product, it doesn't mean the next one will. Unless you have real-time knowledge about all the jots and tittles of operations within the areas likely to be affected in any given organization and have a good grasp on how to minimize the disruption, you could be walking into a buzz saw.*

■ *Work with your "internal champions," getting them to help you think through possible resistance points and identify the individuals most likely to react negatively. You should meet with potential critics early on to invite them to help you think through what an optimal implementation might look like.*

■ *Be humble about your solution. Never let the words, "All you have to do is . . . ." pass your lips. You will immediately be branded as naïve, and you will have to work hard to re-establish your reputation. Avoid absolute statements or implied promises. Remember, some potential clients may not achieve results as dramatic as your demo slides probably project. If, for example, your product could potentially generate FTE reductions, it's possible the health system has already implemented a project that has helped them move part-way toward that goal. Therefore, your chance to reap the low-hanging fruit may not be there, so be careful about over-promising results. Use phrases like, "typically," "in most cases," and "we've seen that many hospitals . . ." If they end up buying your product, this will help keep expectations in check and make it easier for the healthcare organization to view you as a long-term partner instead of someone who sold them something that didn't really work that well. As one CEO put it, "approaching the C-suite with more humility than bravado is often the better way to go."*

■ *Don't assume that your product or approach will solve all the system's problems. Yours will probably not be the company that finally whips the healthcare world into shape. It's best to ask a lot of questions to determine if there is an alignment between the organization's needs and your offering. If there isn't, it's to your advantage to acknowledge that and point them toward a better-suited approach if you know of one. It's better to establish a relationship with future potential than to try jamming a square peg into a round hole and sacrificing both the current customer and other like-minded potential clients who might hear that your product wasn't all it was cracked up to be.*

78. Trying to Sell to a Hospital That Insists on Having All Technology Products or Services Referred to IT (Even If It Isn't Directly Related to IT), Resulting in the Project Being Buried under Multiple Other IT Priorities

The CIO has ultimate operational responsibility to assure smooth IT operations and maximize data security. Having their blessing can be essential, and earning their opposition can be fatal.

Many executives – especially those who are not particularly comfortable with technology – immediately call in the CIO whenever they hear about any project that even smells like technology. This is entirely appropriate. However, many technologies operate with little interface with the organization's IT infrastructure. Examples include point-of-care testing devices, freestanding endoscopes and ultrasound units, audiometers, bladder scanners, and many other clinical and medical devices.

Most IT departments are severely overworked, and their project lists include dozens and dozens of tasks. Landing at the end of the queue can greatly extend the evaluation and decision-making processes. Several technology vendors have told me they do all they can to avoid getting caught up in the IT department quagmire, not because they are trying to disrespect the CIO but because they recognize their product has virtually no effect on the organization's technical infrastructure and they don't want to add months to the decision-making process.

Recommendation:

■ *Fully respect the CIO's and the IT department's roles and avoid getting on their wrong side at all costs. However, if your product has minimal impact on existing technologies, try to steer the evaluation process away from IT. This will undoubtedly speed the process up, and IT will probably appreciate not having to add yet another project to their long task list.*

79. Having to Comply with a Hospital's Requirement That All Vendors Subscribe to a Vendor Clearinghouse before It Will Allow a Presentation

Healthcare accreditation organizations like the Joint Commission and DNV GL Healthcare require provider organizations to know who is entering their facilities and for what purposes. This requirement applies to all vendors. Among the items tracked are whether a vendor has any criminal or federal sanctions against it or is on a government watch list. Additionally, healthcare organizations often add specific health requirements like yearly influenza vaccinations, tuberculosis skin tests, or other types of vaccinations for the individuals themselves.

In order to manage and document these reporting requirements, many hospitals make all outside representatives register with credentialing companies like Vendormate, Symplr, and others. These organizations conduct the necessary back-ground, financial, and compliance checks and create online repositories that ensure up-to-date credentialing documentation so representatives are not denied access because of incomplete or inaccurate information. The credentialing companies often offer dashboards to track which vendor reps fully comply and which do not.

As inconvenient as it may seem to have to register with one of these credentialing companies, it's an unavoidable reality if you want to do business with the healthcare organizations that subscribe to their services. Many vendors and contractors new to the healthcare market are unaware of this requirement.

Recommendation:

- *If you plan to target many healthcare organizations, there is a good chance that at least some of them will work with one of the credentialing companies, so reach out to one of these organizations so you won't be turned away from a potential client's campus.*

80. Encountering an Organization That Prefers to Develop Its Own Technology In-House Instead of Seeking Outside Solutions.

About 20 years ago, many healthcare organizations that saw the growing potential of technology felt energized to develop their own customized computer programs to tailor solutions to their particular needs. Because clinical and management software programs were still in their early stages, some healthcare organization concluded that no program fully met their requirements. Consequently, they decided to design their own.

Four more recent factors have taken some of the steam out of this trend:

1. Technology vendors have greatly upped their games, and commercially available solutions are far more robust. Many vendors now have the resources necessary to conduct the underlying research and advanced programming required to develop state-of-the-art programs.
2. The demands on hospitals' IT departments have grown considerably as the roles of data, IT, and technology have exploded. Furthermore, financial pressures have forced providers to evaluate every FTE position. This means provider IT departments have less and less flexibility to develop new offerings.
3. Software as a Service (SaaS) delivery of software has made the process of updating programs from external vendors far simpler than it used to be.
4. Those provider organizations that developed their own solutions have had first-hand experience with the challenge of continuously having to update programs and applications. Creating software in the first place is a monumental effort, but the task doesn't end on release day. There are inevitably bugs to fix and enhancements to offer. These are never-ending tasks, and experiencing the reality of these demands has caused some healthcare organization would-be IT developers to back away from the "grow your own" strategy.

This means that the desire to do in-house development has subsided a bit, which increases the opportunity for outside companies to fulfill their needs. However, you may still encounter a few organizations that prefer to do things internally.

Recommendations:

■ *If you run into healthcare organizations that want to do their own in-house development, gently remind them of the challenges of creating and maintaining self-developed solutions.*

■ *If your company has the capacity to do so, you can offer to tweak your offering to maximize its utility to prospective clients. This customization would allow you to meet their needs and remove the reason for them to take the process in-house. Just be sure to keep it as affordable as possible.*

81. Encountering Internal End-Users' "Bandwidth" Issues

Physicians, nurses, technicians, other clinical personnel, and executives live busy and hectic professional lives. By now you should agree that the healthcare delivery environment is extremely complex, and, if anything, demands on individuals' time are increasing.

All new technology involves a learning curve, and harried people are not always enthusiastic about interrupting their routines to take on yet another new application. Given the onslaught of new technology being introduced into both the clinical and business sides of healthcare, this could be a fairly significant deterrent. Fortunately, software and app developers are gravitating toward informal industry practices about how apps look, feel, and operate. So, even if users are new to a particular app, they can often figure it out pretty easily.

However, there are only so many programs and apps people are willing to utilize, and the problem is made worse if what you are trying to introduce is not likely to be used a lot. End-users may conclude that adopting to the new technology isn't worth the effort it takes to learn if it only comes into play occasionally.

When I worked at Georgia Hospital Association, one of the jokes was that none of the executives knew how to do anything on our mega-copier except make single copies. And forget about us trying to fix a paper jam. When this happened, our solution was simple: Call one of the support staff. The reason for our ineptitude was that we almost never had to use any of the advanced features or fix a paper jam, and because doing any of those things was fairly complicated, we didn't perform those functions often enough to really internalize the processes. So, anticipated low-volume rates for a new technology can breed indifference or even hostility.

This phenomenon is not unique to healthcare. Every organization is potentially susceptible to this problem. However, there is a major factor within the healthcare environment that makes the situation even more challenging because it sucks up considerable end-user bandwidth. That's the Electronic Health Record (EHR). It's well-known that many physicians and other clinicians detest EHRs, and some who are nearing retirement age have decided to leave early rather than have to embrace EHRs.

Modern Healthcare magazine recently ran a humorous piece in its "Outliers" back page feature spotlighting a satirical Twitter account called "EpicParodyEMR." (Epic is a leading EHR supplier.) Here are some tweets:

- "Myth: Our Epic design team stays up late at night thinking of ways to torture you and make your life harder. Fact: They actually go to bed pretty early."
- "The Epic Help Desk: Helping you adjust to us."
- EPIC is an acronym for "*E*xasperating *P*hysicians *I*nhibiting *C*are"[2]

There is not a single clinician on the planet who decided to enter the field of medicine so they could play with EHRs all day. For many, the emotional bandwidth required to use EHRs has sucked the life out of any desire to adopt yet more technology.

The bottom line is that the perceived benefits of a new technology must exceed the perceived "cost" of learning yet another program, and many in the healthcare world may need extra convincing.

Recommendations:

■ *If your technology has a mainstream-type look and feel, you can showcase the familiarity of its flow with potential clients to help reduce their resistance to learning yet another new tool.*

■ *If a particular use case is apt to be low volume, there's not much you can do to change that. Stress the value your product brings to their issues. Like anything else, even if a particular solution disrupts a workflow or requires some extra effort, people will generally use it if they see it as a net positive.*

82. Encountering Patients' "Bandwidth" Limitations

Clinicians aren't the only ones with limits on how much technology they can handle. Patients can have the same issue. Three factors contribute to this:

1. Patients' level of technology literacy – Even though millennials love technology, many in the Greatest Generation and Baby Boomer demographic groups do not. Many are intimidated by technology, and some even seem to take pride in the fact that they don't understand computers. Fortunately, this group is shrinking as software is becoming more user-friendly.
2. Patients feeling overwhelmed by the number of different technologies they are asked to use – If they have several physicians or other caregivers, each with their own portals, they may resist having to master several portals, websites, and kiosk technologies in addition to having to track the many passwords involved.

3. Just like the clinicians and executives referenced immediately above under Pitfall 81, patients may be infrequent
users, especially if they are asked to interact with several
portals and websites.

Patient-facing apps are typically purchased by healthcare
organizations so their patients can use them. Your contacts in
the healthcare organization may be well-aware of the reasons
some of their patients may not gravitate toward using additional technology. As a result, they may be hesitant to move
forward.

Recommendation:

■ *As discussed under the preceding pitfall about hospital
personnel who are asked to use various technologies, make
sure your technology has as much of an "industry standard feel" as possible, and stress the value of your product
to both the patient and the healthcare organization departments with which they interact.*

83. Suffering Because of Sub-Optimal Implementation of Previous Technologies, Leading to General Skepticism about Technology or, If the Prior Technology Is from Your Own Company, Your Reduced Credibility Which Undercuts Renewals, Cross-Sell Opportunities and Strong References

Some over-zealous healthtech sales executives overlook the
need to thoroughly understand the adequacy – or lack thereof –
of internal operational processes before slapping in a new software program. At its core, much of technology is merely a tool
to greatly streamline or accelerate a certain process or analysis.

If the core activity is a well-oiled machine, automating it can significantly enhance productivity. But if, on the other hand, the underlying systems are flawed, all you've done is helped the flawed way of doing things become more efficient at being flawed. Technology can't fix a practice that is fundamentally defective.

Your objective should be to work with your potential client to document their current approach and determine where it is breaking down. This can be a lengthy undertaking that may take many weeks and involve numerous committee meetings. Only after both you and the client fully grasp the extent of the baseline problems can you determine the best way to deploy your solution.

I discussed technophobia under Pitfall 75. People who resist technology may have gotten there largely because of previous frustrations with other programs or hardware. This makes them reluctant to try yet another new program. The situation is made worse if you happen to work for the same company that sold a previous installation to the same customer and the results were judged to be subpar.

Recommendations:

- *See the recommendations under Pitfall 75 about technophobic users.*
- *If the previous less-than-ideal installation was from a different vendor, you can contrast their implementation process and yours.*
- *If your company is to blame, own your responsibility and extend some kind of free service or concession to help mend a bridge that would have otherwise been burned. Furthermore, you can highlight the improvements your company has made since their previous experience.*
- *A strong users' group should be central to your product support strategy. A users' group provides several advantages:*

- *It helps make sure your clients will take fullest advantage of your product, thereby maximizing their satisfaction.*
- *It fosters cross-pollination of ideas and recommendations among peer organizations. This further cements your product as a valued asset for each user organization.*
- *It alerts you to user concerns long before renewal time, allowing you to take corrective action.*
- *It helps develop esprit-de-corps within a cadre of happy users, greatly boosting your credibility and maximizing the chances of contract renewals.*
- *Feedback from your clients flows into the product improvement process, making your offering better for your entire client base.*
- *It can support cross-sell opportunities if your company has other products.*

84. Encountering Things Beyond Your Control

We all know that bad things happen. A potential client suffers an unexpected financial setback. Your "internal champion" suddenly falls from grace or leaves the organization. New leadership comes in and changes strategic direction. A sale is lost because it turns out the son-in-law of the highest admitting orthopedic surgeon works for a competing vendor. More than one of my clients has run into this type of problem.

Recommendation:

■ *Unfortunately, there is little you can do when this happens. Pick yourself up and move on. Although you will understandably be disappointed, keep the door open and don't do anything to burn bridges. You never know when things might open up again. And never express anger or badmouth the organization to others.*

End Notes

1. Rick Pollack, "How hospitals are redesigning care delivery to serve changing needs," *Modern Healthcare*. September 26, 2015, accessed March 3, 2019.
2. "Epic trolling," *Modern Healthcare*, April 1, 2019, page 44.

Final Thoughts

We've come a long way. I tried in the first part of this book to do three things:

1. Orient you to some of the healthcare field's unusual challenges
2. Suggest some common-sense approaches to make things better
3. Spotlight the incredibly exciting breakthroughs and opportunities healthtech offers

The first two chapters highlight problems, and the entire second part of the book focuses on difficulties you may face as you interact with healthcare organizations. In order to not overwhelm you, I tried in every case to provide practical suggestions for circumventing potential problems. Many of them can be minimized or even eliminated with careful forethought and planning.

I am very glad I had the opportunity to circulate the various chapters to more than two dozen respected industry colleagues for their input and suggestions. That took this book from being just the opinions of one person sitting behind his laptop to representing a consensus of industry leaders. I don't want to imply that every healthcare executive or clinician who reviewed parts of this book endorses every idea in it. I take responsibility for the content, but you can know that these are sound suggestions that reflect the wisdom of people who collectively represent hundreds and hundreds of years of industry experience.

In case you are slightly overwhelmed or even depressed by some of what you've read, let me remind you that the healthtech field is at an unprecedented point of dynamic expansion. I suggest you go back to Chapter 4 and re-read the section called "Explosive Growth" to remind yourself about the incredible opportunity this field offers.

Congratulations on choosing to join the healthtech industry. I trust some of the ideas in this book will help you navigate through the challenges and inspire you succeed in bringing revolutionary products to the market with the end of changing patients' lives.

Index